ST. MARTIN'S GRIFFIN ✖ NEW YORK

The New York Times
BRIDGE BOOK

An Anecdotal History of the
Development, Personalities and Strategies
of the World's Most Popular Card Game

♠ ♥ ♦ ♣

Alan Truscott
AND
Dorothy Truscott

ST. MARTIN'S GRIFFIN ☙ NEW YORK

www.stmartins.com

Design by MMDesign

Library of Congress Cataloging-in-Publication Data

Truscott, Alan.
    The New York times bridge book : an anecdotal history of the development, personalities, and strategies of the world's most popular card game / Alan Truscott and Dorothy Truscott.
        p. cm.
    Includes index (p. 257).
    ISBN 0-312-29090-X (hc)
    ISBN 0-312-33107-X (pbk)
    EAN 978-0312-33107-8
    1. Contract bridge—History. 2. Bridge players—Anecdotes. 3. Contract bridge—Collections of games. I. Truscott, Dorothy Hayden. II. New York times. III. Title.

GV1282.23 .T78 2002
795.41'5—dc21   2002068124

First St. Martin's Griffin Edition: August 2004

10 9 8 7 6 5 4 3 2 1

Introductory Note

Much of this book can be read by nonplayers or beginners. Readers who wish to know more about the basic structure of the game are advised to try any of the following by the same authors:

Basic Bridge in Three Weeks, by Alan Truscott (Putnam, 1987)
Bid Better, Play Better, by Dorothy Truscott (Devyn Press, 1998)
Winning Declarer Play, by Dorothy Truscott (Wilshire, 1969)

Unless otherwise indicated by the context, and except in chapter 17, the first-person "I" in this book refers to Alan Truscott.

The authors wish to thank Phillip Alder and Kenneth Barbour for reading the manuscript and making helpful suggestions.

The authors are also very grateful to Mike Levitas for suggesting the idea for the book and carrying it forward, and to Peter McLennan for accurate copyediting.

Contents

CHAPTER 1

How It All Began

Aristocracy, Waving Flags and Competing

This book could in theory begin with the invention of playing cards, probably in China a millennium ago. The evidence is scanty, and it may have been in India, or even further west. There is a pleasant legend that they were invented by the Emperor Suen-Ho to keep his concubines amused in the year 1120, but he was, it seems, at least 140 years too late to claim the honor. China then disappeared from the history of card playing until 1978, when Deng Xiaoping emerged from the confusion of the Cultural Revolution to take control of the country. One of his first acts was to promote his bridge-playing comrades to top government positions and to encourage the activity. To the end of his long life, he sat up late at night, bidding enthusiastically according to the Precision System. I doubt if he knew that I devised that name and gave considerable help to the Chinese-American, C. C. Wei, who invented it. But the supreme leader of the world's most populous country was happy to have his love of the game publicized. "When the Chinese people see me playing bridge," he declared, "they are reassured as to my mental health."

There are two oddities about the first great name in the history of bridge, a man who lived in London. One is that he still receives mail more than two centuries after his death. The other is he that did not play bridge. What this barrister did was to play the ancestor game of whist, in which there was no bidding or dummy. The trump suit was determined by turning up the last card dealt.

He taught the game efficiently to the wealthy residents of his home city. In 1742 he published a booklet of 86 small pages with a long title: *A Short Treatise on the Game of Whist, Containing the Laws of the Game, and Also Some Rules Whereby a Beginner May, With Due Attention to Them, Attain to the Playing It*

Well. The only extant copy of the first edition is in the Bodleian Library in Oxford. My copy, dated a year later, is nicely bound in leather but is one of many pirated productions.

The laws suggested by him were principally concerned with the penalties for revoking. His "Code of Ethics and Fair Play" was so good that it was carried forward, with minimal changes, into the laws of auction bridge and contract bridge.

His technical advice was sensible. For example, "That you have two Trumps remaining when Adversaries have only one, and it appears to you that your partner has one great Suit, in this case always play a trump; tho' you have the worst, because by removing the Trump out of your Adversary's hands, there can be no obstruction to your Partner's great Suit." This situation is familiar to good bridge players, but novices often fail to deal with it correctly.

Despite the title, this became a best seller, possibly the biggest seller to make its appearance in the 18th century. Later he expanded it to include the rules of other card games. My copy is signed by the author and includes a warning to pirates. All this made his name a household word, and when he died in 1769, at 97, he was the accepted arbiter of law and order in all games.

His name was Edmond Hoyle, which is why we still say, "According to Hoyle" and puzzled players still write to him seeking enlightenment. Because *Hoyle's Rules of Card Games* have been updated regularly ever since, they sometimes receive a reply from the modern authors. Religious works apart, it is surely the book with the longest continuous publishing history.

Another man who put his name firmly in the dictionary, without even a capital letter, was a contemporary of Hoyle. He was frequently First Lord of the Admiralty, and was burdened with the nickname "Jemmy Twitcher." One night he was reluctant to leave the card table to satisfy his hunger and called for a servant to bring him a slice of meat between two pieces of bread. Since he was the fourth Earl of Sandwich, people have been eating sandwiches ever since. Few remember to thank the shade of Jemmy Twitcher.

Whether he was or was not playing whist at the time is not quite clear, but many of his contemporaries were certainly enthusiasts. George Washington played regularly at Mount Vernon for 15 years before the start of the Revolution. Napoleon's celebrated foreign minister, Charles Maurice de Talleyrand-Périgord, once asked a young man if he played whist. When he received a negative reply, he pontificated, "Young man! You do not play whist? What a sad old age you reserve for yourself."

Another Frenchman of stature was Alexandre Louis Honoré Lebreton Deschapelles, who was highly expert at billiards, in spite of having lost an arm in battle. He was at one time, until surpassed by one of his students, the world's best chess player, and he was generally regarded as the world's best whist player. This is an astonishing parlay, even if before the days of formal tournaments in either game. The closest parallel is a modern one: Irina Levitina won world championship medals in chess while representing the Soviet Union, and has been a member of a winning United States women's bridge team in world play.

Deschapelles invented an entry-creating play, named after him, which is extremely difficult even when all four hands are in view.

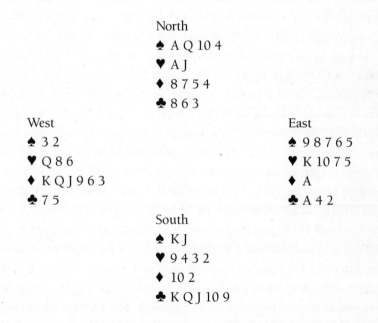

North
♠ A Q 10 4
♥ A J
♦ 8 7 5 4
♣ 8 6 3

West
♠ 3 2
♥ Q 8 6
♦ K Q J 9 6 3
♣ 7 5

East
♠ 9 8 7 6 5
♥ K 10 7 5
♦ A
♣ A 4 2

South
♠ K J
♥ 9 4 3 2
♦ 10 2
♣ K Q J 10 9

Suppose that we are playing bridge, not whist, and that the contract is a highly optimistic three notrump. The diamond king is led, and when East wins with the ace he must look for an entry to partner's hand. The solution is to lead the heart king, a Deschapelles Coup. Whether dummy takes the ace immediately or not, the heart queen becomes an entry to West's diamonds.

On the other side of the English Channel, C. S. Forester's fictional naval hero, Horatio Hornblower, supported himself with modest whist winnings during an unwelcome interlude of peace with France. His skill was based on mathematical understanding, which also served him well in navigation. On the eve of a battle his officers were expected to play whist with him, and some of them found this more terrifying than the broadsides of the enemy.

The Hoyle tradition, calling for respect for the laws and ethical play, continued in London's clubs. The Stratford Club, founded in 1815, the year of Waterloo, found an ingenious way of dealing with a problem created by its own bylaws. These provided no way to expel a member, and one obnoxious individual had made himself highly unpopular. A special general meeting was called, and the members voted to dissolve the club. The group moved to another room and voted to form a new club. All but one of the applications for membership were accepted.

The new club was the Portland, which became the custodian and interpreter of the laws of whist, and later of bridge, from that point on. The new name was derived from the Earls of Portland, a family with many whist enthusiasts. One of them, Lord Henry Bentinck, was a leading witness in the first scandal to afflict the game.

It occurred in 1836 at Graham's Club, the only one that provided for morning play. A rumor circulated there that one of the regular players, a close friend of the Duke of Wellington, "knew how to deal." He was the senior Baron of England, Henry William Lord de Ros, and his title dated back to 1264. He was a successful player, and several members noted that he dealt clumsily, with his hands often below the table. He used marked decks, and regularly contrived to have the final card, which he received, be an ace or a king.

He sued one of the other members for libel, and hired the attorney general of England to appear for him. His chief witness was a doctor who testified that de Ros had arthritic hands and would be unable to carry out the alleged maneuvers. But there were formidable witnesses testifying against him, and some marked cards were produced in evidence. The jury found against him, and he retreated to the Netherlands in considerable embarrassment. When he died three years later at 46, the wits suggested that his tombstone should read, "Here lies de Ros, waiting for the Last Trump."

Bentinck, one of the witnesses against de Ros, was reputed to be the best whist player in England. He made the first important contribution to the theory of the game, and its offshoots are an essential part of the bridge we play today.

His idea was that the play of an unnecessarily high card followed by a low card should convey a message to partner. He called it a Blue Peter, after the signal flag, blue with a white center, traditionally hoisted by a ship about to leave harbor. In effect, it said, "pay attention." The meaning he chose to convey was, "Partner, please lead trumps." That was important in whist, when there is no dummy, no bidding and no clue to the distribution.

This highly creative idea, using irrelevant cards to send messages, became known as a "peter." The term is still used in England, but Americans prefer the dull but descriptive "high-low" or "echo." For modern bridge purposes, there are three quite different principal meanings. (See below p. 8.)

All the modern theories of signaling would no doubt astonish Lord Henry Bentinck. His little thought about playing high-low in whist has had a thousand descendants in bridge.

The Bentinck family had caused some confusion in the English aristocracy by appropriating the name "Cavendish." This already belonged to the Dukes of Devonshire and their clan, which was even more prominent in 19th century England. So when a club named the Cavendish started up, it was claiming connection with two of the greatest families in the land. When the club's most talented member, Henry Jones, decided to use the pseudonym Cavendish in writing about whist, he added to the confusion. Many bridge clubs in modern times have taken the name Cavendish, the most famous of which was in New York City. The name is preserved in the annual Cavendish tournament, now played in Las Vegas. It attracts top players from around the world and has a Calcutta auction in which the total investment frequently tops $1 million.

Jones became the great authority on whist of his century, just as Hoyle had been in his. And he had the same propensity for long titles. His master work, which appeared in 1863, was *The Laws and Principles of Whist Stated and Explained, and its Practice Illustrated on an Original System, by Means of Hands Played Completely Through.* Luckily for him, the public surged to buy *Cavendish on Whist,* which was the publisher's shrewd choice for the spine.

In the area of play, whist is a more difficult game than bridge, because there is no dummy. To test this, try playing *contract whist,* which is up to a point a normal bridge game. But when the bidding is over and the lead is made, all four players play, with all the cards hidden.

Nevertheless, "Cavendish" was able to make plays that are difficult today at the bridge table.

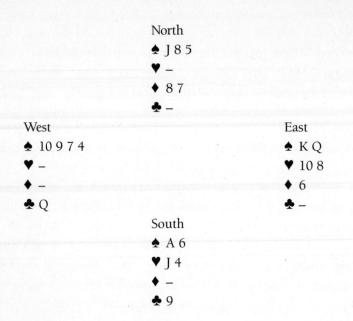

North
♠ J 8 5
♥ –
♦ 8 7
♣ –

West
♠ 10 9 7 4
♥ –
♦ –
♣ Q

East
♠ K Q
♥ 10 8
♦ 6
♣ –

South
♠ A 6
♥ J 4
♦ –
♣ 9

Diamonds were trump in this end position and Cavendish was East. He had two obvious plays when South led a club and North ruffed. One was to throw a spade and the other to throw a heart. In either case, North would draw the missing trump. South would throw the suit that East still guarded and make the remaining tricks.

Cavendish, however surprised the other players by an underruff, throwing the diamond six. This ought not to have saved him, for he would have been squeezed if it had occurred to North to lead his remaining trump. But squeeze play was virtually unknown in whist and North led a spade. South won and cashed his heart jack, but Cavendish made a trick at the finish, thanks to an underruff. His opponents thought he had made a foolish error and were quite unable to follow his explanation.

In 1857, when he was just 26, Jones had a thought that was just as significant, in the long run, as Bentinck's had been a generation earlier. He devised a method of proving that whist was a game of skill. He took four good players and made them play what would now be called a match against four ordinary performers. The good players held the North-South cards at one table, and the East-West cards at the other. A series of deals were played, and by comparing the results he proved his point: The good players had taken considerably more tricks, in total, than the lesser lights.

He had invented the first duplicate game, as well as the method that is still favored for world bridge team championships. The idea was eventually developed for pairs play by John T. Mitchell, a Scot who went to the United States. Whist tournaments were played regularly for half a century, beginning in 1891. And the Mitchell movement, which he devised, is still the cornerstone of duplicate bridge around the world.

Mitchell and his friends did not know it, but the writing was on the wall for whist: A new game was developing in the Near East, in the Ottoman Empire. It is just possible that it was played by some British officers in Constantinople during the Crimean War, 1853–56. They are said to have crossed the old wooden Galata bridge to play cards at a coffeehouse, and were therefore going "to the bridge." It is certain that the new game, with a dummy and rudimentary bidding, was being played in the 1860's and 1870's, and was usually called "britch," or "biritch," or "khedive." Some connect it with the Russian game *vint*.

The dealer's side had the right to name the trump suit and unlimited doubles and redoubles were allowed. This reached England and the United States in the early 1890's, and by 1904 players were ready for the next step.

No. 1 ▸ *Signaling*

The first, and most common, type of signal indicates a desire to have a particular suit continued by partner, or attacked by partner. For example:

Dealer: South

Vulnerable: Both

North
- ♠ Q 10 7 2
- ♥ A 8 4
- ♦ A Q
- ♣ K J 10 8

West
- ♠ A K 9 6
- ♥ 3
- ♦ 10 8 6 2
- ♣ 9 5 4 3

East
- ♠ 8 3
- ♥ J 10 9 2
- ♦ K 9 7 5 3
- ♣ 7 6

South
- ♠ J 5 4
- ♥ K Q 7 6 5
- ♦ J 4
- ♣ A Q 2

South	West	North	East
1 ♥	Pass	1 ♠	Pass
1 N.T.	Pass	4 ♥	Pass
Pass	Pass		

This is a strange deal. North-South have 29 high-card points between them, but cannot make any game against accurate defense. Three notrump and four hearts are both sensible contracts, preferably played by North, and most partnerships would reach the latter.

In the diagramed auction, North has hopes of slam when his partner opens the bidding with one heart, promising a five-card suit. He settles for game when he hears the rebid of one notrump, suggesting a minimum balanced opening. The combined hands are most unlikely to have more than 30 points, well short of the 33 points normally needed with balanced distributions.

So North should simply bid four hearts. There is known to be an eight-card heart fit, and there cannot be an eight-card spade fit since partner did not raise. Some players who like to use gadgets would bid two clubs, which in the modern style asks partner to clarify his distribution. This is called "New Minor Forcing," and makes absolutely no sense here. It will give you information you do not need, and give information to the enemy that may help them. Once you know what the contract should be, bid it immediately.

Even worse would be a bid of three hearts, which might create a disaster. Many players would treat this is an invitation to game and might pass.

This suggests three general points:

1. If you know that the combined hands have the strength for game, you must not make a bid short of game that partner could pass.

2. An area that needs careful partnership agreement is that in which the responding hand jumps at his second turn. If it is a new suit, it is almost always forcing. Half a century ago, most experts played that all such jumps were forcing. The modern style is that they are all invitations to game and can be passed. Some compromises are possible, but it is vital to discuss this. It is perhaps the most important bidding problem to sort out with a strange partner.

3. Some bids are conspicuously ambiguous, with two, or even more, possible meanings. You should, in general, prefer an unambiguous bid. But you should have a general agreement about such situations. I make my partners agree that ambiguous bids should carry the weaker interpretation: nonforcing rather than forcing; weak rather than strong if two strengths seem possible. Many have the opposite agreement. Neither agreement will solve all such problems, but it will improve your batting average.

Now return to the actual deal. West leads the spade king against four hearts. (Many modern players prefer to lead the ace from an A-K combination. That is another matter for partnership discussion.)

South plays low from the dummy. What should you do as East?

If you play the eight it will be, thanks to Bentinck, a peter. Or, if you prefer, a high-low or an echo. It will tell partner that you want him to continue spades.

So he will cash the spade ace next and you will play the three. He will lead another spade, you will trump, and South will be very grateful. Whatever you do, he will draw trump and make four hearts. You will never score a diamond trick, because South will eventually throw a diamond loser on one of dummy's black-suit winners.

And it is all your fault, because you did not use your brains. Bridge requires mental effort, and if you are not willing to make it you will not be popular with your partners.

Any signal, peter or high-low, or anything else, must be used thoughtfully. When your partner leads a king in this situation, you will usually play high with a doubleton, but *usually* does not mean *always*. In this case the one thing you do *not* want is to ruff a spade. That does you no good at all, because you are sure of a trump trick.

What you want, without any doubt at all, is a shift to diamonds. You should therefore play the spade three on the first trick. This tells your partner that you do not want him to continue spades. He will use his brains, we hope, and realize that you can hardly need him to play a club or a trump. He will shift to a diamond, hoping that you have the king and can take a trick. There is nothing South can do: He is doomed to lose two spade tricks, one diamond trick and one trump.

Such signals come in many disguises. When you are making your first discard, you can play a high card to say, "I have strength in this suit and want it led," or a low card to say, "I am weak in this suit and do not want it led."

Normally, you should signal as loudly as possible. For example, if you signal with a seven you never have the eight. It follows that to show a strong honor combination you play the highest of sequential cards. Discarding the queen to show strength would be correct from Q-J-10-9 or A-Q-J-10.

But there are two things to beware of: First, only signal when you think the message will help your partner. Very often a signal will help the opposition and should not be given. This requires judgment, and experience is the only guide. In particular, do not signal to show an ace unless you are sure your partner needs the information. Second, if in doubt, do not signal.

Many modern experts use "upside-down" signals. This means that playing high-low means you do not want this suit led, and playing low-high means the opposite. So on this deal an "upside-down" signaler would play the eight to discourage another spade lead. But upside-down would only apply to a specific partnership agreement. With a partner you do not know, the eight means "please continue spades."

The other two main varieties of signal apply when encourage/discourage makes no sense.

Consider this suit position in a notrump contract:

North

♣ K Q J 10 9

West   East

♣ 8 4 2   ♣ A 7 5

South

♣ 6 3

South has no entries to the North hand in the other suits. He will be able to take four tricks if East makes the mistake of winning when the suit is led for the first time. He will take two tricks if East holds up his ace twice. But he will take only one trick if East holds up his ace exactly once.

In such situations the defender aims to play his ace on the declarer's last card in the suit. And how does he know the number of cards the declarer has?

The answer is that his partner must give him a signal. When the suit is first played, West must pay attention. His cards are unimportant, but he can use them to send a message. A low card, here the two, shows an odd number of cards, in this case three. A high card would show an even number, so the play of the eight would show either two cards or four. (Memory: *low* and *odd* are three-letter words; *high* and *even* are respectable four-letter words.)

The partner of the signaler can nearly always work out what to do. In this case, East does some simple arithmetic when he sees the two. West cannot have five cards, for that would make 14 clubs in the deck. If West has a singleton, East's play does not matter. But if West has three cards, East must hold up once and win the second round.

East's technical problem is easy. But he may have a psychological problem. Does West know how to signal correctly? And is he paying attention? In an expert game the answers to both questions are normally affirmative. In a low-level game it may be harder, and East should probably hold up twice whatever his partner does. This may give away one trick, but it cannot give away three.

So if you are not already trained in this area, get in the habit of saying to yourself when you see a strong suit in the dummy, "Low with odd, and high with even."

Just as with the high-low signal, many experts use this *count* signal the other way round. But you can assume that the normal version applies without specific discussion.

Last, but by no means least, of the standard methods of signaling is the *suit-preference* signal. Suppose that you have a five-card heart suit headed by A-K. You lead your two winners against four spades, and dummy has Q-x-x. Your partner signals high-low, encouraging you to continue. Your remaining cards are the 4-3-2. Which one do you play?

You know that your partner will ruff, and may have a problem about his next play. If you want him to shift to a club, the low-ranking suit, you play your lowest heart, the two. If you want him to play a diamond, the high-ranking of the possible suits, you lead your high heart, the four. And if you are not sure what you want him to do, you lead the three, a neutral card carrying no message at all.

There are many situations, some of them subtle, in which a suit-preference message can be transmitted. Keep looking for them, and you will send and receive more and more signals.

CHAPTER 2

Everyone Bids and
Doubles; Another Signal;
and a Ship

Like most of the steps in the evolution of bridge from whist, the next
one, auction bridge, is wrapped in mystery. About 1904 in England,
someone had the brilliant idea that all four players, not just the dealer
and his partner, should have a chance to name the trump suit or elect to play
without trumps. The issue would be decided in favor of the player who was
willing to promise to take more tricks than his opponents would commit to.

The result was exactly like a commercial auction, although it took some
time to sort out the details. It was easy to decide that a bid of two ranked
higher than a bid of one, and so on. It was not so easy to settle the rank of the
suits. Spades started at the bottom, but then became the top suit, with the
result we know today: in ascending and alphabetical order, clubs, diamonds,
hearts, spades, with notrump outranking them all.

There were bonuses for games and slams, but no requirement to bid to a
high level. If the bidding ended at one heart, the declarer scored game if he
made 10 tricks, a small slam if he made 12 tricks, and a grand slam if he made
13 tricks. So the bidding often ended quickly. Only if both sides had a long suit
or two was the auction vigorous.

It did not take long for someone to realize, as Bentinck had done, that it
was possible to send significant messages. The light dawned simultaneously
and independently in 1912–13. Maj. Charles Patton in New York City and
Bryant McCampbell in St. Louis, Mo., each concluded that there was little
advantage in doubling for penalties when an opponent opened the bidding
with one in a suit. In the unlikely event that a player had sufficient length and
strength in the enemy suit to expect to defeat a one-level contract, his best pol-
icy was, and still is, to lie low. So Patton and McCampbell recommended that

the double should be used to show a good hand, with a desire for partner to choose a suit. That was so sensible that it became standard, and still is. What to name this action was more difficult. After various false starts, the theorists settled for "takeout double."

This simple idea has led to a complex structure of bidding. (See below p. 18.)

Now back to our main story. The two main threads of bridge history, in the Near East and the Anglo-Saxon world, converged in a strange way in 1917. The most remarkable bridge game of the century occurred in the Turkish harbor of Constantinople, now Istanbul. An American gunboat, the *Scorpion*, was attached to the American Embassy there, and it was boarded by the Turks, who were German allies, when the United States entered World War I.

The German Navy, present in force, wanted the *Scorpion* for use as a decoy, but the crew much preferred to be interned under Turkish control. The ship's fate was to be determined by Talat Pasha, the powerful minister of the interior, who happened to be an acquaintance of the ship's captain, Lt. Cmdr. Herbert Babbitt.

Talat, like many of the Turkish magnates, was a bridge enthusiast, and Babbitt had a happy thought. He challenged Talat to a rubber, with the ship as the stake. If he lost, the *Scorpion* would go to the Germans. If he won, the vessel would be interned where she was.

Talat accepted this remarkably creative suggestion, and play began. Everything hinged on the final deal, perhaps the one shown below. (Only the final contract is on record.) This was auction bridge, and nobody was vulnerable. Indeed, nobody would be vulnerable for another eight years. But both sides had scored a game at this point.

North
- ♠ 7 6 5 4
- ♥ 2
- ♦ 8 7 6 5 2
- ♣ A K Q

West
- ♠ 10 2
- ♥ J 9 7 4 3
- ♦ 9 4
- ♣ J 10 8 7

East
- ♠ J 9 8 3
- ♥ A K 8 5
- ♦ K J 3
- ♣ 6 5

South
- ♠ A K Q
- ♥ Q 10 6
- ♦ A Q 10
- ♣ 9 4 3 2

West	North	East	South
		1 ♥	1 N.T.
2 ♥	2 N.T.	Pass	Pass
3 ♥	Pass	Pass	3 N.T.
4 ♥	4 N.T.	Pass	Pass
Pass			

Talat opened the East hand with one heart, and his partner persevered slowly to the four-level. Four hearts could have been doubled effectively, but that would not have ended the rubber and saved the ship. North bid four notrump, relying on Captain Babbitt's reputation as the best player in the United States Navy.

Four notrump was a very rare contract in the auction game. Slam bonuses were scored whether or not the slam was bid, so a slam exploration that stopped short did not exist. The captain began with the knowledge that nearly all the missing high-card strength was on his right.

Talat tried a small deception by winning the heart lead with the ace and returning the five. Babbitt was not fooled. He put up the queen, and when this won he could count nine tricks, since the diamond queen was a sure winner. For his tenth, he could have pinned his hopes on finding East with the diamond jack as well as the king, but it seemed likely that one of the black suits would break favorably.

He therefore cashed his spade winners, finding that East was guarding the suit. He then cashed two club winners, reaching this ending:

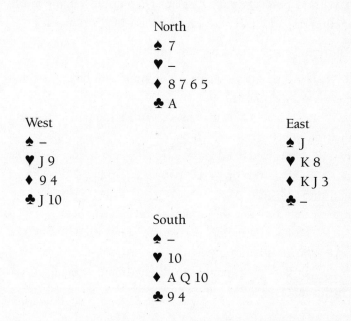

North
♠ 7
♥ —
♦ 8 7 6 5
♣ A

West
♠ —
♥ J 9
♦ 9 4
♣ J 10

East
♠ J
♥ K 8
♦ K J 3
♣ —

South
♠ —
♥ 10
♦ A Q 10
♣ 9 4

Babbitt could have survived by risking a finesse of the diamond ten, but he cashed the club ace, hoping for a split. Talat should have unblocked his heart king, but he fell from grace by throwing the eight. Now Babbitt finessed the diamond ten and led a heart, scoring two diamond tricks at the finish to make his contract and save the ship.

Talat kept his word, and the *Scorpion* and her crew remained in Turkish waters till the war was over. For the rest of his naval career her captain was known as Four Notrump Babbitt.

No. 2 ▸ *The Takeout Double*

The following assumes an opening suit bid at the one-level.

1. The doubler shows an opening bid or better, and tends to be short in the opponent's suit. With fewer than 17 high-card points, he is expected to have at least three cards in each unbid suit. With 17 points or more he plans to continue bidding over a minimum response and may have a variety of distributions.

2. The doubler's partner has many options.

a. With 0–8 points he makes a minimum suit bid, at a pinch choosing a three-card suit.

b. With 9–11 points he may make a single jump in a new suit, inviting game.

c. With a balanced hand and some values in the enemy suit he can bid one notrump (7–10), two notrump (10–12), or three notrump (13–16).

d. He can bid a game if he knows which one to bid.

e. He can bid the opponent's suit to show strength and ask partner to keep bidding.

f. He can pass for penalties with length and strength in the enemy suit.

3. The opener's partner has many options. He may:

a. raise the opening bid with weak hands, usually to the two-level with three cards, higher levels with four or more.

b. bid a new suit with moderate values (at the one-level, usually played as a one-round force).

c. bid one notrump with moderate values (7-10 points).

d. redouble with almost all good hands (10 or more points).

e. jump in a new suit, which in the modern style shows a strong suit and a fit with opener.

f. There are two popular conventional possibilities: first two notrump with any good hand (10+ points) and at least four-card support (invented by me in 1949) and second, two clubs to show a strong single raise with three-card support, sometimes coupled with three diamonds to show the same with four-card support.

The following deal was played in 1974, in a competition to select the United States world championship team.

	North	
Dealer: South	♠ A Q 9	
Vulnerable: East-West	♥ Q 10 6 2	
	♦ 9 4	
	♣ A K Q 8	

West		East
♠ K 3		♠ J 7 6 5 2
♥ A 9 8		♥ J 7 3
♦ A Q 10 8 2		♦ 6
♣ 6 5 3		♣ J 9 7 2

	South	
	♠ 10 8 4	
	♥ K 5 4	
	♦ K J 7 5 3	
	♣ 10 4	

South	West	North	East
Pass	1 ♦	Dbl.	Pass
1 N.T.	Pass	3 N.T.	Pass
Pass	Pass		

Half a century after it was invented, North used the takeout double. South responded one notrump, showing something in diamonds and roughly 7-10 high-card points. His partner ventured three notrump, knowing that his partner would have the advantage of knowing that West held virtually all the missing high cards.

A black-suit lead would have been good for the defense, but West was guessing. He chose the diamond two, hoping his partner held an honor, but was disappointed: South won with the seven. Declarer seized the opportunity to finesse the heart ten, and it was his turn to be disappointed. East won with the jack and shifted to a spade; West's king forcing the ace. A heart was led to the king and ace, leaving this tricky position:

North
♠ Q 9
♥ Q 6
♦ 9
♣ A K Q 8

West
♠ 3
♥ 9
♦ A Q 10 8
♣ 6 5 3

East
♠ J 7 6 2
♥ 7
♦ –
♣ J 9 7 2

South
♠ 10 8
♥ 5
♦ K J 5 3
♣ 10 4

There was a panel of expert commentators explaining the proceedings to a large audience watching in a Vugraph theater. They confidently predicted that South was about to make his three notrump contract. West would return a spade, and South would take dummy's winners. That would leave a three-card ending in which West and South would have nothing but diamonds. South would then lead dummy's diamond nine and score his ninth trick in that suit at the finish.

But the West player, Steve Goldberg of Marietta, Ga., outwitted his opponents and the commentators. He made the strange and unexpected play of cashing the diamond ace before leading his spade three. Dummy won with the queen, and South cashed the two heart tricks.

East was forced to save his four clubs, and he had to come down to one spade winner. South led that suit, attempting to endplay the East player, Lou Bluhm of Atlanta. But East found the right counter. He returned the club jack, and South had to choose between allowing West to take the last trick with a diamond or East to take the last trick with the club nine.

South was left to reflect that he could have made a more successful decision in the bidding. If he had made a penalty pass when his partner doubled one diamond, he would have defeated West by two or three tricks, collecting 500 or 800 points. This penalty pass is not used enough. It has the advantage that the score is quite small if the contract succeeds, and if that is the case the doubling side may be due for a minus score in any event.

Takeout doubles occur in many situations, and it is vital to know when they apply. They are always doubles of suit contracts below the game level. Doubles of notrump are for penalty and do not ask partner to bid. If partner has already acted, a double is usually for penalty. One important exception occurs when the opponents have raised a suit. Another is the negative double. (See page 130.)

Penalty doubles are indicated at a low level when the opponents do not seem to have a good fit and your side has most of the high cards points. At a high level, double in a competitive auction when in doubt. The opponents are probably saving, i.e., overbidding to prevent you from making your contract. They expect to be doubled, so do not disappoint them.

CHAPTER 3

A Yachtsman Goes on a Cruise

It began with whist, a servants' game that moved upstairs to entertain the aristocracy. Perhaps the children learned it from the maids. It then became bridge, the prototype game. The third step was auction bridge, and the fourth was not long in coming.

In 1912, just as Patton and McCampbell were thinking about takeout doubles, four British officials serving the British Raj in India had an interesting thought. One was Hugh Clayton, who later became a member of the Indian Council of State and was knighted. He and his three friends developed SACC, using their initials to name their new game. It encouraged players to bid to the level their hands warranted by giving bonuses for a game, a five-level effort (demislam), a small slam, and a grand slam. Penalties were heavy, to discourage sacrificing, which was then called flag-flying.

This did not attract much attention, although a letter from Clayton to *The London Times* appeared in 1914. A few years later, as World War I came to an end in 1918, French players adopted the same principle, apparently independently. Bidders were encouraged by the scoring table to climb to their *plafond*, or ceiling. The English name was *contract*. In *Ashenden*, Somerset Maugham's semifictional recollections of wartime spying for Britain in Switzerland, he reported playing "contract, a game with which I was not very familiar." He took bridge very seriously, and is unlikely to have distorted his facts.

The steps that led to the game we all play today are almost all obscure, but there is one date that is well documented. It is October 31, 1925, and it saw the birth of contract bridge. (I was just in time for it, but Dorothy missed by three days.)

The place was the *S.S. Finland*, which had been on the front pages of the newspapers 13 years earlier: It had been the floating hotel which carried the highly successful United States contingent to the 1912 Olympic Games in Stockholm.

The ship was in the middle of a cruise from California through the Panama Canal when it reached Balboa. The passengers were not pleased when they were told that could not go ashore for quarantine reasons.

There was a group of four Americans, and one of them suggested playing bridge. His name was Harold Stirling Vanderbilt, scion of a famous family of enormous wealth. (His grandfather, who had Dutch ancestors, was "the Commodore," Cornelius Vanderbilt.) He worked intermittently for the family business, the New York Central Railroad, but he had many other interests.

One of these was yachting. In the next 12 years he led the Americans to victory over the English in the America's Cup three times. He codified the rules of the road for sailing vessels, which are still known as the Vanderbilt Rules. Another interest was auction bridge. His partnership with Waldemar von Zedtwitz was one of the best, and they had many successes in tournaments. But he had heard about *plafond* and other experiments with the idea of bidding hands to the ceiling.

So he developed a scoring table that was almost perfectly balanced. It was so good that only minor modifications have been made in the past 75 years. The one substantial change was intended to discourage sacrifices.

The other three men were delighted, and they played for two nights. Vanderbilt was quite irritated when a young woman insisted on joining the game on the second evening, but she had a contribution to make. She suggested the word "vulnerable" for the state of having a game, with greater penalties in the event of an unsuccessful contract. And we have all been vulnerable ever since.

To celebrate the 40th anniversary of this significant occasion, I wrote about it in my *New York Times* column. It seemed important to include the names of the three companions who played the first game of contract bridge in its modern form, so I did some careful research. In 1929 Vanderbilt dedicated his first book to F. A., F. B. and D. A., and I needed to know for whom the initials stood. The *Finland* had been sent to the scrapheap soon after the cruise, but remarkably, the shipping line still had the passenger lists. Inspecting them, I was able to name Frederic Allen, Francis Bacon and Dudley Pickman. It now occurs to me that I could have saved myself some trouble by telephoning Vanderbilt and asking him the question. He still had five years to live; dying at 86.

When the cruise was over, Vanderbilt circulated his rules to a few friends in Newport and New York City. He had not invented contract bridge, as many have suggested, and he never claimed to have done so. There were several references to an embryonic form of the game in books in the period 1920-22. But he had made it an attractive package. The idea spread like wildfire, and within three years contract-bridge tournaments were being played, pushing auction into the background.

Vanderbilt took three other important steps.

He invented the first bridge system and called it the Club Convention—everyone else called it the Vanderbilt Club. This required an artificial opening bid of one club with virtually all strong hands. He offered the following as an entertaining example of its use:

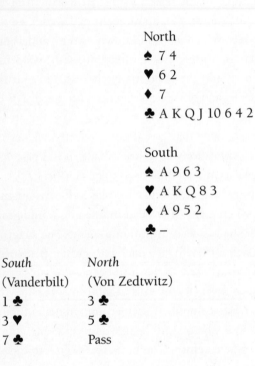

North
♠ 7 4
♥ 6 2
♦ 7
♣ A K Q J 10 6 4 2

South
♠ A 9 6 3
♥ A K Q 8 3
♦ A 9 5 2
♣ —

South	North
(Vanderbilt)	*(Von Zedtwitz)*
1 ♣	3 ♣
3 ♥	5 ♣
7 ♣	Pass

One club was strong, and three clubs showed a solid suit. The jump to five clubs showed extra length, implying at least a seven-card suit. Vanderbilt bid the grand slam with confidence, and many years later asked the question, "How many times, I wonder, in the history of contract bridge, has a player bid a successful grand slam with a void in trumps?"

If this deal were played in a modern pair tournament, few would solve the bidding problem. North might try Blackwood at some point, but would be in trouble if South showed two aces: He would have to worry about two quick losers in spades, or even in hearts.

His second step was to write the first significant book on the game he had devised. It was entitled *Contract Bridge: Bidding and the Club Convention*. Hardly anyone played it, which was a pity. He was ahead of his time, and his idea eventually had many imitators. Most of the world championships of the past 50 years have been won by players using a strong-club system. But as we shall see, the rest of the world was about to head down the wrong track.

Vanderbilt's third step was to inaugurate the Vanderbilt Knockout Team Championship, which has been one of the most coveted titles in the game ever since. At first it was a separate event, but it was eventually merged into the Spring National Championships. Almost all the greatest American players have won it at one time or another. He endowed the competition sufficiently to give each winner, in perpetuity, a silver replica of the trophy, and won it himself on two occasions.

The first victory came in 1932, and had a remarkable denouement.

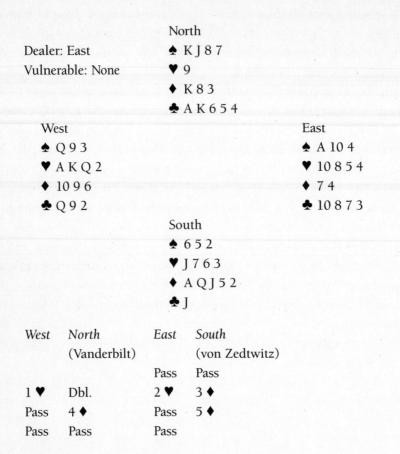

Dealer: East
Vulnerable: None

North
♠ K J 8 7
♥ 9
♦ K 8 3
♣ A K 6 5 4

West
♠ Q 9 3
♥ A K Q 2
♦ 10 9 6
♣ Q 9 2

East
♠ A 10 4
♥ 10 8 5 4
♦ 7 4
♣ 10 8 7 3

South
♠ 6 5 2
♥ J 7 6 3
♦ A Q J 5 2
♣ J

West	North (Vanderbilt)	East	South (von Zedtwitz)
		Pass	Pass
1 ♥	Dbl.	2 ♥	3 ♦
Pass	4 ♦	Pass	5 ♦
Pass	Pass	Pass	

This was the final deal. Holding opening values and length in the unbid suits, Vanderbilt was happy to use the takeout double that Patton and McCampbell had created two decades earlier. His action on the next round was decidedly optimistic. With little in reserve, he should have passed, but he raised to four diamonds. Waldemar Von Zedtwitz carried on to five and was not at all pleased when West led the heart king and the dummy appeared.

West should now have shifted to a trump with decisive effect. Better still, he could have led a trump originally. But he led a spade at the second trick, and there was a long, long pause.

Outside the playing room there was much whispering. The other room had finished play some time earlier, and word came through that "the baron" was in five diamonds. (He had renounced his title, but the bridge world continued to use it.)

The players knew that the championship was on the line, and were sure the contract would fail. Von Zedtwitz was always a slow player, but this time he took a full 20 minutes. He then called for the spade jack, and felt better when East won with the ace.

A heart was returned, and ruffed in dummy. The club ace was cashed, a club was ruffed, and another heart was ruffed in dummy. Another club was ruffed, and trumps were drawn. At the finish, dummy's spade king was the entry for two club winners, and the contract made. Vanderbilt had won his own championship, but he would not have won if the defense had been better. West would have prevailed if he had considered the impending heart ruffs and shifted to a trump at the second trick.

Both of Vanderbilt's Vanderbilt triumphs were with von Zedtwitz, who was a multilingual Renaissance man. At the age of 1 he became a baron after his German father was killed in a yachting accident. His mother was a Caldwell from Kentucky, and his great-grandfather, John C. Breckenridge, was vice president of the United States from 1857 to 1861 and later Confederate secretary of war.

Von Zedtwitz was studying in Germany when World War I began and was drafted into the German Army. After it was over, he had a long but ultimately successful battle to recover his Caldwell inheritance, which had been confiscated because he was an enemy alien. For the next 50 years he lived in New York City, in a Park Avenue apartment with walls adorned with old masters, including a Rembrandt. He used his linguistic talents to work as a lexicographer.

He was involved in bridge in every possible way. He developed the theory of bidding and many of his ideas became standard. He helped Vanderbilt and others devise the laws of the game. (His old friend therefore had a unique distinction: He was a top performer and a major lawmaker in two quite distinct activities, yachting and bridge.) He became president of the American Contract Bridge League, carrying out a major reorganization when that body was in difficulty. In addition, he represented the United States in the councils of the World Bridge Federation.

Von Zedtwitz was a perfectionist, and always a very slow player. I found that to be true when I played with him in the 1960s. And he liked to have something to do while he was thinking. Early in his career he used to pull on an earlobe with his free hand. A doctor said this might induce cancer, so he switched to pulling on a lock of hair. At an international tournament, a Frenchwoman asked her partner, "Should I offer the poor man a bobby pin?" She was highly embarrassed when the baron told her, in perfect French, that he did not think it would be necessary.

In old age his sight failed badly, and he could only see the cards by holding them close to his face. He used a powerful lens, and the cards in the dummy were announced to him. But this did not hamper him. In 1970, at 74, he won the first World Mixed Pairs Championship in Stockholm. His partner was Barbara Brier, and three years later they won another significant title: The Reisinger Knockout Teams in Manhattan, which is almost as old as the Vanderbilt Teams and has always attracted the top players. This was a notable deal from that final:

	North	
Dealer: North	♠ K J 8 4	
Vulnerable: None	♥ K J 3	
	♦ Q 6	
	♣ A 9 5 2	

West		East
♠ 7 6 3		♠ Q 10 9
♥ 10 8 2		♥ 9 7 6
♦ 9 7 3		♦ A J 10 5 4 2
♣ K Q J 10		♣ 4

	South	
	♠ A 5 2	
	♥ A Q 5 4	
	♦ K 8	
	♣ 8 7 6 3	

South	West	North	East
(von Zedtwitz)		(Brier)	
		1 ♣	2 ♦
Dbl.	3 ♦	3 ♠	Pass
3 N.T.	Pass	Pass	Pass

With the passing of the years, the first artificial use of a double, now 60 years old, had been extended in many ways. (See below p. 122.) The most important was the negative double, which called for a double by opener's partner to be for takeout, rather than penalty, when an opening suit bid of one was overcalled with another suit.

Von Zedtwitz was happy to use this when his partner's one-club bid was followed by a weak jump to two diamonds. The double suggests, but does not guarantee in this context, at least four cards in any unbid major. Brier therefore bid her spade suit, but subsided when her partner bid three notrump.

This was the best available game contract, and would have been easy to make if West had held the spade queen. As it was, a diamond lead would have settled matters in favor of the defense. To lead partner's known long suit against notrump was usual practice. But West allowed himself to be seduced by the strength of his clubs into leading the king of that suit.

This gave South a chance, and he seized it. He won the club ace immediately, since holding up would have permitted a shift to diamonds. He led a spade from the dummy, and won with the ace when the ten appeared on his right. The spade jack was finessed, losing to the queen.

East was reluctant to shift to diamonds, since that would have given South a trick in the unlikely event that he held K-x-x. He therefore led a heart, which was won in dummy. South led the diamond queen, which was won with the ace.

East returned the jack, and after winning with the king South cashed all his remaining hearts. This was the position:

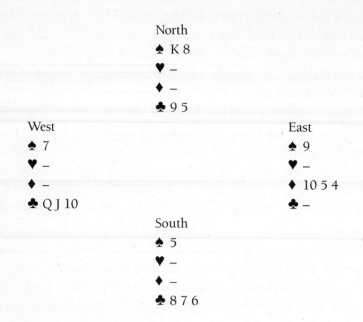

North
♠ K 8
♥ –
♦ –
♣ 9 5

West
♠ 7
♥ –
♦ –
♣ Q J 10

East
♠ 9
♥ –
♦ 10 5 4
♣ –

South
♠ 5
♥ –
♦ –
♣ 8 7 6

Now the baron had to solve the spade position. The eight represented his ninth trick. Should he finesse or not?

As usual, he took his time. There were two approaches.

The first required him to work out the distribution of the spades from the information he had about the other three suits. He was now counting, which is the vital skill that separates the experts from the lesser lights. (See below p. 31.)

He knew that East had begun with exactly three hearts, and the bidding and play made it virtually certain that he had begun with six diamonds. That meant that he had begun with four black cards, and the singleton club was another virtual certainty. West would not have led a three-card club suit in preference to a diamond, and East had failed to return the suit.

He concluded that East's original distribution must have been 3-3-6-1, and von Zedtwitz led confidently to the spade king, collected the nine, and made his game.

In this case the count was clear to the baron. But it is not always so. The declarer's information about the length of the other suits may be insufficient, and in that case he must look for other clues. It was fortunate for him that he did not need one, for the available clue would have pointed in the wrong direction.

The clue is called "restricted choice." (See below p. 34.) This states that a player should be assumed to have had no choice, rather than have exercised a choice in a particular way. So East was much more likely to have begun with Q-10 doubleton of spades rather than have played the ten from Q-10-9. With that holding he might have chosen the nine.

No. 3 ▸ *Counting*

There is one vital skill that separates the expert from the nonexpert. It is called counting, and a player who does not master it can never reach the top levels of the game. This concerns the distribution of the cards around the table, and these mirror the distribution of the hand held by a player. They are simply different ways of dividing 13 cards into four groups, and can be called patterns.

The commonest pattern is 4-4-3-2, which means that a player has two four-card suits, a tripleton and a doubleton. Almost as common are 5-3-3-2 and 4-3-3-3. These hands are "balanced."

There are slightly unbalanced patterns: 5-4-2-2; 4-4-4-1; and 6-3-2-2. More unbalanced are 5-4-3-1; 5-5-2-1; 6-4-2-1; and many others.

These patterns should become old friends. An inexperienced player should think about the pattern whenever he picks up a hand. He should reach the point at which an unfamiliar pattern will cause him to know immediately that he has the wrong number of cards: Somebody has dealt him 12 or 14.

An elementary skill concerns the trump suit. There are three ways to count trumps:

1. Wait until halfway through the deal and start counting. The mental process may be, "There were two rounds of trumps, and somebody did not follow. He trumped once, and I can still see two trumps in my hand and one in the dummy. Take that away from 13, and I may get the number of trumps still in the opposing hands."

And you may not. This is a recipe for disaster, and players who use it often complete a hand without knowing what the trump position was. There are two vastly superior methods.

2. When the dummy appears, count the number of trumps in your hand and the dummy. Subtract from 13 to get the number of trumps the enemy possesses. Five will be the commonest number. Remember that number, and mentally check off the enemy trumps as they appear. At each point you should know how many trumps are still out.

3. Think about the patterns. If you have a 4-4 trump fit, the likely pattern is 4-4-3-2. An odd number of cards usually divide evenly, so 3-2 is what you expect. If someone shows out on the second round, he began with one card and the pattern is 4-4-4-1. The other defender began with four trumps and has two more.

An even number of cards is likely to break unevenly. So six trumps will split 4-2 more often than 3-3, and four trumps tend to be 3-1 rather than 2-2.

These counting methods can be applied equally well to any crucial suit.

The reason you should think about patterns is that it becomes vital when you reach the next and more difficult stage: counting the whole deal.

North
♠ 7 3
♥ K 8 6 5
♦ K Q 8 3
♣ K 7 2

South
♠ A K 5
♥ A Q J 7 2
♦ A
♣ J 10 6 4

North	South
Pass	1 ♥
3 ♥	6 ♥
Pass	

North's jump to three hearts, after an original pass, shows a hand just short of an opening bid. (For a modern way to bid this, see Drury, page 195.) South's leap to six hearts is a reasonable shot.

The spade jack is led, and South can see that he will eventually have a club problem. He will be able to discard two clubs on dummy's diamond winners, but will still, apparently, need to find West with a club honor and guess what to do.

But if South counts carefully he may have an epiphany. He wins with the spade ace, and cashes the ace and queen of hearts. Both opponents follow suit. He takes the diamond ace and the spade king, and then ruffs a spade. To his surprise, East discards a club on the third round of spades, which means that West began with six spades.

Two clubs are thrown on the K-Q of diamonds, and both opponents follow. But when South plays the last diamond from dummy, East throws a club. Now is the time to think.

East began with two spades, two hearts and three diamonds. He must have begun with six clubs, and West therefore with none. West's original distribution must have been 6-2-5-0, and East's 2-2-3-6. Ruffing is hopeless, for East is sure to have the A-Q of clubs. The position before this trick must have been:

North
♠ –
♥ K
♦ 8
♣ K 7 2

West
♠ 10 9 8
♥ –
♦ J 9
♣ –

East
♠ –
♥ –
♦ –
♣ A Q 9 8 5

South
♠ –
♥ J 7 2
♦ –
♣ J 10

Light dawns. If you simply discard a club, West will be trapped. He will have to give you a ruff-and-sluff. Whatever he does, you will ruff in the dummy and discard your last club, making the slam.

That sort of play become routine if you are in the habit of counting all the suits. Sometimes, as here, counting will give a surefire answer. Often it will simply provide a good indication. Most of the time counting will not help, but if you develop the habit you can use the skill when it matters.

Another type of counting concerns high-card points. If the bidding has shown that an opponent has a particular strength, counting will often show that he has, or has not, a crucial card.

No. 4 ▸ *Restricted Choice*

When I started contributing articles to magazines in the early 1950's, I wrote about the following common suit combination:

North
♠ K 10 7 6 2

South
♠ A 5 4 3

If South plays the ace, what should he do next if the queen or jack appears on his right?

Lead another round, and a low card appears on the left. Is this a guess? At that time, players thought so. I pointed out that there are strong reasons to finesse.

One way to think about it is to consider the significant original distributions. If you always finesse, you will succeed whenever your right-hand opponent began with a singleton jack or a singleton queen. Playing the king will only succeed if he started with Q-J doubleton. The odds are roughly two to one in favor of the finesse.

Many players find this confusing. The point to consider is that if East began with the Q-J doubleton, he might have played either card. If he began with a singleton, he had no choice.

This became known as the Principle of Restricted Choice. Always assume that your opponent had no choice, rather than assume that he exercised a choice in a particular way.

Here is a more complicated example.

North
♠ A 8 4 2

South
♠ K Q 3

You start out hoping that the suit divides 3-3, in which case dummy's last card will be a winner when the king, queen and ace have been cashed. But when you play the king and queen, West plays two low cards and East contributes the nine and jack.

You lead the three and West follows low. Should you play the ace? Or should you finesse the eight?

Other things being equal, the odds clearly favor the finesse. If your right-hand opponent began with J-10-9 he could have hung on to the nine, the ten or the jack. If he began with a doubleton (J-10, J-9 or 10-9) he had no choice. The odds are roughly three to one in favor of the finesse.

So make up your mind before you start playing the suit that you intend to finesse if the opportunity arises. You will then win in three doubleton situations, and lose in one tripleton situation. In general, if the fall of the opposing cards opens up a finesse possibility, you should usually take it.

CHAPTER 4

The Great Entrepreneur;
and a Murder

♠ ♥
♦ ♣ Vanderbilt and von Zedtwitz were larger-than-life figures, but the next character in the story was larger still. His name was Ely Culbertson, and Bertrand Russell later described him as "The most remarkable, or at any rate the most psychologically interesting, man it has ever been my good fortune to know . . ."

Culbertson was born in Romania in 1891. He was a trial to his American father, a successful oil prospector, and his Russian mother, daughter of a Cossack general. At the age of 16 he was an enthusiastic revolutionary and under arrest in Sochi, on the Black Sea coast. He played *vint* with a group of condemned men, and was released thanks to his mother's efforts. He was sent to Yale, but quickly wandered off, first to the Bowery, then to Canada, where he led a strike of railroad construction workers. He rode the rails to San Francisco as a hobo, and briefly enrolled at Stanford, reading the works of the Russian anarchists. He became a revolutionary in Mexico, then in Spain, finally reaching Paris and becoming a student of politics and government.

He spent time in Germany, Switzerland and Italy, having many encounters with women, who did not matter to him, and with auction bridge players, who did. He lost money with the first group but balanced his accounts with the second. Through a fluke he had a windfall success at roulette; when he left the table to settle an argument, he won 40,000 francs when his money stayed on the table with repeated good results. When World War I ended he tried London, Berlin, Danzig and Brussels. The Belgians expelled him for being a bridge teacher, and he worked his passage back to New York as an able-bodied seaman. His family was there, but, thanks to the Russian Revolution, there was no money.

So he played bridge, working his way up to the five-cent game at the Knickerbocker Whist Club, where he developed a scientific approach to the game. There he met Josephine Murphy Dillon, who was beautiful and talented. He persuaded "Jo" to adopt his system and eventually to marry him. Lacking money in in New York, they ventured to Hollywood and won $6,000 in a set game against the owner of a casino. And in 1927, in Santa Barbara, he met his destiny: contract bridge.

Back in New York, still with no money, he presented some potential backers with his grand plan to create "Ely the Celebrity." Using the emotive language of the movie industry, he would project himself to the public in every possible way as the great authority on the new game. The backers balked, but he went ahead anyway. Jo would provide romantic appeal.

His first move was to start a magazine, and the first issue of *The Bridge World* appeared in October 1929. That was the month of the Great Crash on Wall Street, but, surprisingly, it did not slow him down. He stirred up controversy by attacking Wilbur Whitehead and Milton C. Work, his main rivals for the ear of the bridge public.

He recruited an impressive stable of contributing editors, including Sidney Lenz and Theodore Lightner, and stated the aims of the magazine, "*The Bridge World* tells you how to win. It gives you a cross-section of the minds of the masters who do not lose. It gives you the best methods." (See below p. 41.)

It also gave the best gossip. The second issue carried the news of the first (and last so far as we know) bridge-table murder. It occurred in Kansas City, Mo., where a young perfume salesman named John Bennett lived with his wife, Myrtle. On September 29, 1929, they planned to go to the movies with their neighbors, Charles and Myrna Hoffman but, facing bad weather, decided to play bridge instead.

As married couples sometimes do, the Bennetts became quite upset with each other. She raised an opening bid of one spade to four spades with a hand that justified only two spades. When he duly failed, she called him a "bum bridge player" and he slapped her. She left the room, and he suggested that the Hoffmans leave. They hesitated, perhaps because they had not yet collected their large winnings at a tiny stake.

Myrtle reappeared carrying her mother's loaded gun, and John quickly locked himself in a handy bathroom. This proved insufficient protection, for she got off two effective shots. He staggered out, and she fired two more shots.

He slumped into a chair, muttering as he died, "She got me." The police found her bent over the body, sobbing wildly, and took her to jail.

Culbertson produced a deal and demonstrated that John could have made four spades and saved his life by skillful play. But it was total fiction. Not surprisingly, none of the three surviving players could remember the details. At the trial 17 months later, Myrtle was defended by Senator James A. Reed. Weeping copious tears, she explained that John had intended to go to St. Joseph. Mo., the next morning, and she had brought the gun down so that he could pack it. She stumbled over a chair, and the gun fired twice. Two more shots went off when he fell forward, twisting her arm.

This did not explain the bathroom door, and it was fortunate for her that her first and conflicting statement to the police was excluded by the judge. The jury deliberated for eight hours, partly because they insisted on learning how to play bridge, and finally acquitted her. They had perhaps decided that John was indeed a bum bridge player and deserved what he got. She is said to have collected a large sum of money from a dazed life insurance company. Alexander Woollcott, who described the episode in *While Rome Burns,* claims that she eventually found a partner who did not know her story. When he put down an inadequate dummy and announced, "Partner, you'll probably want to shoot me for this," she fainted.

Mrs. Bennett faded from history, her role ended, but Culbertson was just getting started. He had two aims for 1930 and managed to combine them. One was to write a major book on bidding, *The Blue Book,* and the other was to play a challenge match in England. An English bridge expert, Lt. Col. Walter Buller, had asserted that a good English team would beat any American team "sky-high." Culbertson offered to bring a team at his own expense, and play a 300-board match at Portland Club rules for any stake Colonel Buller should choose.

Jo was furious, since they had no money at all. Ely had to play rubber bridge to raise cash to pay *The Bridge World* staff. How would they pay for the trip? And what if they lost? He claimed that he had formed a syndicate to back the team, and that their teammates, Lightner and von Zedtwitz, would pay their own way. He would raise money from the sale of *The Blue Book,* of which not a word had yet been written.

The May issue of *The Bridge World* offered readers *The Blue Book* at a bargain price of $1.50. Money poured in, and he set up a publishing company. He made a deal with the French Line to provide tournaments and lecturers on every trans-Atlantic voyage. This was worth $1,000 a month. The Culbertson team won a major tournament in Asbury Park, N.J., in July, but in mid-August he still had not written a word.

The forthcoming match was attracting attention. The Thomas Cook travel company, somewhat confused, suggested their branches arrange transportation for bridge-builders and architects for the forthcoming international bridge congress in London.

At last Ely began dictating, 18 hours a day, to a relay of three secretaries. After one chapter, however, he was rushed to hospital with a recurrence of an old stomach ulcer problem. After surgery, he continued dictating. Jo checked everything and supervised the proofs. He finished dictating in the taxi en route to the ship.

As the gangplank was lowered, his publisher shouted from the dockside, "How about the dedication?"

"To my wife and favorite partner," bellowed Ely.

There were 4,000 advance orders, and the print order was 6,000. They were all due for a surprise.

In London, Ely was asked what chance the English had. "Not a chance in the world," he told the reporters. "They're lousy players."

He had no idea, of course, because he had never seen his opponents play. But it was all good publicity.

Ely had brought a set of duplicate boards, but the hosts did not like them. They insisted on dealing, playing, recording, and using envelopes to pass the cards to the other room. This slowed things down, and a planned five days for 200 boards stretched to seven.

After the first day's play the English led narrowly, but they were destroyed on the second day. On what they called "Black Tuesday" they lost nearly 4,000 points. Buller suffered this disaster:

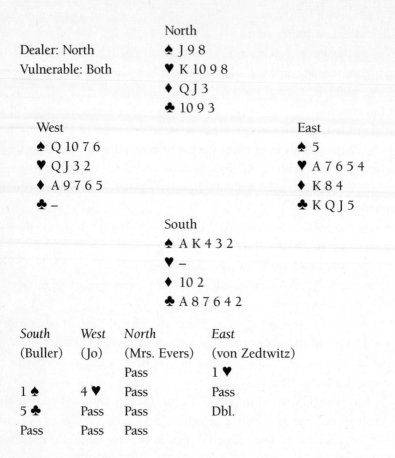

Dealer: North
Vulnerable: Both

North
♠ J 9 8
♥ K 10 9 8
♦ Q J 3
♣ 10 9 3

West
♠ Q 10 7 6
♥ Q J 3 2
♦ A 9 7 6 5
♣ –

East
♠ 5
♥ A 7 6 5 4
♦ K 8 4
♣ K Q J 5

South
♠ A K 4 3 2
♥ –
♦ 10 2
♣ A 8 7 6 4 2

South	West	North	East
(Buller)	(Jo)	(Mrs. Evers)	(von Zedtwitz)
		Pass	1 ♥
1 ♠	4 ♥	Pass	Pass
5 ♣	Pass	Pass	Dbl.
Pass	Pass	Pass	

The result was down four, for a penalty of 1400 according to the scoring table then in use. This was a phantom save, since in four hearts East would have lost a spade trick, a diamond trick and two trump tricks. (Unless South foolishly led the club ace.)

Buller explained that he was sure that four hearts would make and he was trying to recoup after several bad results. This showed a total misunderstanding of match strategy. There were still 150 boards to be played, and it was no time to panic.

Buller's methods did not include any forcing bids, and as a consequence of this his teammates played an easy slam in a part-score. Both teams bid a grand slam missing a cashing ace, but the English succeeded thanks to a misguessed lead. Nevertheless, the final score in favor of the visitors was 4,445 total points.

The English generally agreed that the American bidding methods were superior, although Buller insisted that he had been unlucky. An English critic, pushing his own methods, subsequently pointed out that the Americans had missed 30 game contracts and 11 slams. He also counted 31 instances in which Ely broke the rules he had laid down in *The Blue Book*.

In talking to the press, Jo maintained that the average woman was better than the average man. "Why? Simply because a man is all vanity. He knows so much that he will not bother to learn or study. He takes things for granted, and there is next to nothing you can take for granted at the bridge table."

In America, bridge was popular because women could play on equal terms with men. The game, she suggested, taught patience, fortitude, courage and the ability to make decisions quickly and accurately. She was a superb spokesperson for the game.

Before they left there was news from New York about *The Blue Book*. "Success enormous. You are rich."

Ely the Celebrity had arrived.

No. 5 ▸ *The Culbertson System*

The nucleus of the Culbertson System was the one-over-one forcing response to an opening bid of a suit. Almost all of it is familiar to modern players:

1. A one-over-one suit response had a wide range and was forcing for one round.

2. A single raise of opener's suit showed moderate strength and at least Q-x-x in the trump suit.

3. A double raise was practically forcing, leaving partner the option of passing with an absolute minimum hand.

4. A one-notrump response showed a weak hand, and might have trump support.

5. A two-notrump response was strongly invitational.

6. The rebids after a one-over-one response were much as those used today: single jumps invitational unless in a new suit.

All this seems very reasonable to a modern bidder. *But:*

1. A two-over-one response was not forcing and suggested a final contract. (Six years later the system apparently changed, but there was confusion. Whether a response at the two-level was or was not forcing was undisclosed.)

2. Opening bids could be quite weak. A flat hand with A-Q-x-x in one suit and an ace in another was acceptable because it had two and a half honor tricks. (See below, page 50.)

CHAPTER 5

The First Feud

Culbertson had won his international challenge match, admittedly against weak opponents who thought that simple, natural methods were all that the game required. He had a successful magazine, a best-selling book and a national reputation. He needed to build on the momentum, and he did it with successful marketing techniques and an understanding of mass psychology.

He set up a bridge laboratory with analysts ready to answer letters and look for possible improvements in the System. More important, he established the Culbertson National Studios, with a chain of teachers. They were usually intelligent women, often wives of doctors and lawyers, who were prominent in their communities. He himself was a first-rate lecturer.

Within a few months the statistics were amazing. *The Bridge World's* circulation was 40,000. Market researchers estimated that there were 20 million players in the country, and that 84 percent of them played the Culbertson System.

In his path stood a group of established authorities who had made their reputations in the days of auction bridge and its predecessor game. Their leader was the veteran Milton C. Work, who had initiated the first game of duplicate bridge in North America 35 years earlier. In 1929 he had rushed into print with a book, *Contract Bridge for All,* at the same time as Vanderbilt's effort and a year before *The Blue Book.* Work sneered at the use of forcing bids, and allowed for only one: a jump from one notrump, which was a minimum opening, to three of a suit. But in some respects, as we shall see, he was ahead of Culbertson.

In July 1931, Work joined with a group of other well-known figures, including Wilbur Whitehead, Sidney Lenz, George Reith and E. V. Shepard, to establish the Official System. They had all made their names before contract bridge was introduced. (See below p. 50.)

Whitehead had given the Culbertsons a great deal of help in their days of poverty, and Lenz was Jo's first teacher. But some response was needed, and Ely took the initiative. He announced in *The New York Herald Tribune* that he had placed $10,000 in escrow as his stake in a challenge match against any four members of the Official Group. They would only have to put up $1,000. Alternatively, he would play against two of them, staking $5,000 to $1,000. When this got no response, he offered to play against Lenz and any partner he chose, with the winnings going to charity.

He then took Jo on a two-month trip to Europe. It was a whirlwind vacation, which took them to Paris, Italy, Poland, the Ukraine and the Caucasus. He found an old aunt living in poverty, and she refused his offer to take her to America. Finally they arrived in Moscow, and he had a surprise. When he offered to promote bridge in the Soviet Union the reply from the director of the Card Trust was, "Our aim is not to sell as many cards as possible, but as few as we can. Cards remind our workers of the old days of kings and queens and bourgeois society."

Back in New York, he continued to maneuver for a challenge match. He had chosen an opponent with a remarkable history. Sidney Lenz was born in Chicago, but spent his childhood in Vienna. By the time he was 27 he had made a fortune in the timber business and devoted himself to a wide range of activities. He had spent a year in India studying Oriental philosophy and Hindu magic. He was a highly skilled card manipulator, and the first amateur to be elected a member of the American Society of Magicians. He was a scratch golfer, who shot his age when he was 69. He played tennis on even terms with top professionals. He once held a national record at lawn bowls, was a table-tennis champion, and played chess with the world champion José Capablanca.

Many thought him the best auction-bridge player, and he was a prolific writer on the game. He coined the term "squeeze," borrowing it from baseball, and originated many standard plays. Later in life, he was known as the Grand Old Man of Bridge.

After much goading by Culbertson, he finally accepted the challenge, choosing as his partner a man of great talent who was 29 years his junior. Oswald Jacoby was born in Brooklyn and served in the closing stages of World War I. He studied briefly at Columbia University and at 21 was a qualified actuary, the youngest person ever to pass the rigorous examinations. He had a string of bridge successes, at auction and contract, including the first Goldman Pairs in Manhattan in 1929. He was at the start of one the greatest careers in the game.

Jacoby's weakness, in the view of some critics, was a penchant for psychic bids, bluffs that were liable to give trouble to partners as well as opponents. The term had been invented by Dorothy Rice Sims as a result of a deal on which she opened one club holding 5–5 in the major suits. She wanted to call it a "psychological" bid, but her spelling could only manage "sycic."

The prematch publicity was extraordinary. Culbertson virtually guaranteed extensive and favorable coverage by giving lessons himself to a group of media moguls, including the president of the Bell newspaper syndicate. He and Jo were portrayed as the young couple doing battle with the jealous Old Guard, even though Jacoby was the youngest player. Celebrities lined up to be allowed a 15-minute glimpse of the play in the Chatham Hotel.

It all began on December 7, a date that would later be famous for other reasons. After a sumptuous dinner, play began at 10 p.m., two hours late. Lenz and Jacoby were blessed with all the high cards and won the first rubber in spite of this deal:

	North	
Dealer: East	♠ Q J	
Vulnerable: North-South	♥ K 2	
	♦ K 8 7	
	♣ K Q 7 6 5 3	

West		East
♠ 10 7 2		♠ K 9 8 5 4 3
♥ J 10 8 7 6 5		♥ 9 4 3
♦ J		♦ 5 4
♣ A J 2		♣ 10 8

	South	
	♠ A 6	
	♥ A Q	
	♦ A Q 10 9 6 3 2	
	♣ 9 4	

It can be seen that six diamonds by South is a virtual certainty. However, the bidding was:

West	North	East	South
(Jo)	(Jacoby)	(Ely)	(Lenz)
		Pass	2 ♦
Pass	3 ♣	Pass	3 N.T.
Pass	4 N.T.	Pass	Pass
Pass			

Jacoby was surprised by the pass of four no-trump. He might have bid six notrump, which would have been successful. At any rate, one would think that this deal would end the rubber.

But when the dummy appeared, Lenz noted that six diamonds would have been highly desirable. He now had diamonds in his head and forgot that he was actually playing in notrump. The result was that instead of making 12 tricks he won 8 and the rubber went on. I eventually asked the North player what had caused this remarkable lapse at the start of a match that was being reported on front pages of every newspaper in the country.

"He was drunk," snarled Jacoby, still irritated half a century later. So the sumptuous prematch banquet, planned by Culbertson, had had an impact. This episode was the main reason the wire services reported that the first rubber featured some of the worst bridge ever played by experts. Soon after, Jo led out of turn and presented her opponents with a small slam.

Lenz and Jacoby had practiced in preparation, but had never played together in competition. This was a substantial disadvantage. The older man had a passion for playing in notrump, which was the normal strategy in auction bridge.

Jacoby arrived late on one occasion, having been bitten by a dog he had attempted to rescue. Ely annoyed both Lenz and Jo by arriving late for almost every session and then ordering a steak to eat at the table. In a modern setting, the conditions of contest would have provided penalties for late arrival. The tournament director was Alfred Maximilian Gruenther, a uniformed Army officer who lectured at West Point and was later to become famous for other reasons. He should surely have issued a warning for the first late arrival and announced penalties for future sessions.

After four sessions, Lenz and Jacoby led by 5,650 total points. But when Jo took time off at Christmas to shop and be with the children, the tide turned. Lightner took her place and held a series of big hands. Culbertson took the lead and never relinquished it.

The most controversial deal of all was this one:

                                    North
Dealer: South   ♠ A Q 10 3
Vulnerable: Both   ♥ A
                                   ♦ A Q 9 7
                                   ♣ A 7 5 2

West   East
♠ 9 8 5   ♠ 6 2
♥ K 6   ♥ 10 3 2
♦ 5 4 3 2   ♦ K J 10 8 6
♣ K J 9 8   ♣ Q 10 3

                                    South
                                   ♠ K J 7 4
                                   ♥ Q J 9 8 7 5 4
                                   ♦ –
                                   ♣ 6 4

South	West	North	East
(Jacoby)	(Ely)	(Lenz)	(Lightner)
1 ♥	Pass	3 N.T.	Pass
4 ♥	Pass	4 N.T.	Pass
5 ♥	Pass	6 N.T.	Pass
Pass	Dbl.	Pass	Pass
7 ♥	Dbl.	Pass	Pass
Pass			

Jacoby thought of opening four hearts but did not wish to miss a spade fit. However, his decision to bid a semipsychic one heart did not, as it turned out, prevent that outcome.

Lenz was now in trouble because of the Milton Work theory: No response to one of a suit is forcing, not even a jump shift. In that light, his jump to three notrump, which appears ridiculous, is understandable.

Jacoby thought he was ending the bidding with four hearts, but he did not bargain for Lenz's notrump addiction. The chance of scoring 150 for aces was irresistible and he persevered with four notrump. Five hearts was bid in the hope of buying the contract, but Lenz was unstoppable. To his partner's fury, he went on to slam. Six hearts would have been just fine, but he bid six notrump.

Culbertson was proud of his double, which aimed to push Jacoby into seven hearts. It succeeded, and the contract failed by one trick.

What would have happened if the bidding had ended in six notrump, doubled or undoubled? We shall never know, for everything would have hinged on the opening lead. With little to guide him, Lightner would have had to lead a club to beat the contract. After anything else, Lenz would have been able to establish and use dummy's hearts, with two entries available in spades. Lightner had not yet invented his slam double, which will be discussed later, and even if he had it would not have helped him. It would, however, have prevented his partner from doubling six notrump.

And it did not occur to anyone that seven spades would have been unbeatable. That was the suit that neither player had managed to show, although Jacoby had had no real opportunity to do so.

This is one of the few deals from the match that can be considered a system triumph. A Culbertson partnership would have been able, in response to one heart, to bid one spade, a one-round force, or two spades, a strong jump shift.

Culbertson continued to be irritating. At times he played very slowly, sending Lenz to sleep, and when he was dummy he rushed off to chat in the press room. Gruenther was regularly dispatched to bring him back.

Lenz accused Culbertson of failing to follow his own system, bringing this heated reply: "Why don't you read my *Blue Book*? Every sucker in the country has read it except you."

"I haven't," came a voice from a kibitzing chair, dissolving the tension. It was Chico Marx, always ready to entertain.

Play moved to the Waldorf Hotel, where Culbertson came close to fighting with a large, aggressive Englishman, Sir Derrick Wernher. Meanwhile Lenz, who was clearly responsible for many of the difficulties of his partnership, took to criticizing his partner publicly. Eventually Jacoby could stand it no longer. He withdrew from the match, sending a graceful letter citing radically distinct differences of bridge method. He thanked Lenz for the high honor he had done him by selecting him as a partner, and praised Culbertson as one of the truly great practical and analytical players in the world.

Jacoby was replaced by Cmdr. Winfield Liggett, a World War I veteran. He was a good player, though not in Jacoby's class. The Culbertson lead climbed to over 20,000, but then Lenz and Commander Liggett held phenomenal cards, and the final margin was 8,980.

Culbertson was satisfied. His name had been on the front pages of the newspapers for a month. He was now broke again, because he rented space for the match and fed lines of spectators and newspapermen. But the money rolled in. In one day, orders came in for 5,000 copies of *The Blue Book* and 11,000 copies of his *Contract Bridge Summary*. These two books were the best sellers, both fiction and nonfiction, for the whole of 1931.

Culbertson became so famous that he was asked to do endorsements. With Wrigley as a sponsor, he made a profitable series of radio broadcasts about bridge. Chesterfield cigarettes distributed small booklets on bridge in their packets, and paid $10,000 for the privilege of using the Culbertson names. He and Jo were summoned to Hollywood and paid $270,000 for making six short movies. He lectured to 3,000 at the Oakland Auditorium.

Ely the Celebrity was now a household word. He had an instinctive feel for advertising and self-promotion. When a New York newspaper asked its readers to choose "the world's biggest bore," he asked his army of bridge teachers to vote for him and won easily.

Culbertson had achieved an astonishing feat. In a period of two years, he had persuaded millions that it was socially unacceptable *not* to play bridge. Several times each week couples would sit down with their neighbors—like the Bennetts and the Hoffmans, but with less melodramatic results—to enjoy themselves at the card tables. It was an ideal occupation for married couples during the Depression, when there was no television and money was short for restaurants and theaters.

No. 6 ▸ *Differences Between the Culbertson and Official Systems*

CULBERTSON		OFFICIAL
1. Valuation		Point count for notrump
Honor tricks		Ace 4
K-x or Q-J-x	half	King 3
A or K-Q	one	Queen 2
A-Q	one and a half	
A-K	two	
A vague system that was difficult for ordinary players.		Jack 1 Two tens 1 (Devised by Milton Work)
2. Opening two-bids Forcing two. All openings of two in a suit promise a game, with two notrump as a negative response.		Two clubs on any game-forcing hand, with two diamonds as the negative response. Other two bids strong, with a strong suit (the forerunner of the Acol two-bid).
3. Forcing bids in general One-over-one by responder forcing. (Whether Culbertson originated this is unclear.)		Adopted the Culbertson method, with one-over-one forcing.
4. One notrump opening bid To be avoided. If used, Not vulnerable: minimum hand Vulnerable: 4 honor tricks		12–15 points

CULBERTSON	OFFICIAL
5. Opening three-bids	Very strong.
Strong. Seven or 8 winners	
not vulnerable, 8 winners	
if vulnerable. Between 2	
and 3 honor tricks. In a	
minor, long and solid with	
queens and jacks outside.	

With hindsight, the Official System theorists were generally right and Culbertson was generally wrong, but Culbertson had the ear of the public.

There was no slam bidding machinery in either method, and the results were pathetic. Culbertson was slightly better off because he had forcing bids available and could "approach" slowly.

So in two important areas, valuation and the opening bid with game-going hands, the verdict of history has favored Culbertson's rivals. But nobody read their book.

CHAPTER 6

Slams

Culbertson was now the king of the bridge world, not to mention *The Bridge World* magazine, and his subjects were eager to listen to any words of wisdom that fell from the royal lips. They had already accepted his method of valuation by honor tricks, which was confusing and inaccurate. An A-K combination was worth 2, but the same cards in opposite hands were worth 1½. There was no constant total of honor tricks in the deck. It took 20 years for the public to switch to the simple and superior 4-3-2-1 count devised by Milton Work and recommended by the Official System.

Now Culbertson wanted to improve his methods of slam bidding. He was fully aware that his bidding at the six- and seven-level, both in England and in the Lenz match, had been decidedly inferior. He therefore invented the Culbertson Four-Five Notrump, which was quite complicated. After a suit was agreed, a four notrump bid showed either three aces, or two aces and the king of a bid suit. There was an array of responses, with five no-trump promising two aces or all the bid kings. The idea of using four notrump, a bid not normally needed, for conventional purposes was significant and was to have a sequel.

The American public was not enthusiastic, but there were two strong reactions in England. First, the Portland Club in London, which prepared and issued the laws of the game, declared that the convention was illegal. It was tantamount, said the lawmakers, to taking a card, or cards, out of your hand and showing it to partner. Culbertson and the Americans rejected this hotly, and their position eventually prevailed. This was just as well, for the Portland rule would have stifled the development of bidding for the rest of the century.

Second, most of the top British players, spurning the pooh-bahs of the

Portland, adopted the four-five notrump convention, and played it for a quarter of a century or more. I played it in the fifties, and looked down on the lesser players who used "Blackwood."

Easley Blackwood was an insurance executive in Indianapolis who was a bridge enthusiast. He wrote several books and a column, and late in life became the executive secretary of the American Contract Bridge League. His name is known worldwide because of a thought he had in 1933. He suggested that a bid of four notrump should simply ask partner how many aces he holds, with responses on a step system. (See below p. 58.)

Blackwood wrote a letter to *The Bridge World* accompanied by an article describing his slam convention. He received a polite reply from the editor, which still survives, explaining that the public would not be interested in this strange idea and everyone preferred the Culbertson Four-Five Notrump. In hindsight, this was about on a par with President Cleveland, who, on being shown an early telephone, called it a nice toy, but said, "Nobody would want to own one."

Few players would consider the possibility of using Blackwood on the following deal:

```
                          North
Dealer: South.            ♠ —
Vulnerable: Both          ♥ A K Q J 10 6 4 3
                          ♦ 8 7 2
                          ♣ Q 8
        West                              East
        ♠ 9 2                             ♠ 8 7 5
        ♥ 9 8 7 2                         ♥ 5
        ♦ J 10 9 6 5 4 3                  ♦ —
        ♣ —                               ♣ J 10 9 7 6 5 4 3 2
                          South
                          ♠ A K Q J 10 6 4 3
                          ♥ —
                          ♦ A K Q
                          ♣ A K
```

South	*West*	*North*	*East*
7 ♠	Pass	Pass	Pass

To pick up the hand of a lifetime and wind up with a minus score is a deflating experience for anyone, but the ignominy increases substantially if partner is able to point out that a slightly more thoughtful approach would have left the partnership better off to the extent of about 2,700 points.

This deal was played many years ago in a duplicate game in Asheville, N.C., and recorded for posterity by J. D. Vanderwart of that city. The South player was noted for making abrupt decisions, and opened the bidding confidently with seven spades.

He enjoyed the stunned silence that ensued around the table, but his enjoyment faded rapidly when everyone passed and West led the diamond jack. East ruffed and returned a club, and by the time the smoke had cleared the defense had taken the first five tricks for a penalty of 500.

One would sympathize with South's opening bid at rubber bridge, for it seems quite reasonable, even if disastrous in the outcome, to try for 150 honors as well as the grand slam. But this was duplicate, so the honors did not count, and there was a positive advantage in playing in seven notrump, for the extra ten points, if North held the heart ace.

If an opening four notrump is Blackwood, that bid could be used effectively here. But the traditional meaning is a balanced hand and about 28 high-card points, and there are other possible interpretations. So the safest procedure for South is to make a forcing opening and bid Blackwood eventually, ignoring the guideline that frowns on the use of that convention when holding a void.

"Why didn't you bid seven notrump?" demanded South in the postmortem, seeking to shift responsibility for the disaster.

"Because you might have had two voids," retorted North. "You can think yourself lucky that the ruffs did not cost you anything. Since everyone else bid and made seven notrump, we'd have had the same bottom if you had made seven spades."

Culbertson, who prided himself on his understanding of mass psychology, did not appreciate that a vast majority of his readers were ordinary folk who wanted simplicity. Like the Bennetts, they wanted to have a little fun with the neighbors and were not interested in sophisticated scientific bidding. So they were not in the least interested in the Master's next offering: Asking Bids. (See below p. 60.)

The idea was that, after suit agreement, a new-suit bid should ask about partner's holding in that suit. There was a complex series of responses, indicating controls in other suits when the responder had something useful in the asked suit. This concept was explained at length in the 1936 *Gold Book,* which covered bidding and play, but readers yawned. There was more interest in Europe, Australia and South Africa. I was an asking-bid enthusiast a decade after the idea was born.

There were two other ideas that were more popular because they were simpler. One was the Five Notrump Grand Slam Force. (See below p. 60.) The other was the Lightner Slam Double. Theodore Lightner, who was one of Culbertson's regular partners on major occasions, had a brilliant conception. He argued that a double of a freely bid slam should request an unusual lead. The leader should consider dummy's suit, or a suit in which he has considerable length in the light of the bidding. The doubler will often have a void and be looking for a quick ruff. This could frequently defeat a slam that was otherwise due to succeed.

A normal penalty double of a slam is mathematically unsound: It aims for a small profit and risks a large loss, since the opponents may redouble. So a secondary advantage of the Lightner Double was that it prevented partners from being foolishly greedy.

The Lightner Double is of course a warning to the opponents, who can occasionally beat a retreat to a safer spot. This opened the door to an extraordinary double cross on the following deal.

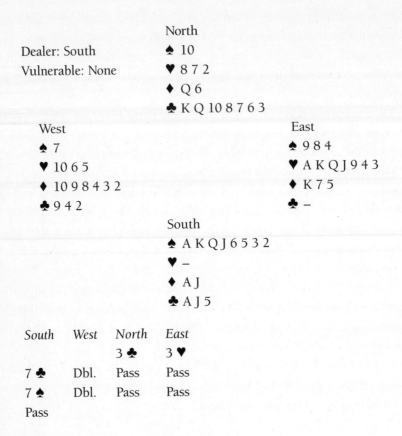

North
Dealer: South   ♠ 10
Vulnerable: None   ♥ 8 7 2
                         ♦ Q 6
                         ♣ K Q 10 8 7 6 3

West   East
♠ 7   ♠ 9 8 4
♥ 10 6 5   ♥ A K Q J 9 4 3
♦ 10 9 8 4 3 2   ♦ K 7 5
♣ 9 4 2   ♣ –

                         South
                         ♠ A K Q J 6 5 3 2
                         ♥ –
                         ♦ A J
                         ♣ A J 5

South	West	North	East
		3 ♣	3 ♥
7 ♣	Dbl.	Pass	Pass
7 ♠	Dbl.	Pass	Pass
Pass			

This occurred in the Reisinger Knockout Teams in New York in 1983, and
the hero in the West seat was John Lowenthal, a player noted for his bursts of
creative imagination. It was no surprise to him that his opponents bid a slam,
but it was a shock to find them at the seven-level before he had a chance to
pass. An opening three-club bid had been raised to a grand slam after East had
bid hearts.

Lowenthal never liked to pass, and after a little thought he came forth with
a double. It might seem that he had no hope of defeating the contract, and
indeed he had not. But he had worked out the likely layout of the cards around
the table and had a subtle thought.

To justify his bid, South had to have some good club support, presumably
three cards, and all the other suits controlled. Somebody had to have spades,

and there was good reason to think that South held length and strength, offering the prospect of discards. And it was highly probable that North-South had ten clubs between them, leaving East with a void.

When the double came around to South, he thought what Lowenthal hoped he would think. The double was a Lightner action, asking for an unusual lead. West must be void in spades, and was trying to encourage his partner to find a lead in that suit for the decisive ruff.

Not knowing that West had come up with a psychic Lightner double, South beat a retreat, not unnaturally, to seven spades. Lowenthal doubled again, putting great faith in his analysis of the situation. He then led a club.

South was a large, aggressive character. He put his cards face up on the table and glared at East. Snarling, he said: "If you're going to ruff this, I'm going to kick you."

East was small and nervous, with a strong sense of self-preservation. He produced a trump to beat the grand slam, got up from the table and set off at a great pace for the horizon.

Unfortunately, the first use of this slam double in the Culbertson-Lightner partnership happened to have a disastrous result, and Ely indignantly refused to have anything more to do with it. This slowed the spread of an excellent idea, but it is now used universally. It is one of the two significant conventions (the Grand Slam Force is the other) to survive from the Culbertson group, and the Master was against it: It did not appear in *The Blue Book* or *The Gold Book*.

From this point on, Culbertson paid little attention to the vast business he had established, which included a national organization competing with the American Contract Bridge League. He had the knack of recruiting talented lieutenants, and four of them made a mark on the game. One was Albert Morehead, his chief of staff, who organized Culbertson books, wrote *The New York Times* column for 30 years, and produced dictionaries late in life. Another was Alphonse Moyse Jr., who edited *The Bridge World* and was famous for his advocacy of the 4-3 trump fit. A third was Alfred Sheinwold, who wrote the Culbertson newspaper columns and eventually had a syndicated column of his own. And the fourth was Alexander Sobel, who became the country's top tournament director. A curious outcome was that Culbertson could shout "Al" and any one of the four could come running.

No. 7 ▸ *The Blackwood Convention*

The Blackwood convention began as something quite simple, which appealed to the average player. When four notrump was bid artificially, the usual responses were by steps:

RESPONSE	MEANING
Five clubs	No ace
Five diamonds	One ace
Five hearts	Two aces
Five spades	Three aces

This was easy enough, but there were some tricks to remember, and still are:

1. Five clubs was the response used in the wildly unlikely event that the responder held four aces. That would mean that the Blackwood bidder was trying for a slam with an aceless hand. It was assumed that the four notrump bidder would be able to tell, from his hand and the previous bidding, whether he was facing no ace or four aces. (That assumption was not totally valid. See below, pages 177–178.)

2. Blackwood was not advisable with two quick losers in any side suit. Nor was it appropriate with a void suit, because the ace of that suit in partner's hand would not be helpful. For a strange exception to the second of these guidelines, see page 56 above.

3. If the responder held a void, he had a difficult problem. Counting it is as an ace could lead to disaster. The following consensus gradually developed: bid five clubs with a void and no ace; bid five notrump with a void and two aces; bid six of a suit below the trump suit with that void and one ace; bid six of the agreed trump suit with one ace and a higher-ranking void.

4. Blackwood had to be used carefully if intending to play in clubs. Making the bid with one ace would lead to disaster if partner bid five diamonds, showing that he also had one ace.

5. Blackwood followed by five notrump asked for kings on the same principle. This showed interest in a grand slam and guaranteed that the partnership possessed all the aces. The responder might choose to bid seven himself holding a long running suit or some other appropriate hand.

6. A complication is that four notrump is not always an artificial request for aces. If there has been no natural suit bid, and sometimes if there has been one, the bid is a natural invitation to six notrump. A raise of one notrump or two notrump to four notrump is natural, and in such positions Gerber is available: Four clubs asks for aces on the Blackwood principle.

7. This original version of Blackwood is still widely used. But modern experts have introduced a different version. It is called Roman Keycard Blackwood, usually shortened to RKCB or RKC. The king of the agreed trump suit is considered the equivalent of an ace, and there are thus five key cards. The responses to four notrump are:

RESPONSE	KEY CARD
Five clubs	Zero or three key cards
Five diamonds	One or four key cards (The five-club and five-diamond responses may be inverted by agreement.)
Five hearts	Two key cards without the trump queen
Five spades	Two key cards plus the trump queen

On the next round, the cheapest meaningless bid asks for a cue bid to show a useful high card. That may be a trump queen, if not already shown, or a side king. Many modern experts use Kickback, in which, after suit agreement, the cheapest suit bid is used as a substitute for four notrump.

No. 8 ▸ *Asking Bids*

Culbertson's complex asking bids, which he viewed as a technical triumph, never achieved any popularity. Similar bids, however, are used in specialized systems.

There is one area in which a type of asking bid is favored by some experts. It occurs after an opening bid of three or four of a suit. A new-suit bid (with the exception of four hearts in response to three spades) is an asking bid, attempting to determine the opener's holding in the suit asked about. The responses are:

First step: At least two losers.

Second step: Second-round control, king or singleton.

Third step: First-round control, ace or void.

No. 9 ▸ *Five Notrump Grand Slam Force*

A jump to five notrump was given a special meaning by Culbertson. He called it the Grand Slam Force. In its original version, it called for partner to bid a grand slam holding two of the top three trump honors, A-K, A-Q, or K-Q. In Europe it is often called Josephine, out of a mistaken belief that Josephine Culbertson invented it.

Eventually it was realized that the convention can be used to locate a single top honor. Assuming that hearts is the agreed trump suit, a sensible table of responses is:

RESPONSE	MEANING
Six clubs	Ace or king
Six diamonds	Queen (or two extra trumps)
Six hearts	No top honor
Seven hearts	Two top honors (a better bid is seven clubs)

After a six-club response, a six-diamond bid can be a further ask, with the message: Bid seven if you have an extra trump.

If diamonds is the trump suit, then a six-club response promises one top trump.

Many modern experts have a different use for a bid of five notrump when investigating a slam. If it is not a jump, it requests partner to select a suit slam at the level of six.

No. 10 ▸ Cue-Bidding

Cue-bids, like stage cues, point in a particular direction. They come in two varieties.

If the partnership is committed to a particular game and a slam is in prospect, the cue-bid shows a control in the suit bid. The modern term is *control bid*.

West	East
1 ♠	3 ♠
4 ♣ (or ♦, or ♥)	

These bids show a control, which is almost certain to be the ace, and hint at six spades. It is normal to cue-bid cheaply, so four diamonds denies the club ace. East can sign off in four spades, or cooperate by making a cue-bid of his own, or bid Blackwood or bid slam directly. A subsequent cue-bid in a suit that has already been cue-bid suggests a second-round control, a king or a singleton.

Above the game level, the cue-bidder shows a strong desire to reach slam and will often have a weakness in an unbid suit that inhibited the use of Blackwood. These cue-bids apply when a suit has been agreed upon, either directly, by being bid and raised, or by inference.

A low-level cue-bid is a completely different animal. See below, page 194.

For another slam device of major importance, see the Splinter Bid, pages 239–240.

CHAPTER 7

International Play and Another Feud

In 1930, Ely Culbertson had established the idea of playing international matches. These were private challenges, a method that worked well for him. Charles M. Schwab presented a trophy for competition, which was contested in 1933 and 1934 in London, between the Americans and the British. Schwab was the head of Bethlehem Steel, and was the first wealthy man to help in the promotion of the game. Another, even more significant, was Ira Corn, Jr. (See below p. 174.)

The first Schwab Cup match, against an English team of limited ability, was an easy American victory by a margin of 10,900 total points after 300 deals. The most remarkable feature was that a book of the match with all the deals and bidding, plus a few crumbs of commentary, appeared 36 hours after play ended. Modern world championship books, with commentary in depth, sometimes take a year.

Before going to London, the Americans visited Paris and played a match with *plafond* scoring, at which they were at a disadvantage. It paid to bid to the limit of the hand, but there was no vulnerability and little advantage in bidding a slam. There was a strange denouement. The score was virtually tied near the end, when this apparently innocuous deal appeared:

Dealer: West

North
- ♠ 10 5 4
- ♥ 10 8 4 3
- ♦ Q 10 6 4
- ♣ Q 7

West
- ♠ A Q 9
- ♥ J 5
- ♦ K 5 3 2
- ♣ K 4 3 2

East
- ♠ K 8 6 3 2
- ♥ A 9 6 2
- ♦ 8
- ♣ 10 9 8

South
- ♠ J 7
- ♥ K Q 7
- ♦ A J 9 7
- ♣ A J 6 5

West	North	East	South
(Ely)	(Albarran)	(Jo)	(Venizelos)
Pass	Pass	Pass	1 N.T.
Pass	Pass	Pass	

Pierre Albarran, North, was the dominant player and theorist on the French bridge scene. His partner, Sofocle Venizelos, was a member of a famous Greek family whose father was President of the country. In 1950, 17 years later, Venizelos became Prime Minister.

Culbertson produced the diamond deuce with what a French commentator called his "usual air of terrible suffering." This was, it can be seen, the traditional fourth-highest of his longest and strongest. But only just.

Venizelos was gratified by this development. He won with the jack and returned the seven. Ely won with the king, with Jo discarding the heart deuce, and later commented, "I am famous for my mistakes, but this time I produced one of the brilliant plays of which I am sometimes capable. I played the ace of spades. My wife signalled with the eight and we took poor Venizelos for a 300-point ride." The result should have been down two, but the discarding was bad.

In the excitement, the board was then returned to the table with a fatal 90-degree shift. (That rarely happens today, because the players are required to leave the board on the table during the play.) In the replay, Theodore Lightner and Mike Gottlieb, Culbertson's teammates, had the East-West cards, bidding and making two spades with the same cards on which Culbertson had collected 300.

In a modern tournament, the board would be automatically discarded and a replacement deal substituted. After much argument, a committee decided that the Culbertson score should stand, but that the French should be credited with the American score in the replay. That was not as weird as it sounds. They did not wish to throw out the good American result, and gave an estimated normal result for the replay.

More furious argument ensued, after which it was agreed that the match should be agreed a draw with six deals still unplayed. Neither side wished to lose face by losing. The French claimed a moral victory, because they had a small lead when play was abandoned.

The following year was a different story. The Culbertson team consisted of Josephine Culbertson, Lightner, and his chief of staff, 25-year-old Albert Morehead. The British team was much stronger than before: Richard Lederer, William Rose, Stanley Hughes and Henry St. J. Ingram. The British team led in the early stages, but the Americans surged back with help from this deal:

	North	
Dealer: East	♠ A K 2	
Vulnerable: North-South	♥ A J 4 2	
	♦ J 9	
	♣ K Q 10 2	

West		East
♠ 10 6		♠ J 7 5 3
♥ Q 7 3		♥ K 10 9
♦ K Q 10 7 5 4		♦ 8 6 3 2
♣ 9 4		♣ A J

	South	
	♠ Q 9 8 4	
	♥ 8 6 5	
	♦ A	
	♣ 8 7 6 5 3	

From the earliest days, psychic or semipsychic bids in third seat were popular, especially at favorable vulnerability. It is not altogether surprising, therefore, that both West players opened the bidding. Hughes and Lightner each
chose one notrump, relatively safe when the weak notrump was part of the system: East was most unlikely to be interested in game.

The British pair, Lederer and Rose, climbed to five clubs and had to fail by
one trick. In the other room the bidding was:

East	South	West	North
(Ingram)	(Morehead)	(Hughes)	(Josephine)
Pass	Pass	1 N.T.	Dbl.
Pass	2 ♠	Pass	3 ♠
Pass	4 ♠	Pass	Pass
Pass			

At that time, a double of one notrump was regarded as a takeout move,
just as over a suit. In time, players realized that this made no sense: A player
could hardly be prepared for all four suits and not be willing to defend.

A modern player would therefore treat the double as penalty, and remove it
only in the rare situation in which he has a very weak hand and a long suit. In
this case, a pass by South would force West to escape and North-South would
go from there.

As it was, Morehead followed a principle of the Culbertson System: In
responding to a takeout double, choose a major rather than a minor. Instead of
bidding clubs and landing in the five-four club fit, he found himself in four
spades with a four-three fit. He did not feel confident when the diamond king
was led and the dummy appeared, and proceeded to play the hand very, very
slowly. He had, indeed, much to think about, and the play took as long as three
normal deals.

After winning with the diamond ace, he led a club to the queen and ace.
When East returned a diamond, he threw a heart loser, refusing to be forced.
West won, and could have defeated the game by playing a third diamond. That
would have given South a hopeless task wherever he chose to ruff.

Instead West led a heart and Morehead took full advantage of the reprieve.
He won with the heart ace and cashed the ace and king of spades. He followed

with the club king, collecting the jack. When he led a spade and East played the seven, the moment of truth had arrived.

Morehead was now sure that the opening bid was psychic, but that did not say much about the location of the spade jack. He had not heard of restricted choice, which was still 19 years away, but he did the right thing by finessing the spade nine. Perhaps it was instinct. He drew the last trump, cashed his clubs and made his game. (Soon after this, Morehead became the bridge editor of *The New York Times* and held that position until 1963. I succeeded him, and there have been only two holders of this post in 66 years.)

The Americans won by 3,600 total points, a relatively small margin after 300 boards, and left England for the last time. They had won three out of three against the British, but it had been a harder task at the end.

The Culbertson teams were successful in Europe because the players on the other side of the Atlantic were not well developed technically. The self-elected leaders of the English establishment believed in natural methods, and were not up to the challenge. They were improving, however, and showed it in 1934.

Back in the United States, however, Culbertson did not do well. Oswald Jacoby, who had suffered as Lenz's partner in 1930–31, was winning tournaments with a variety of partners. He and three equally brilliant young men, Howard Schenken, Michael Gottlieb and David Burnstine (later Bruce), formed themselves into a team, called themselves the Four Aces, and won almost every contest they entered. In an 18-month period they won 11 major championships out of a possible 13. When Culbertson entered a team, as he did in the 1935 Grand National, he lost to the Four Aces by 5,280 points. Luckily for him, the public paid no attention to tournament results and his reputation remained high.

When Ely played the Four Aces there was always tension. In one celebrated episode, Burnstine was able to take advantage of a well-known habit of Culbertson's. When dummy, he would invariably leave the table, with someone else turning his cards. (In modern times he would be barred from doing this, unless he had a serious reason for leaving).

Burnstine had to make a crucial lead, and while deep in thought opened a packet of chewing gum. Culbertson, the future dummy, was waiting nervously, poised for departure. At long last Burnstine threw something on the table and Culbertson instantaneously spread his cards. He snatched them up again when he realized, just too late, that Burnstine had led his gum wrapper. Having had a glimpse of the dummy, the crafty Ace was able to find the killing lead and defeat the contract. Ever since, this has been known as the Gum Wrapper Coup.

The Four Aces wrote a book about their methods, expounding another valuation method: 3-2-1-½. This was technically sensible, as were their other ideas, which included a prepared opening in a minor with a three-card suit. They offered the first discussion of psychic bidding. But the only person to make money from the book was Culbertson. He bet the authors that they would not sell 1,000 copies and won the wager.

One of the great personalities of the game in this period was P. Hal Sims, a giant of a man who entertained many of the experts at his home in Deal, N.J. In 1931–32 he won a series of tournaments with Schenken, Jacoby and Gottlieb, under the label "The Four Horsemen." When Burnstine joined the team in place of Sims, it became the Four Aces.

Sims was proud of his psychological insight, and claimed that in a two-way finesse situation he could always guess the location of the queen by studying the demeanor of the opponents.

North
♠ A 10 8 2

South
♠ K J 9 3

Some of his friends decided to play a trick on him and made him sit at the table with a deal featuring this as the trump suit. He gazed from side to side with growing irritation and then announced, "Goddamn—it, they've both got the queen!"

And he was right! His "friends" had given both opponents the queen, so that the one he did not select could produce the card and prove him to be wrong. So his record stayed intact. For more about two-way finesses, see below p. 75.

Sims challenged Culbertson to a rubber-bridge match, in which he and his wife would face Ely and Josephine. This was duly played in 1935 and attracted some attention, although not nearly as much as Culbertson-Lenz. The Culbertsons won easily, by 16,130 points, largely because Dorothy Sims was much weaker than the other three players.

There were two serious international events in prospect. The first was a match played at the end of 1935 between the European champions, who happened to be France, and the American champions, the Four Aces. The match began in Madison Square Garden with much hoopla, but competitive interest soon disappeared. The French were outclassed, and the Americans built a massive lead, eventually slowing down deliberately to maintain some public enthusiasm.

This was billed as a world championship, but was in fact the equivalent of golf's Ryder Cup where just two teams compete. The real thing was coming up in 1937. An International Bridge League, with the European Bridge League and Culbertson's United States Bridge Association as its component parts, announced that its first competition would be in Budapest.

Culbertson expected his team to go, but the Grand National Teams, designated for selection, was won easily by the Four Aces: Schenken, Jacoby, Gottlieb and Burnstine. Culbertson's magazine, *The Bridge World,* reported this without mentioning the names of the winners. He then outmaneuvered them by announcing that the team would go as the representatives of the Culbertson System. The Four Aces indignantly refused to accept this condition and withdrew, to Culbertson's delight. In hindsight, they should have made the trip and then repudiated the methods of their celebrated rival.

That did not solve Culbertson's problem, since a Minneapolis team finished second and his own group was not qualified. He therefore announced that the United States would send two teams, the Minneapolis squad and his own. He and Josephine set off with Charles Vogelhofer, a good New York club player, and Helen Sobel, a bright young talent. She was a chorus girl whose stage credits included appearing with the Marx Brothers in *Animal Crackers,* and she had just married Al Sobel. As his foursome included two women, he took three more women to play in the Women's Teams. The fact that the events would be played simultaneously was foolishly overlooked, and the unfortunate threesome had to recruit an American tourist as their fourth. Predictably, their result was bad. Austria, who had the young Rixi Markus, took the first world women's team title.

In the open event, there were 18 teams, 16 from Europe. They were divided into four groups, with the four winners to play in the quarterfinals against a second-place team from another group. The European favorites were Austria and Hungary, which advanced easily to the semifinal stage. The American teams struggled through, both playing extra boards, required by a rule that more than 300 total points were needed to win.

In the semifinal matches, Culbertson beat Hungary, and Austria beat Minneapolis, setting up a 96-deal final. The European players were Karl Schneider, Hans Jellinek, Udo von Meissl, Eduard Frischauer, Walter Herbert and Carl von Bluhdorn.

There were several strange features about the play. The new Culbertson Asking Bids were used frequently, and successfully, by the Austrians. The Americans missed good opportunities to use them, and on the one occasion that they were used a disastrous muddle resulted: Jo passed an asking bid, and a grand slam was played in game.

The Americans never opened one notrump, perhaps because, in pre-Stayman days, they did not know how to respond to it. Helen Sobel had:

♠ A K 6
♥ K 5 3
♦ K 8 4 3
♣ A 9 8

She bid one diamond, and did the same on a similar hand. Both were entirely typical one-notrump bids in Culbertson's methods at that date.

In the early stages of the 96-board match the Austrians had a series of accidents. On consecutive deals von Meissl miscounted his tricks and confused the club ace with the spade ace. Von Bluhdorn led out of turn. Jellinek intended to sign off in five spades but jumped to six, missing two aces. When Schneider intended to bid five clubs and said five spades by mistake, he reached an accidental slam that was virtually a laydown.

With the game still in its infancy, it is not surprising that the standard of play was low.

Dealer: East

Vulnerable: Both

North
♠ A K J 6 5 4
♥ A 9
♦ A 6 4
♣ A J

West
♠ 9 7
♥ Q 8 6
♦ J 7 5 2
♣ 10 7 6 5

East
♠ Q 10 8 2
♥ K 7 3 2
♦ Q 3
♣ K 8 4

South
♠ 3
♥ J 10 5 4
♦ K 10 9 8
♣ Q 9 3 2

West	North (Josephine)	East	South (Ely)
		Pass	Pass
Pass	2 ♠	Pass	2 N.T.
Pass	3 ♠	Pass	3 N.T.
Pass	Pass	Pass	

A diamond was led to the queen and king. The diamond ten was led and covered by the jack. This was a serious error and gave South an obvious road to nine tricks by leading the ace and jack of clubs. Instead he cashed his diamonds, squeezing the dummy, and took a spade finesse, eventually going down one.

Austria made the same contract playing from the North side. The commentator said nothing about the two errors but claimed that the Culbertson System was at fault: The negative two notrump response resulted in the contract being played from the weak side.

Ely Culbertson, who had played little for several years, was clearly the weakest player on the American team. His frequent semipsychic actions and undisciplined bids had produced one good result but also several poor ones.

However, he bid out of turn in one case, so preventing his partner from bidding a slam that would have failed. Vogelhofer and Sobel were not perfect, but they held up pretty well and were clearly the better American partnership.

Nevertheless the match was close for 80 boards. With 16 remaining, Austria led by 890 total points, which was far from decisive. But Austria surged to victory by 4,740. Board 81 was a killer for the Americans.

		North	
Dealer: South		♠ A 4	
Vulnerable: East-West		♥ K 10 4	
		♦ A	
		♣ A 8 7 5 4 3 2	

West		East
♠ 8 7 5		♠ Q 10 9 3
♥ J 8 7 6 5 3		♥ Q
♦ 10 4 3		♦ K Q 8 7 6 2
♣ J		♣ Q 6

South
♠ K J 6 2
♥ A 9 2
♦ J 9 5
♣ K 10 9

The right contract for North-South is surely six clubs. But:

South (Frischauer)	North (Herbert)
1 ♣	1 N.T.
2 N.T.	3 ♣
3 ♠	4 ♣
5 ♣	7 ♣
Pass	

Dr. Paul Stern, the author of the book of the match, claimed this as a triumph for the Austrian System which he himself had invented. One club was usually the equivalent of a weak notrump opening, and the one-notrump response was a strong random game-force.

Seven clubs needed a 2-1 club split and in all likelihood a winning spade finesse or, better, a squeeze. Best, after drawing trumps, is to play three rounds of spades, ruffing the third. If the queen does not appear, there are some complicated squeeze possibilities. As it happened, a heart lead allowed South to score his 13th trick in that suit. The grand slam chance was slightly inferior, but Stern produced a rationalization, "At this stage of the match, moreover, it seemed advisable to bid the grand slam, as it could be assumed that the Culbertsons at Table 2 would take the same risk."

This was a dubious argument. The most likely way to lose the match was for Austria to bid a grand and fail by one trick. As it turned out, the Culbertsons rested cautiously in game:

South	North
(Josephine)	(Ely)
Pass	1 ♣
1 ♠	2 ♣
2 N.T.	3 N.T.
Pass	

The Americans lost 920 total points, and were headed down a slippery slope to defeat. It would have been different, one may suppose, if the Four Aces had made the trip, as they should have done.

The most curious feature of this last deal is East's silence in both rooms. This was understandable when Vogelhofer was in that position. Both his opponents had shown strength, and he would have had to bid at the two-level at unfavorable vulnerability.

But Schneider's silence over a standard one-club opening is extraordinary. A suspicious person might infer that West had passed a secret message, "I have a very weak hand." The same person would find confirmation on another deal on which the Culbertsons again missed a good slam:

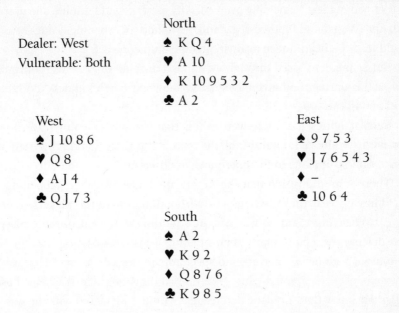

Dealer: West
Vulnerable: Both

North
♠ K Q 4
♥ A 10
♦ K 10 9 5 3 2
♣ A 2

West
♠ J 10 8 6
♥ Q 8
♦ A J 4
♣ Q J 7 3

East
♠ 9 7 5 3
♥ J 7 6 5 4 3
♦ –
♣ 10 6 4

South
♠ A 2
♥ K 9 2
♦ Q 8 7 6
♣ K 9 8 5

The Austrian North-South bid six diamonds, and North made the winning guess by leading a low trump from his hand. This solved the problem of the jack of diamonds. But in the replay:

West	North	East	South
(Schneider)	(Ely)	(Jellinek)	(Josephine)
Pass	1 ♦	1 ♥	1 N.T.
Pass	3 N.T.	Pass	Pass
Pass			

South must be blamed for the considerable underbid of one notrump. However, two notrump or three diamonds would have been forcing to game. The Culbertson System, which used the inaccurate honor-trick valuation method, always had trouble in handling 11- and 12-point hands.

But consider what East-West were up to. First, East made a vulnerable over-call with one jack, causing Stern to say in his book, "East's intervening bid on a trickless hand discouraged any aspirations towards a slam in North and South."

What he did not mention was the strange behavior of Schneider, whose partner had made a vulnerable overcall. Any expert would double one notrump with the West hand, showing a hand just short of opening values. And he would lead the heart queen against any notrump contract.

But Schneider passed throughout and led the club three. This is only explicable if his partner had given a signal to show extreme weakness, both in the hand and in the suit.

Such activities, and there were others that involved opening leads, may or may not have affected the result of the match. But there could have been other goings-on less obvious to the post-mortem observer.

There is no indication that the Americans knew what was happening, but the following year the Austrians visited London, where the players were not naive. "What impressed us was not their bidding, nor their dummy play, but their defense. And particularly their opening leads. 'Devastating' was the word unanimously coined by players and spectators to describe them." That was the comment of S. J. Simon in his groundbreaking bestseller *Why You Lose at Bridge*. He knew that sophisticated readers would understand what he was saying. Players who cheat are regularly more successful in opening leads than are their opponents. Sixty-five years later, the verdict of history must be that the Austrians should be disqualified and the Americans were entitled to reign as world champions.

Culbertson's interest in bridge now ended, and he never played in a serious event again. Soon after, he and Jo were divorced. He was not an easy man to live with, and pursued women outside marriage. His organization continued productively with negligible help from its leader.

Culbertson was more interested in international politics. He pressed for a world federation, and after World War II for United Nations reform. With support from many others, including Dorothy Thompson, he pushed for "a real world authority under a higher law, with a world judge and a world policeman." Support came from many quarters, and in 1948 his ABC plan had support from 16 senators and 14 congressmen, including Estes Kefauver, Richard Nixon and Mike Mansfield. Senate hearings were held dealing with United Nations reform. John Foster Dulles was in favor, but the effort was swallowed up in the election campaign and the next administration had other concerns.

The involvement of the Austrians in international bridge ended when Hitler took over their country. Frischauer and Herbert came to the United States. Jellinek died in a concentration camp. Schneider survived and was to be heard of later.

No. 11 ▸ *The Two-Way Finesse*

North
♠ A 10 8 2

South
♠ K J 9 3

When there is a two-way finesse possibility, such as the one shown for Sims, there are four legitimate ways of improving the odds:

1. Consider what is known about the lengths of the other suits. The player who has the majority of unknown cards will tend to have the queen.

2. Consider the high-card points. What a player has bid, or has not bid, may indicate whether or not he has the crucial queen.

3. When all the intermediate spots are held, as in the diagram, lead the jack from the closed hand and watch your left-hand opponent closely. If he plays the queen or hesitates, the problem is solved. If he plays low promptly, win in dummy and play your right-hand opponent for the queen.

4. With no clue, play your left-hand opponent for the queen. The fact that he did not lead the suit originally is a slight suggestion that he has the queen.

A fifth way is popular but foolish: Assume that the queen lies over the jack. This has a tenuous validity at rubber bridge, where the queen may have captured the jack in a previous deal and not been separated in the shuffle, but none whatever at duplicate.

There are two illegitimate ways of improving the odds. Do not use them, but beware of the player who tries them against you.

1. Think for a long time and then lead rapidly from the wrong hand. The player who objects probably has the queen, because he is paying attention to what you do.

2. In rubber bridge, the following is possible:

North
♠ K 3 2

South
♠ A J 10 9 8

Before playing the suit, announce 100 honors and note the behavior of the opponents. But an elderly Frenchman, sitting on the left, found the correct counter. He held the queen and knew that the claim was false. But he wrote down 100 on his scorepad, causing South to misjudge the situation. West produced his queen to defeat the contract, announced "one down, no honors," and crossed them off his pad.

CHAPTER 8

A Formidable Foursome

 When Culbertson played his three matches in England in the period 1930–34, his opponents were mostly elderly, self-elected and incompetent. That quickly changed.

By a happy coincidence, four brilliant young men were in the habit of playing at a small bridge club in Hampstead, North London. It was on Acol Road, so it was called the Acol Club. The system they developed there became known as the Acol System, and it has been widely played in Britain and other parts of the world ever since. (See below p. 82.)

The oldest of the group and its acknowledged leader was Maurice Harrison Gray, who had been a dispatch rider in World War I. He was tall, bald, mustached and impressive, and was all those things when I was his partner two decades later. Unexpectedly, he was a serious lepidopterist. Part of his cottage home was the breeding ground of interesting moths, many unknown in England, which the visitor was not allowed to disturb. His mail dealt not only with bridge but with such questions as, "How do you encourage the love life of the lesser Manchurian spotted hawk?"

His working life was spent at a typewriter, from which he ejected daily articles for a newspaper, weekly articles for *Country Life,* occasional articles for bridge magazines and answers to readers' questions on match points and moths.

Among his many superb efforts at the bridge table, the following is perhaps the most memorable:

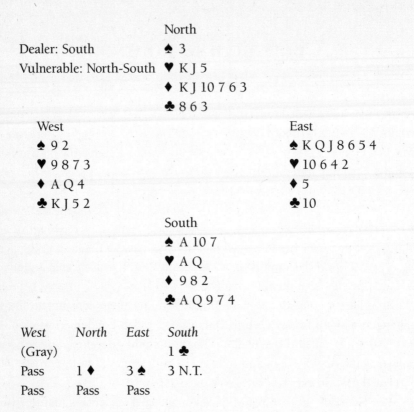

Dealer: South

Vulnerable: North-South

North
♠ 3
♥ K J 5
♦ K J 10 7 6 3
♣ 8 6 3

West
♠ 9 2
♥ 9 8 7 3
♦ A Q 4
♣ K J 5 2

East
♠ K Q J 8 6 5 4
♥ 10 6 4 2
♦ 5
♣ 10

South
♠ A 10 7
♥ A Q
♦ 9 8 2
♣ A Q 9 7 4

West (Gray)	North	East	South
			1 ♣
Pass	1 ♦	3 ♠	3 N.T.
Pass	Pass	Pass	

The spade nine was led. Unsure whether East held six spades or seven, South held up his ace until the third round. If he had won the second trick there would have been no story.

Looking at all four hands, it is easy to see that South can make ten tricks by leading the diamond nine and finessing. But the declarer was not unnaturally nervous. He did not wish to lose to a hypothetical diamond queen in the East hand.

South was ready to make the right technical play: Lead to the diamond king. This guards against a singleton or doubleton queen in the East hand, and if West has both missing honors he is welcome to take them. As can be seen, this line of play was due to succeed.

But an extraordinary thing happened. On the third round of spades Gray had to make a discard, and his diamond ace hit the table. South was not pleased. It appeared to him that West had made an entry-creating discard with a doubleton ace. That would promote his partner's queen to a trick, and South would not be able to establish diamonds without allowing East to score spade tricks.

South could now have made 11 tricks by finessing in diamonds, but Gray had created an effective illusion. Shooting a venomous look at his lefthand opponent, South decided to rely on clubs. He crossed to dummy by overtaking the heart queen with the king, and finessed the club queen. This lost to the king, and Gray led the diamond four. Still in the grip of the illusion, South put up dummy's king and continued clubs. He was not at all pleased when Gray produced the diamond queen to score the setting trick.

Gray's partner was an extraordinary character who would startle the stuffy members of Crockfords Club by appearing in a ragged shirt and filthy gray trousers with a gap between them. Simon's name had been Simon Skidelsky, which soon became amended to Skid Simon, and he was a chain-smoking genius. His talent showed itself not simply in bridge but in writing comic novels. In partnership with Caryl Brahms, he wrote 12 novels in which he provided the comedy and she supplied the research and background. Their first was *Bullet in the Ballet,* and one of the others, *Trottie True,* became a successful movie. Anyone who has not read them has missed a treat.

One of Simon's three bridge books, *Why You Lose at Bridge,* became an instant classic and is still popular. In it, he stressed the psychological side of the game: Try for the best result possible, not the best possible result. It is no use making a clever bid, aimed at reaching a perfect contract, if you have a partner who will not understand it. He also formulated an important guideline in competitive bidding: If both sides have a good fit, bid one more for luck when in doubt. This may result in a small loss, but it will avoid the disasters that occur when both sides are due to succeed in their contracts.

Gray and Simon were cartooned in a magazine as Don Quixote and Sancho Panza. By 1939 they were members of the British team at the European Championships in The Hague, Netherlands, but, with relatively weak teammates, did not win.

A memorable hand that they played together on another occasion was the following. It has a distinctly modern flavor.

North

Dealer: North

Vulnerable: East-West

♠ K 8 6 5 2
♥ J
♦ J 8 6 4 3
♣ 7 4

West

♠ Q 4
♥ K 9 8 6 3 2
♦ Q 10 7 5
♣ Q

East

♠ A J
♥ A Q 7
♦ A K 9 2
♣ A 10 8 3

South

♠ 10 9 7 3
♥ 10 5 4
♦ —
♣ K J 9 6 5 2

South (Gray)	West	North (Simon)	East
		Pass	1 ♣
Pass	1 ♥	Dbl.	Redbl.
4 ♠	Pass	Pass	Dbl.
Pass	Pass	Pass	

In the English style of the time, and the standard method anywhere today, East should certainly have opened two notrump or, holding all the aces, a strong artificial two clubs. That would have provided a good description, kept his opponents at bay, and made reaching an easy six hearts the likely result.

But East decided to be fancy and bid one club, which allowed Simon to interject a double of the one-heart response, trading on the favorable vulnerability. By the standards of the time this was highly daring, with four working high-card points. A modern expert might venture one notrump, showing, as a passed hand, great length in the unbid suits. But that was an idea still in the future.

The redouble showed considerable extra high-card strength, which East certainly had, and it was Gray's turn to be imaginative. With only a four-card suit he leaped to four spades. He expected this to be a good result against an enemy four-heart contract, with a crossruff in the red suits likely to develop. This "advance save" concept received its theoretical underpinning half a century later, with the development of the Law of Total Tricks. (See page 189.)

West should no doubt have bid five hearts, immediately or on the next round, but he both passed and accepted his partner's double. North-South had already won the bidding, and things got better. The club queen was led and won with the ace, but East did not place his partner with a singleton. Instead of giving a club ruff, which would have resulted in a two-trick defeat, East decided to stop the crossruff. He led the ace of spades followed by the jack, which gave Gray no pain at all. He won with the spade king, finessed the club nine, and made an overtrick. Dummy's heart was discarded and there was a crossruff at the finish.

The other founders of the Acol System were less well known to the bridge public. One of them, however, was headed for fame on a wider stage. He was a Scotsman named Iain Macleod, who was on the verge of qualifying to represent Britain in the 1939 European Championships, together with Gray and Simon, when an attack of flu removed him from the selection process. A few weeks later the European War began and he immediately joined the British Army. He was the most junior officer—he had been commissioned four days earlier—when he arrived in France, and was wounded in the leg before the escape from Dunkirk. Later he helped plan the invasion of Normandy and landed in France, once again, on D-Day.

After the war his bridge activity was limited. He wrote a weekly newspaper column, wrote one significant book, and captained the British team in Venice in 1951. But politics claimed Macleod, first as a member of Parliament, then as minister of health, and finally as chancellor of the exchequer. He was widely viewed as a potential prime minister when he died prematurely at 57.

The fourth member of the team was the theorist. His name was Jack Marx; he put the ideas of the group into concise form, improving and polishing. He was a shy man with health problems, but he was to outlive all his teammates. He put forward an idea of major importance. (See below page 115.)

When international bridge resumed after World War II, the Acol group went into action. England won three straight European titles, with Gray as the playing captain, the only successful playing captain in bridge history. Simon was his partner in 1948 and 1949, but an early death removed him from the scene. Marx took his place in 1950, helping to win the title.

No. 12 ▸ *The Acol System*

The Culbertson (and later Goren) bidding methods that spread around the world in the 1930's and 40's had many weaknesses. The Acol group looked for the flaws and found solutions. They had the advantage, along with nearly all the British players, that they were already using the Work 4-3-2-1 point-count. Many Americans were still counting honor tricks, which had no fixed total. Trying to total honor tricks in the later rounds of bidding to decide whether or not to bid game or slam was like attempting to add scrambled eggs and Jell-O.

1. The one notrump opening.

Culbertson began by recommending a weak notrump opening, but then shifted to a strong notrump. But he advised his readers to prefer auctions starting with a suit bid in the interests of efficiency. He took his own advice, and he and his group rarely opened one notrump. In the 1937 World Championship they never opened one notrump, even when the hand was entirely suitable.

The Acol players had no such qualms, and succeeded in having it both ways. They adopted a weak notrump when not vulnerable, since the risk of suffering a serious penalty was small. When vulnerable the notrump opening was strong. The ranges were originally 13–15 and 16–18, but were eventually diluted to 12–14 and 15–17.

2. Responding to one notrump.

Culbertson avoided opening one notrump because he did not know how to respond to it. The Acol players were perhaps the first to realize that the responder to one notrump was in control of the auction and must be able to choose a suit contract at the two-level. If he did so, he announced a total lack of interest in game and the opener was required to pass. This became known as a "weak takeout," and eventually, in social American games, as a "drop-dead" bid. If the responder wished to be in game, he would bid something else. Gray's dictum was "Bid What

You Think You Can Make," and this encouraged direct leaps to three notrump or a major-suit game. Jumps in a suit to the three-level were available for strong hands that needed exploration. The next steps in efficient notrump bidding came later, and will be described in subsequent chapters.

3. Limit Bidding.

As soon as convenient, one member of the partnership should describe his hand accurately. His partner could then work out the combined assets and usually make a final decision.

The most obvious example of this was the one notrump opening. Another was the limit raise, such as three hearts in response to one heart. This showed at least four-card support with about 11 high-card points, or slightly fewer with good distribution. Acol never adopted the forcing jump raise favored by Culbertson, and eventually the Americans came to realize that the English had the right idea. Virtually no American expert has used the forcing jump raise for more than 30 years.

This solved the problem of the hand worth a limit raise, for which Culbertson had no solution. It created a problem with the hand worth a forcing raise, perhaps 13–15 points in high cards. The Acol solution was to bid a new suit and then jump to game in the original suit. Other solutions were eventually forthcoming. (See below, pages 195, 239.)

4. The two notrump response.

Another limit response that came from the Acol group was the jump response of two notrump to a suit opening. It showed 11–12 points, and the opener was expected to pass with a minimum balanced hand. Half a century later many American experts adopted it when responding to a minor-suit opening, and in that context it is the standard modern treatment on both sides of the Atlantic.

5. Second-round jumps by responder.

Hands worth about 11 points, not quite enough to insist on a game, also presented problems for responder on the second round after a one-over-one response. Culbertson had largely failed in this area, and the American experts continued to have trouble. Consider this sequence:

West	East
1 ♣	1 ♥
1 ♠	?

In the Culbertson-Goren tradition, jumps in a bid suit (3♣, 3♥ or 3♠ were always forcing. Two notrump was not well defined, but the experts treated it as forcing. The 11-point hand remained in limbo.

Acol laid down that all these jumps were natural, nonforcing limit bids showing about 11 high-card points or the equivalent. But this left some problems when the responder's hand was stronger.

If the responder had four-card spade support and values for game he could bid four spades. If he had six strong hearts or better, with values for game, he could bid four hearts. And if he had game values, no fit, and at least one stopper in the unbid diamond suit, he could bid three notrump.

6. The Fourth Suit.

This, however, left many problem hands with game-going values. One was the hand with good support for opener's original minor suit. Another occurred, in a slightly different auction, when the responder responded in diamonds and had six of them. These could be dealt with in America by using a forcing second-round jump. But there were still many difficult hands, particularly those lacking a stopper in the unbid suit.

The solution came eventually from the Acol group's chief rivals in England, who were headed by Leo Baron and included Adam (Plum) Meredith, Nico Gardener and Norman Squire. The Baron System introduced several important ideas: any four-card suit was biddable, irrespective of quality; four-card suits should be bid up the line, which called for a one-heart response with both majors, for example; and a two-heart response to one spade should promise a five-card suit. A Baron convention still popular in Britain is the two notrump jump response to show a strong balanced hand, at least 16 high-card points.

In the mid-50's, in a series of magazine articles followed by a major book, Squire pointed out the advantage of using a bid in the fourth suit as artificial. In the above sequence, with three suits bid at the one-level, a bid of two diamonds has little value as a natural bid. If responder has diamonds, he will usually choose to bid two or three no-trump. So two diamonds is an "idle bid," and can be used to convey this message, "I have a good hand, partner, but do not know what to do."

This could be used, for example, with a hand holding good club support that will be shown on the next round. Or with a hand such as this:

♠ K 4 2
♥ A Q 7 6 2
♦ 9 4 3
♣ A J

After 1♣ 1♥ 1♠, the player with this hand has no sensible natural bid. He therefore bids two diamonds, asking the opener to describe his hand further. As this does not promise anything in diamonds, the opener should not bid no-trump without a diamond stopper.

This became known as Fourth Suit Forcing, which is shorthand for Fourth Suit Forcing and Artificial. Nobody, or almost nobody, played that the fourth-suit was nonforcing. The idea that it should be artificial was the contribution of Squire and his teammates.

All these English ideas spread around the world, and eventually became standard in North America and elsewhere. Modern American experts owe a considerable debt to the English theorists, although they rarely recognize the fact.

7. Other Acol ideas.

There were two other important Acol ideas that did not catch on outside England. One was the Acol two-bid, showing a long, strong suit and a hand just short of game values. Another was the Acol three notrump opening, showing a long solid minor suit with stoppers in at least two of the side suits. This was eventually modified in the United States and became the Gambling Three Notrump. It shows a long, solid suit with little outside strength, and partner acts appropriately: If he bids clubs at any level, the opener corrects to diamonds if that is his suit.

CHAPTER 9

Mr. Bridge

♠ ♥ ♦ ♣ Back in 1923, when the game of choice was auction, a young hostess in Montreal laughed merrily at the pathetic bridge performance of one of her guests. He was a 22-year-old law student at McGill University, who went home blushing with embarrassment and determined never to suffer in such fashion again. He was, however, intrigued by the game, and grabbed every book he could find, laying out cards to follow the play. Many of the books were by Milton C. Work, who had begun duplicate bridge some 30 years earlier.

This started one of the great careers in the game, for the young man was Charles H. Goren. He went home to Philadelphia, where Work reigned over a busy bridge scene, and continued to study without going near a card table. "It was a case," he said later, "of the fellow who wouldn't go near the water until he was an expert swimmer."

After winning $10 in a newspaper competition, he decided that the time was ripe. He and a friend entered a public duplicate game and won first prize, erasing his embarrassing memory of Montreal. Other successes followed, and he soon put aside his intention to practice as a lawyer. He signed up as a technical assistant to Work, helping prepare books, lectures and columns. He became familiar with the Work 4-3-2-1 point count, originated by Bryant McCampbell in 1913 and popularized by the "Grand Old Man" from 1923 on. This was entirely sensible, but was overshadowed in the early years by Culbertson, whose unsound honor-trick method monopolized the space in the American bookstores.

Goren developed a partnership with Work's chief assistant, a fine player

named Olive Peterson. The following deal from a team game provided them
with Kipling's two imposters: triumph and disaster.

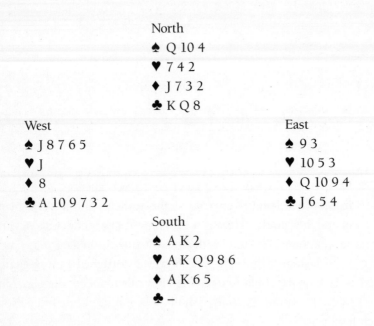

North
♠ Q 10 4
♥ 7 4 2
♦ J 7 3 2
♣ K Q 8

West
♠ J 8 7 6 5
♥ J
♦ 8
♣ A 10 9 7 3 2

East
♠ 9 3
♥ 10 5 3
♦ Q 10 9 4
♣ J 6 5 4

South
♠ A K 2
♥ A K Q 9 8 6
♦ A K 6 5
♣ —

Goren, South, and Peterson, North, reached the correct contract of six
hearts with bidding that has been lost in the mists of time. The opening lead
was the heart jack, and trumps were drawn.

Goren cashed the ace and king of diamonds, and was dismayed by the outcome. He now seemed doomed to lose two tricks in the suit, but he kept his
head and made a surprising move. He cashed the spade ace, and, holding his
breath, led the spade two to dummy's ten. When this decidedly abnormal
finesse succeeded he was happy. He led the club king from the dummy and discarded the spade king. With the club ace in the West hand, there was no
defense. If West had ducked, a diamond would have been thrown on the spade
queen. West chose to win, and had to concede two tricks to dummy, allowing
the diamond losers in the closed hand to disappear.

Goren looked forward to explaining this brilliant performance to his teammates when the time came to compare scores. He was soon deflated. The rival
North-South pair had overbid foolishly to seven hearts and West had placed the
club ace on the table. This was the only disastrous card—even a low club

would not have been fatal—and South had quickly made 13 tricks. Dummy's clubs provided discards for the diamond losers. The game of bridge, as Goren knew well, is full of disappointments. The winning method, as he knew, is to arrange for your *opponents* to be disappointed whenever possible.

	North	
Dealer: South	♠ Q 5	
Vulnerable: North-South	♥ Q 3	
Part Score: 60	♦ Q J 8 7 5 4	
	♣ A J 9	

West		East
♠ K 9		♠ 6 4
♥ A K 9 8 4		♥ 10 7 6 5
♦ K 9 3		♦ 10 6
♣ 10 6 2		♣ Q 8 7 4 3

	South
	♠ A J 10 8 7 3 2
	♥ J 2
	♦ A 2
	♣ K 5

South	West	North	East
	(Goren)		
1 ♠	Dbl.	Redbl.	2 ♥
2 ♠	3 ♥	3 ♠	Pass
Pass	4 ♥	Pass	Pass
4 ♠	Pass	Pass	Pass

In usual circumstances, the West hand would be worth an overcall or a takeout double, but no more. In that light, Goren's bidding seems quite out of character for a man who was known as an accurate, disciplined bidder. But the circumstances were not normal.

The North-South part score meant that one notrump or any higher contract would end the rubber. If East-West suffered a penalty of 300, the price would be worth paying. But 500 would be too much. It would prevent a 700 rubber bonus, but that would not be the right comparison: North-South would still be well-placed with a game and a 60 part score. The game has an unwritten value of 350, which is cashed when the partnership collects a 700-bonus.

Knowing from North's redouble that East had virtually no high-card strength, West pushed and pushed again. He hoped that he would have a chance against four spades, but that was in theory unbeatable.

Goren cashed his two heart winners, but was now endplayed, something that rarely happens at the third trick. A lead away from one of the remaining kings would be immediately fatal. A heart would give a ruff-and-sluff, on which South's diamond loser would disappear. A club would sooner or later give South a crucial third trick in that suit. When dummy's nine was played East could do no better than duck. Then South would cash the club king, and play ace and another spade, catching West again and making four spades.

Faced with these disagreeable alternatives, Goren nonchalantly threw the spade nine on the table. Thinking this marked East with the spade king, South put up dummy's queen and then played a spade to his jack. After winning with the king, Goren could lead a heart safely and the contract had to fail.

Goren was clearly on thin ice. Consider what would have happened if North-South had doubled four hearts. Since the hearts break, and South has both the ace of spades and the ace of diamonds, East would have escaped for down two. That would be 300-a-price that East-West were willing to pay. But the risk of losing 500 or more was not as great as might appear: Goren had judged correctly that South was in no mood to settle for a penalty.

Unlike most of his contemporaries, Goren played happily and successfully with woman partners. Peterson was the first. Sally Young, who is now in the Bridge Hall of Fame, was the second. The third and greatest was Helen Sobel, also a Hall of Famer. Once, while playing with Goren, Sobel was asked by an intrusive journalist, "What does it feels like to play with a really great player?" Pointing across the table, she retorted, "Ask him."

While working for Work, Goren began teaching on his own, emphasizing natural tactics rather than artificial conventions. He was struggling, but making progress, at writing and lecturing as well as teaching. In 1936, two years after Work's death, his first book was published, and he became the syndicated columnist for The Chicago Tribune and The New York Daily News. That meant financial security.

The Four Aces, based in New York, dominated the major championships, but Goren was contending. He won two major titles in 1933 and in 1937 won the forerunner of the Spingold Knockout Teams. For this, he was recruited by three of the Aces when one was not available. He was the top master-point winner in that year, and was to win the title seven more times. He headed the career master-point ranking list from 1944–62. By the time he retired he had won the Spingold six times, the Vanderbilt Knockout twice, and 24 other major titles. He became a world champion in 1950 when international play resumed following World War II.

The Goren career built steadily, taking advantage of the retirement of Culbertson. The first of his major books, focusing on card play, was *Better Bridge for Better Players,* which appeared in 1942. This had an introduction by George S. Kaufman, a celebrated playwright who was responsible for some memorable witticisms. When a young woman performed dreadfully as his partner, he sweetly inquired, "Tell me, my dear, when did you learn? I know it was today, but what time today?"

For Goren, he wrote, "This book is as clear and thorough a statement of the game as anyone could ask . . . anyone who cannot play bridge after digesting this book had better quietly give up the game. (And I'll furnish a list of names on request.)"

He hinted at a solution to the perennial problem of selecting the winning seats, "Some highly promising results have been obtained with rabbits." He also suggested that the problem of reaching the best contract could be solved if the partners sat side by side on a small bench. "At one time I experimented with transparent cards, but this penalized the nearsighted."

Another Goren landmark was *The Standard Book of Bidding,* which appeared in 1944. Internal evidence suggests that the author consulted some Culbertson texts in doing the work: One common auction, ending in a jump to two notrump after the partnership has bid three suits, was overlooked by Culbertson and then omitted from this and other Goren books.

This time, he recruited an even greater figure from the world of literature to write the introduction: Somerset Maugham. The novelist and short-story writer accepted because he wished to disembarrass himself of a sense of guilt.

"Charles Goren is an amiable man, and I have aroused in the breasts of those with whom I habitually play bridge a cordial dislike of him."

On putting up a jack in dummy and winning the first trick, Maugham murmured, "Charles Goren does not recommend the lead from the queen."

This innocent remark disorganized the defense, and similar quotations from Goren proved useful weapons in the war of nerves.

Maugham exacted a price for his contribution, "But having a practical side to an otherwise idealistic nature, I told him that I had better let him know at once what my terms were. He blanched but agreed to them. They were that he should dine and play bridge with me. Of course, I knew that I should lose my money, but I was convinced that the fun it would be would make whatever it cost well worth it."

Ironically, Maugham did lose a little money on the following deal for a surprising reason. He should have made a small fortune, but he was partnering Goren. The great expert, as he confessed later, misplayed a grand slam.

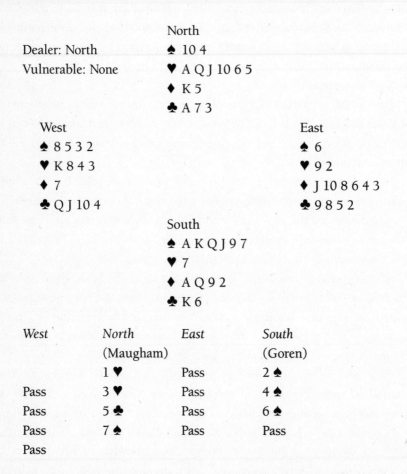

	North		
Dealer: North	♠ 10 4		
Vulnerable: None	♥ A Q J 10 6 5		
	♦ K 5		
	♣ A 7 3		

West
♠ 8 5 3 2
♥ K 8 4 3
♦ 7
♣ Q J 10 4

East
♠ 6
♥ 9 2
♦ J 10 8 6 4 3
♣ 9 8 5 2

South
♠ A K Q J 9 7
♥ 7
♦ A Q 9 2
♣ K 6

West	North	East	South
	(Maugham)		(Goren)
	1 ♥	Pass	2 ♠
Pass	3 ♥	Pass	4 ♠
Pass	5 ♣	Pass	6 ♠
Pass	7 ♠	Pass	Pass
Pass			

South's eventual jump to six spades strongly suggested a solid suit, and Maugham's raise to seven was justified by his fitting diamond king.

When the club queen was led and the dummy appeared, Goren saw a line of play that was almost certain to succeed. He won with the club king and attempted to cash the king and ace of diamonds. If this 93 percent chance had succeeded he would have claimed the grand slam, announcing a diamond ruff with the spade ten.

But alas the actual distribution belonged to the missing 7 percent: West was able to ruff the second round. Looking at the deal later, Goren saw that he could have made the slam. His comment was, "The expert's foot slipped a little on this one. A better plan would have been to win with the king of clubs, play to the ace of hearts, ruff a heart, enter dummy with the ten of trumps and ruff still another heart. If the king falls, all is over. Failing that I test the trumps, and if they are three-two another heart can be ruffed. If the trumps are 4-1, I play the trumps for a double squeeze. West has to hold the king of hearts and East his diamonds and neither can hold clubs . . . It would have been a nice demonstration for Maugham."

Goren had this ending in mind:

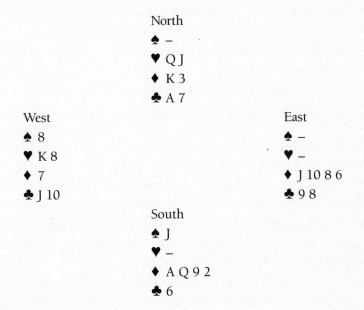

North
♠ –
♥ Q J
♦ K 3
♣ A 7

West
♠ 8
♥ K 8
♦ 7
♣ J 10

East
♠ –
♥ –
♦ J 10 8 6
♣ 9 8

South
♠ J
♥ –
♦ A Q 9 2
♣ 6

On the last trump, dummy gives up a heart and East reluctantly parts with a club. Then three rounds of diamonds destroy West, who must throw a club to keep the heart king. The club seven wins the last trick. (For squeeze plays, see below p. 95.)

In this "confession," Goren was being hard on himself. The more complex line of play, which attempts to establish dummy's hearts or generate a squeeze, is not quite a sure thing, and only marginally better than the play he actually chose. There is no time in a social game for complex percentage calculations. He might have done otherwise in a Vanderbilt match, which offers time for deep thought.

The Goren career continued to build in the forties. It reached a climax when he developed a suggestion made by a Canadian, William Anderson of Toronto. The idea was to give a value to distribution, and help the average player to decide when to open the bidding and when to bid games and slams. (For details, and two alternative methods, see below p. 97.)

The result was *Point Count Bidding at Contract Bridge,* published in 1949 by Simon & Schuster. With a cover price of $1, it became a bestseller and converted the American bridge public from honor tricks to point count. Many were accustomed to using the 4-3-2-1 count for notrump bidding, but now they could employ it for suits as well.

For the world at large, Goren was now "Mr. Bridge," with the fame that Ely Culbertson had had two decades earlier. His *Contract Bridge Complete* was another best seller, taking the place of Culbertson's *Gold Book* and running through 12 editions. His books were translated into 12 languages. For five years he hosted a television program, *Championship Bridge With Charles Goren.*

Goren was a tireless worker, but it was all too much for one man, and like Culbertson, he had to delegate much of the work. Harold Ogust ran "Travel with Goren," taking thousands of enthusiasts on cruises. Richard Frey, a top player and writer, provided *Sports Illustrated* and *McCalls* with bridge articles under the Goren byline. The syndicated newspaper column sometimes used recycled material, which led to an embarrassing coincidence: The two Philadelphia newspapers had the same column on the same day, with identical descriptions, because Charles Solomon, who had no backlog of his own, was also recycling old Goren columns.

By the late sixties, it was clear that Goren was in decline: He had developed what would now be recognized as Alzheimer's disease. He had never married, and needed care. His lawyer and good friend, Lee Hazen, made a sensible arrangement. For the rest of his life, "Mr. Bridge" would be looked after by a nephew, another Goren, who would receive a substantial monthly check while the patient was alive, but nothing thereafter.

Goren lived until he was just 90, outlasting nearly all his old friends. In

1991 I received a message from a Mr. Goren, and I knew what that meant. I returned the call, and as I expected, Mr. Bridge had died. But there was a surprise. I was the first person to be told, and I discovered that the death had occurred two weeks earlier. In the obituary, I did not speculate about a disturbing theory: that the old man might have died and been propped up in bed for two weeks while the nephew awaited the arrival of the monthly check.

No. 13 ▸ *Squeeze Play*

Many books have been written about squeezes, which can be very complex. The great majority, however, fall into three types that the average player needs to be familiar with:

THE AUTOMATIC SQUEEZE

```
                        North
                        ♠ A J 2
                        ♥ –
                        ♦ –
                        ♣
      West                                    East
      ♠ 3                                      ♠ K Q
      ♥ –                                      ♥ A
      ♦ 3 2                                    ♦ –
      ♣ –                                      ♣ –
                        South
                        ♠ 4
                        ♥ K
                        ♦ –
                        ♣ 2
```

South leads his club winner, and East cannot protect both major suits. Switch the East-West hands, and the squeeze still works. That is why it is automatic.

Three points to note:

1. There must be a link between the hand playing the squeeze card (the club two) and the opposite hand. Here the link is the spade suit.

2. The declarer must have lost all the tricks he is willing to lose, so that only the last trick is in doubt. (True for nearly all squeezes.)

3. One opponent (perhaps both) must be threatened or menaced in two suits. In this case, there are menaces in spades and hearts. Here, the menace is a high card. More often, the menace will be based on length. For example, a player who has x-x facing A-K-Q-x knows that only one of his opponents, the one with the majority of the missing cards, can guard the suit.

THE POSITIONAL SQUEEZE

North
♠ A 2
♥ K
♦ –
♣ –

West
♠ K 3
♥ A
♦ –
♣ –

East
♠ J 10
♥ 3
♦ –
♣ –

South
♠ Q 4
♥ –
♦ –
♣ 2

South leads the winning club, and West is squeezed. But this would not work against East, so it is positional.

THE DOUBLE SQUEEZE.

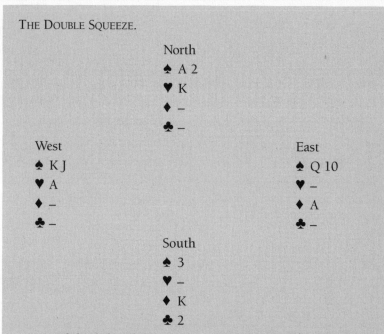

North
♠ A 2
♥ K
♦ –
♣ –

West
♠ K J
♥ A
♦ –
♣ –

East
♠ Q 10
♥ –
♦ A
♣ –

South
♠ 3
♥ –
♦ K
♣ 2

South leads his club winner, and West must throw a spade to guard against the heart king. That card is discarded from dummy, and East must save his diamond ace. Neither defender can hold spades, and dummy's deuce takes the last trick.

This only works because it is West who is trying to guard against dummy's heart menace, and East who is trying to guard against South's diamond menace. Switch the East-West cards and the squeeze does not work.

Look again at the Goren ending in seven spades. If that ending came about in a notrump contract, South could cash the king, ace and queen of diamonds to reach the standard double-squeeze position. The spade jack is then the squeeze card.

No. 14 ▸ *Valuation*

Distributional counts. All of the following three methods of valuation begin with the basic Work count: ace = 4 points; king = 3 points; queen = 2 points; jack = 1 point. All devalue some singleton honors: Deduct one point for a singleton king, queen or jack unless in partner's suit.

In all cases bid a game if the partnership is sure to have a combined 26 points, and stop short if 26 points is impossible.

Similarly, bid a small slam when the combined hands have 33 points, and a grand slam if the combined hands have 37 points.

This point count slightly undervalues aces and does not give a value to tens. So a hand with several aces and/or tens is worth slightly more than its apparent value, and a hand with none of those cards slightly less.

1. Goren count is based on short suits.

> Add to the basic count:
> **a.** One point for a doubleton
> **b.** Two points for a singleton
> **c.** Three points for a void

Deduct one point for an unguarded king, queen or jack unless in partner's suit. Deduct one point for an aceless hand.

A total of 14 points is a mandatory opening. A 13-point hand is an optional opening.

Complicated adjustments are made when raising partner's suit, or when your own suit has been raised.

2. The Karpin count is based on long suits. (It was used for half a century by William Root and other top teachers).

> Add to the basic count:
> **a.** One point for a five-card suit
> **b.** Two points for a six-card suit
> **c.** And so on

Short suits count in the Goren fashion in revaluing the hand after a good fit has been found.

14-point hands always open; 13-point hands nearly always open; 12-point hands sometimes open.

3. Assets are based on long suits and short suits. This valuation method is inevitably recommended by the authors of this book, who invented it.

Add to the basic count:

a. One point for a singleton

b. Two points for a void

c. One point for any suit of five cards or longer.

These are *assets*.

Open all 13-point hands.

Automatic revaluation in the later bidding, at every point by both members of the partnership, in the following manner:

i. If there is no sign of an eight-card fit:	assets count zero
ii. If an 8-card fit is known:	assets count normally
iii. If a 9-card fit is known:	assets double
iv. If a 10-card fit is known:	assets triple

Example:
♠ 2
♥ A J 4 3 2
♦ J 5 4 3 2
♣ J 2

You have 7 high-card points and three assets. If your partner opens one heart, showing a 5-card suit, you know that there is a 10-card fit. Your assets triple to nine and you have more than enough to bid four hearts.

If your partner opens one spade, there is no sign of a fit. Your assets are worthless, and you respond one notrump. This shows 6-9 points, perhaps 10. Your partner bids two hearts, showing a secondary suit of at least four cards. You now know that there is a nine-card fit, so your assets come back to life and are doubled. You bid four hearts. If you raise to three hearts, with a slightly weaker hand, your partner will now double his assets if he has a five-card heart suit: He will know that there is a nine-card fit.

CHAPTER 10

War

As Europe was lurching toward war in 1938, many celebrities were gathered on the French Riviera. Somerset Maugham had a villa there, and his guests regularly played bridge. The game was of mixed standards and he sat South, playing with an American, on the following deal:

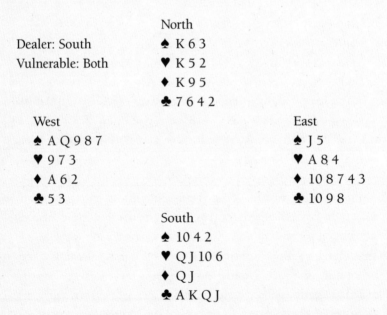

North

Dealer: South
Vulnerable: Both

♠ K 6 3
♥ K 5 2
♦ K 9 5
♣ 7 6 4 2

West

♠ A Q 9 8 7
♥ 9 7 3
♦ A 6 2
♣ 5 3

East

♠ J 5
♥ A 8 4
♦ 10 8 7 4 3
♣ 10 9 8

South

♠ 10 4 2
♥ Q J 10 6
♦ Q J
♣ A K Q J

Maugham bid one notrump, and the bidding ended. West, a weak player who was often confused, led the spade queen.

South was surprised to find dummy with a good hand, but was not unhappy to be playing for just seven tricks. He did not know where the spade ace was, but he was sure the jack was on his left. He played low confidently, and played low again when West followed with the seven. He was distinctly disconcerted when East produced the jack.

East tried the club ten, and South played the ace instantaneously. There was no point in cashing more club tricks, which would simply have given useful information to the defense. Instead he led a low heart to the king, losing to East's ace.

The moment of truth had arrived. Another club lead, or a less plausible heart, would have allowed South to take seven tricks. On paper it is easy to lead a diamond, permitting West to take four tricks. But it was not so easy at the table. It was true that West had played the club three under the ace, but this was not necessarily discouraging: He might have begun with K-J-3 or K-Q-3.

With little to guide him, East relied on a psychological clue. South's rapid play of the club ace earlier suggested that he had no choice in the suit. Lacking the king, he might have thought a bit. So East did the right thing by shifting to a diamond, and West took his ace and three spade winners for down one.

Everyone had something to say in the post-mortem, and East, a good player, began the proceedings.

"That was a remarkable lead, partner," he commented. "I've never seen one quite like it before."

"I just led the fourth highest of my longest and strongest," protested West, who was confused as usual.

"It was actually your fourth-lowest," pointed out his partner, "but I'm not complaining."

South was worried about the bidding. "Why didn't you respond with that hand, partner?" he inquired.

"You would have liked to be higher?" was the retort. "You didn't even make one notrump."

"I don't go by results," persisted Maugham. "You should have raised me with three kings."

North had the last word.

"My kings never take tricks," explained the former Wallis Warfield Simpson, then Duchess of Windsor. "They only abdicate."

That controversial lady was not the first member of the British royal family to play bridge. Her husband's grandfather, Edward VII, was an enthusiast, and played regularly at dinner parties. One of them was at the Bellamy household in a memorable episode of *Upstairs, Downstairs*.

King Edward's youngest cabinet minister also played bridge, but very badly: First Lord of the Admiralty Winston Churchill was the despair of his partners. In 1912, one of them was British Prime Minister Herbert Asquith, and they cruised happily in the blue waters of the Mediterranean aboard the admiralty yacht *Enchantress*. Asquith's daughter, Violet, later recorded the scene:

> My father was an eager and execrable player. Winston was even more dangerous, for he played a romantic game, untrammeled by conventions, codes or rules. When playing together, they made a happy, carefree and catastrophic combination.
>
> But to cut with Winston was to both of his private secretaries a severe ordeal. Masterton was a really good bridge player and treated the game with respect. Moreover, though the stakes were low, he could not afford to lose overmuch. He used to sit in agony while Winston declared, doubled and redoubled with wild recklessness, watching his every discard and building reasonable conjectures on the play, only to be disillusioned and dumbfounded again and again.
>
> "But, First Lord, you discarded the knave . . ."
>
> "The cards I throw away are not worthy of observation or I should not discard them. It is the cards I *play* on which you should concentrate your attention."

The other secretary, Marsh, was deeply pained when Churchill as his partner wasted a king, and was not consoled by the majestic explanation, "Nothing is here for tears. The king cannot fall unworthily if it falls to the sword of the ace."

One deal was approximately this:

North

Dealer: South	♠ Q 5 2
Vulnerable: None	♥ 10 8 5
	♦ J 5
	♣ A Q 8 5 4

West

♠ 8 7 4
♥ A 4 2
♦ 9 7 6 2
♣ K 7 3

East

♠ 10 9 3
♥ K J 9 7
♦ A 10 8 3
♣ 10 2

South

♠ A K J 6
♥ Q 6 3
♦ K Q 4
♣ J 9 6

South	West	North	East
(Asquith)	(Marsh)	(Masterton)	(Churchill)
1 N.T.	Pass	Pass	Pass

Nobody was vulnerable, because nobody would be vulnerable until 1925. One might expect North to raise one notrump to game, but that was not necessary because the game was auction, not contract. It was necessary to make nine tricks to make a game, and that was South's target.

The diamond deuce was led by Marsh, and Churchill as East won with the ace and returned the suit. Asquith won with the king and proceeded to guess correctly in clubs. He led the jack, which was covered by the king and ace, and continued with queen. This play was slightly against the odds, but it succeeded. The ten fell, and he made 11 tricks.

Churchill was furious with his partner because he had led the diamond deuce from a weak suit. Later in the bathroom, away from the overpowering presence of the First Lord, Marsh asked Masterton to endorse his choice of lead and rule whether East was right or wrong.

"You've always told me," he said plaintively, "that in notrump it is right to lead the fourth-highest of my longest suit."

Masterton approved the lead and concluded that the diamond return was unlikely to hold South to eight tricks, whatever the position in that suit. And he doubted whether the great man would have risen to the occasion with a decisive shift to the heart jack, even if he had known that diamonds offered no hope. This heart play is sometimes named for a much earlier First Lord of the Admiralty. (See below p. 111.)

Nowadays many experts would lead the diamond seven in West's position, since they would be afraid that the lead of the deuce would suggest some honor strength. So, although Churchill was undoubtedly a bad bridge player, in his opinion about a low lead from four small cards—as in many matters of wider importance—he was years ahead of his time.

In 1914, Churchill was sitting in the Admiralty in London, playing bridge and waiting for news. When word came that war had been declared, he left the game abruptly to mobilize the fleet. And that was, apparently, the last time he played bridge.

A quarter of a century later, he was back in the Admiralty at the start of an even bigger war in which he was to play an even bigger role. Thousands of bridge players in the 20-35 age bracket went to war around the world, including some who were to become famous. In Britain, for example, Iain MacLeod, a future chancellor of the exchequer, became an officer in a Highland regiment. The Sharples twins, who were leading figures in the game for 40 years, gave the marines and the navy one recruit each. Tony Priday, a future European champion, was in the army throughout. One leading figure who stayed home and played bridge was Terence Reese, who was nominally in a small business that made blackout curtains. His future partner, Boris Schapiro, continued in a family meat business in Smithfield market. (I was in the navy at the end of the war, but too late to see any action.)

When the Japanese bombed Pearl Harbor in December 1941, the news was announced at a tournament in Richmond, Va. Oswald Jacoby rose dramatically, leaving his partner in some difficulty, and went off to take an army intelligence post. He had served for a few months in World War I, and was to serve again in Korea. Alfred Sheinwold left the Culbertson stable and also did intelligence work: He used his wits to demonstrate to a series of complacent commanding officers that their security arrangements were highly insecure. Another American serviceman was John Crawford, a future winner of three world titles. He put his talents to unusual use, instructing other soldiers in how to avoid being cheated at poker and other gambling activities.

Many servicemen found ways to play bridge in prison camps. The strongest game seems to have been in Bandoeng, West Java, where a large number of Dutch officers were confined by the Japanese. The full story was described later by C. Th. de Booy, a Dutch lieutenant commander.

Scene: The open air in the crowded Tjimahi camp.

Time: 7:30 a.m.

Cast: Thirty-two hungry and lean bridge addicts, mostly clad in tatters but all in an optimistic mood, caused by good news from the Pacific battlefront, received in the early morning over a carefully hidden radio.

Props: Sixteen packs of hard-worn cards, eight improvised tables, 32 things to sit on.

This was a memorable deal from a duplicate game.

	North	
Dealer: East	♠ 10 8 7 3	
Vulnerable: Both	♥ 9 6 4 2	
	♦ A 8 3	
	♣ 7 4	

West		East
♠ 5 2		♠ Q
♥ 5		♥ K Q J 10 8
♦ 7		♦ K Q J 10 6 4
♣ K Q J 10 8 6 5 3 2		♣ 9

	South	
	♠ A K J 9 6 4	
	♥ A 7 3	
	♦ 9 5 2	
	♣ A	

West	North	East	South
		1 ♦	Dbl.
4 ♣	Pass	4 ♥	4 ♠
Pass	Pass	Pass	

On the diagramed deal, four West players reached five clubs doubled, losing 800 when the defenders prevented a spade ruff in the dummy.

Four South players were in four spades, and one found a way home in spite
of the fact that there appear to be two sure losers in each red suit. The bidding
provided a valuable clue: West was sure to have great length in clubs, and East
a red two-suiter.

One South won the club ace, drew trumps, and cashed the heart ace and
the diamond ace to end in the dummy. He then led the club seven, and threw a
heart from his hand. West was now on lead in this position:

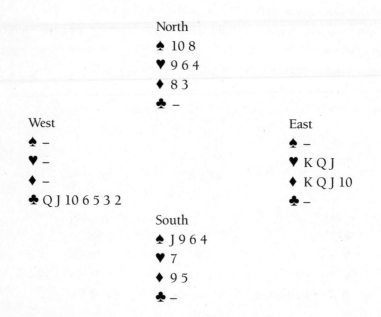

North
♠ 10 8
♥ 9 6 4
♦ 8 3
♣ –

West
♠ –
♥ –
♦ –
♣ Q J 10 6 5 3 2

East
♠ –
♥ K Q J
♦ K Q J 10
♣ –

South
♠ J 9 6 4
♥ 7
♦ 9 5
♣ –

On the forced club return South threw a diamond from the dummy and
the last heart from his hand, a double discard rarely seen outside books. On the
next club lead, South threw dummy's remaining diamond, ruffed in his hand
and made an improbable overtrick. (For a discussion of this type of play, see
below p. 112.) This would be a spectacular play at any time, and South was
playing in the open air in a Japanese prison camp.

Leading the fight to end the European part of the war, and eventually
release all the prisoners, was another bridge enthusiast: General Dwight David
Eisenhower. On November 7, 1942, he relaxed at the card table while waiting
for news of the landing at Casablanca in North Africa. One of the other players
was General Alfred Gruenther, last heard of directing the Culbertson-Lenz

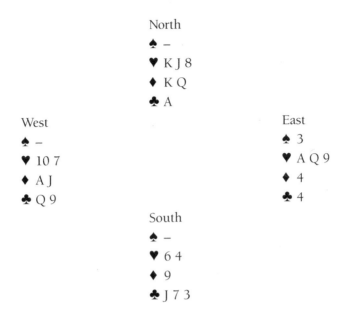

North
♠ —
♥ K J 8
♦ K Q
♣ A

West
♠ —
♥ 10 7
♦ A J
♣ Q 9

East
♠ 3
♥ A Q 9
♦ 4
♣ 4

South
♠ —
♥ 6 4
♦ 9
♣ J 7 3

On East's last spade, West threw a heart. Dummy was now squeezed. If South had thrown a club or a diamond, the dummy would have been squeezed again and the declarer would have made no tricks at all. South did the best he could by throwing a heart, and East led his diamond. West won with the ace and returned his heart ten, giving his partner three tricks in the suit. Dummy made a club trick at the end, for his only trick and a penalty of 3400. The two generals had the biggest score of their bridge careers, and were happy with the thought that their opponents could well afford their deserved financial loss.

At an earlier time, the Eisenhower-Gruenther bridge friendship had an impact on world history. In 1948 the former commander of the invading armies in Europe had a nonmilitary job for the first time in his life: president of Columbia University. This undemanding assignment in Manhattan suited him well, because he could go to his office in the morning and play bridge at his club in the afternoon.

One day he was at the card table and was told by a club servant that he was wanted on the telephone. He was not at all pleased at being disturbed, and grumbled off. He returned looking black, and his young partner, Dan Caulkins, dared to asked what the story was.

"Who was that?"

"It was the president." (Truman)

"What did he want?"

"He wants me to go to Paris as head of NATO."

"Will you go?"

With a shrug, "If the president says go, you go."

"Who will you take as your number two?"

"Well, I ought to take Bedell Smith. But I think I'll take Gruenther because he's a better bridge player."

Which is how General Alfred Maximilian Gruenther subsequently became head of NATO when Eisenhower returned to the United States to run for the presidency. Bridge expertise can help a career.

Eisenhower and Gruenther are not the only world figures who have played the game. Deng Xiaopeng of China and Winston Churchill of Britain have already been mentioned. Mahatma Gandhi, the greatest figure in the history of India, played bridge as a young man. F.W. de Klerk of South Africa, who shared the 1993 Nobel Peace Prize, is also a player.

George Burns, the veteran actor, played bridge at a country club outside Los Angeles whenever he was not working on stage or screen. When he was 95 he arrived to play, intent on puffing his usual cigar at his opponents, and was furious to discover a new "No Smoking" sign. He complained bitterly, and when he arrived the next day the sign read: "No Smoking except for those over 90."

Omar Sharif, star of *Dr. Zhivago* and other great movies, regularly plays with world champions in top competitions and holds his own.

In Washington, D.C., Supreme Court Justice John Paul Stevens is a life master with much tournament experience. Two of his colleagues, Chief Justice William Rehnquist and Associate Justice Sandra Day O'Connor, are also players. Amalya Kearse, a United States Court of Appeals Circuit Judge in New York City, won the World Women's Pairs in 1986, owns six national titles, and has written two books on the game.

There are three enthusiasts in the world of finance. James Cayne, president of the brokerage house of Bear, Stearns, has won several national titles and contends at world level. Warren Buffett, a legendary investor, has played all his life and sometimes appears in tournaments. And Bill Gates, head of Microsoft and the world's wealthiest man, keeps bridge books on his desk and is rapidly improving. In 2000 he competed in a major championship in the Summer Nationals in Anaheim, Calif.

No. 15 ▸ *Sandwich Play*

In the Churchill deal shown (p. 103), the winning play was to return the heart jack, scoring four tricks in the suit. This is sometimes called a sandwich play, recalling the first lord of the Admiralty in the 18th Century. (See page 2 above.) East's J-9 of hearts are sandwiching dummy's ten, and he must have the ace or king of the suit. The more popular name is "surrounding play."

Similar situations are:

North
♥ J 3 2
East
♥ A Q 10 9

East leads the queen. If South has the king he can win, but a later lead from West will be effective.

North
♥ 9 3 2
East
♥ K 10 8

East leads the ten. This is essential if South has A-J-4 or something similar.

Such plays can also be made from the other side of the table, when the sandwiched card is hidden in the declarer's hand. For example:

North
♥ Q 3 2
West
♥ K J 9 4

West leads the jack, sandwiching a hypothetical ten in the South hand. If East has the ace, all goes well. If he does not, the choice of card to lead is not significant.

North
♥ A J 2
West
♥ Q 10 8 5

West leads the ten, sandwiching a hypothetical nine in the South hand. West assumes his partner has the king. If he does not, nothing matters.

ast one trump in
endgame. Try to
he opponents the
ad a suit you pre-

ch your chances
ad them for you.

    KJ6
    A94

mp, or when you

d. The safe line is
move, or strip, or
ing in the North
atever East plays.
ful. If he leads a
w the remaining

EXAMPLE 2

North
* Q 10 9 3
♥ A 10
♦ 6 4 3 2
♣ 6 4 2

South
* A K J 8 5
♥ K 7 6
♦ J 9
♣ A Q 3

South	West	North	East
1 ♠	2 ♦	2 ♠	Pass
4 ♠	Pass	Pass	Pass

West leads three diamond winners and South ruffs the third. Trumps are drawn, both opponents following twice. Now the contract is safe. The declarer plays hearts, ruffing the third round. Once that unimportant suit has been stripped, South leads the last diamond from dummy and throws his club three. West must win and do something helpful. A club shift solves the problem in that suit, and a red-suit lead allows South to ruff in dummy and throw the club queen. The declarer has avoided the club finesse, which was likely to lose.

Now you too can be a stripper.

No. 17 ► *Redoubling*

There are five common types of redouble:

1. If an opening suit bid is doubled, opener's partner redoubles with almost any hand containing 10 points or more. As in the Eisenhower deal, this signals to partner that the opponents may be in trouble. When they make a bid, the next player will normally double in search of a penalty, or pass to give partner the opportunity to double.

2. If a low bid is doubled for penalties, a redouble is normally an SOS, demanding that partner look for another contract.

3. A redouble of a high-level contract is for penalties, suggesting that the opponents have erred in doubling. The mathematics favor the redouble: The profit from success is much greater than the loss from failing by a trick. One conclusion: Be reluctant to double a voluntarily bid high-level contract.

4. A special case occurs when a one notrump opening bid is doubled. Traditionally, redouble is for penalties, indicating that the opening side has the balance of strength. But the redouble can have a special meaning by partnership agreement.

5. If a control-showing cue-bid is doubled, a redouble shows second-round control, either the king or a singleton.

CHAPTER 11

New Ideas in America

In mathematics and science, there are two cases of simultaneous creation of an important concept. One is the calculus, which was devised by Isaac Newton and by Gottfried Wilhelm von Leibniz, using different notations. Another is the theory of natural selection, a key element in evolution, which is regularly credited to Charles Darwin, but Alfred Russel Wallace had the same idea.

There are three such cases in bridge history. The first is the takeout double, originated by Bryant McCampbell and Charles Patton. The second is the Stayman convention, and there are three claimants. (For the third, see later in this chapter.)

The first claimant is Jack Marx of London, England, who was one of the principal inventors of the Acol System discussed in Chapter 8. In 1939 he thought of a way for the responder to uncover major-suit fits following an opening one notrump bid. Two clubs would be entirely artificial and ask for a major suit.

He distributed notes on his idea to several friends, but the start of World War II prevented publication. It appeared as an article in the first bridge magazine to appear in England after hostilities ended: Issue number one of *The Contract Bridge Journal*, edited by M. Harrison Gray.

The second claimant is George Rapee of New York, one of the best American players for half a century. In 1944 it occurred to him that a two-club response to one notrump could be used to search for a major-suit fit. Rapee described the idea to his partner, Sam Stayman, and they experimented with it. It worked well, and Stayman wrote an article for *The Bridge World*, giving his partner credit. It appeared in April 1945, and was, therefore, the first printed

version, one year before the Marx article. It became known as Stayman, which
left Rapee quite disgruntled.

A curious coincidence was that the English and American ideas had identical structures. (Marx served in the British Army in Iceland during the war,
and there were many Americans there. It is theoretically possible that the two-
club idea leaked to New York City by word of mouth, but there is no evidence.)
When the opener had no major suit, he was expected to bid two diamonds
with a minimum hand and two notrump with a maximum. This feature of the
convention disappeared rapidly. In England, Simon simplified the idea that his
teammate, Marx, had put forward. With no major suit, he suggested, the
opener should automatically bid two diamonds. This was obviously sensible,
and the Stayman convention has been used in that way ever since in all parts of
the world. For more details about the use of the convention, see below p. 128.

The new convention quickly became so popular that it was soon adopted
worldwide by thousands of users. Many had no idea that Stayman was a person, and some were confused about the name. He and his wife crossed the
Atlantic on an Italian cruise ship, and were required to play bridge with the
captain each night. "I only play two conventions," he announced, "Blackwood
and Sternberg." And they did.

Rapee and Stayman were regular members of the United States team when
world championships resumed in 1950. Their group, all from New York City
and Philadelphia, won three consecutive titles, the first of them in a three-
cornered event against a British team and a European team. The second was in
Naples against Italy. And the third was in New York against a Swedish team.

One of the Americans who defeated Sweden was Theodore Lightner, the
veteran who had helped Culbertson win three victories in England in the early
thirties. The Lightner Double he invented proved a great help to Stayman on a
later occasion. His opponents used it, and it backfired.

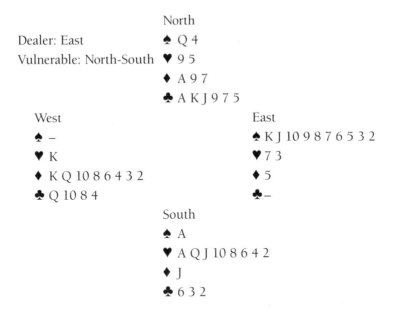

Dealer: East

Vulnerable: North-South

North

♠ Q 4

♥ 9 5

♦ A 9 7

♣ A K J 9 7 5

West

♠ –

♥ K

♦ K Q 10 8 6 4 3 2

♣ Q 10 8 4

East

♠ K J 10 9 8 7 6 5 3 2

♥ 7 3

♦ 5

♣ –

South

♠ A

♥ A Q J 10 8 6 4 2

♦ J

♣ 6 3 2

The chance of picking up a 10-card suit is about one in a million, but the prospects improve considerably when new decks are used and the shuffle is inadequate. That was the case here, at the start of the 1964 World Team Olympiad in Manhattan. Victor Mitchell had become Stayman's regular partner at this time.

West	North	East	South
	(Mitchell)		(Stayman)
		3 ♠	4 ♥
Pass	6 ♥	Dbl.	Pass
Pass	Pass		

A three-spade opening is usually based on a seven-card suit, so East's action was decidedly pusillanimous. Paradoxically, however, it made life slightly harder for North-South than a normal four spades would have done. In raising the four-heart overcall to six, Mitchell had to worry about the chance of two immediate spade losers. That danger would have been much less if the bidding had begun four spades-five hearts.

East's Lightner Double, asking for an unusual lead, strongly suggested that he was void in one of the minor suits. A club lead would have allowed the defense to score all three trumps for down two. Unfortunately, West led the diamond king, since East's void was highly likely to be in that suit.

Stayman knew what the double meant, and after winning the first trick with dummy's diamond ace he simply led to the heart ace. He knew that a normal trump finesse might give the defense a second chance for a decisive club ruff. He was quite content to lose one trump trick, and as it happened he collected a fortuitous overtrick. He drew a second round of trumps and eventually took a marked finesse in clubs. His team gained 17 imps, for in the replay the American East escaped for down two in five spades doubled.

The other players who shared in all three postwar victories were John Crawford and Howard Schenken. Of the prewar Four Aces team, Burnstine and Gottlieb had retired, and Jacoby had moved to Texas. But Schenken was still a force. He devised his own Strong Club system, playing it successfully with Peter Leventritt. His cardplay was legendary. The following example is from rubber bridge.

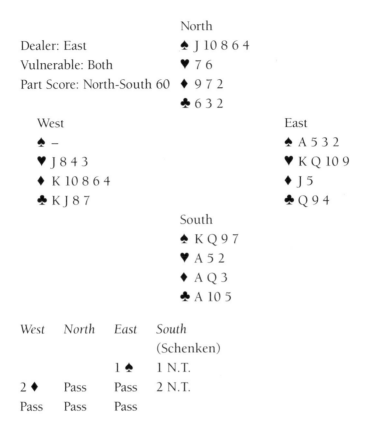

Dealer: East

Vulnerable: Both

Part Score: North-South 60

North
♠ J 10 8 6 4
♥ 7 6
♦ 9 7 2
♣ 6 3 2

West
♠ –
♥ J 8 4 3
♦ K 10 8 6 4
♣ K J 8 7

East
♠ A 5 3 2
♥ K Q 10 9
♦ J 5
♣ Q 9 4

South
♠ K Q 9 7
♥ A 5 2
♦ A Q 3
♣ A 10 5

West	North	East	South
			(Schenken)
		1 ♠	1 N.T.
2 ♦	Pass	Pass	2 N.T.
Pass	Pass	Pass	

This hand certainly "belongs" to East-West. They can make four hearts, rather luckily, and one spade is the limit for North-South against best defense.

But this was in the days when four-card major openings were standard, and East bid one spade. Schenken contented himself with one notrump, enough to convert his part-score to game, and tried again with two notrump when he heard two diamonds on his left.

West led a diamond, giving South a trick and a chance. On the face of it, he had four spade tricks and four tricks in the other suits. But he knew from the opening bid that he would not have four spade tricks: East would be able to hold up his ace for three rounds, and the last spade in dummy would wither on the vine.

So after winning the first diamond trick with the queen over the jack, Schenken did something weird: At the second trick he returned the diamond three. West won with the ten and happily played a third round to establish his suit.

East had to discard, and, as Schenken hoped, he parted with a spade. The spades were quickly established, and eight tricks were claimed, bringing home a rubber that could have gone to East-West.

Jacoby was living in Dallas, but was always on the move. After he returned from service in the Korean War, he set about overtaking Goren as the top master-point winner of all time. In a 60-year bridge career he played some quarter of a million deals, and the following is surely the most sensational of them.

North

Dealer: North
Vulnerable: Both

♠ Q J 8 5 4
♥ 5 2
♦ –
♣ K Q J 10 9 8

West

♠ –
♥ A K Q 10 9 8 7 6
♦ A K Q 4 2
♣ –

East

♠ 10 7 3 2
♥ J
♦ J 9 8 7 3
♣ 4 3 2

South

♠ A K 9 6
♥ 4 3
♦ 10 6 5
♣ A 7 6 5

West	North	East	South (Jacoby)
	Pass	Pass	1 ♠
Dbl.	4 ♠	Pass	Pass
5 ♥	5 ♠	Pass	Pass
6 ♥	Pass	Pass	Dbl.
Redbl.	Pass	Pass	6 ♠
7 ♥	Pass	Pass	7 ♠
Dbl.	Pass	Pass	Pass

West was looking at the hand of a lifetime, and bid it well, up to a point. He made a cunning takeout double of the opening one-spade bid, and bid his hearts gently at the five-level and the six-level.

This was good tactical bidding. The important thing with totally freak hands is to be the declarer, and the exact level is of secondary importance. But at the six-level West became foolishly greedy. When he was doubled he redoubled, and Jacoby worked out what was happening. He retreated to six spades, and took out insurance by bidding seven spades over seven hearts, not an obvious decision with a balanced hand containing two aces.

West doubled in rage, and could have cashed two heart tricks. Not unnaturally, however, it seemed to him that the diamond ace was a better bet for an opening lead.

The play to the first trick was crucial, and Jacoby, with plenty of clues to the distribution, made no mistake. He ruffed with dummy's spade eight and led the spade five. When East played low, Jacoby finessed the six, a remarkable way to play the first round of trumps in a grand slam.

A diamond was ruffed with the spade jack, and the spade nine was finessed. The last diamond in the closed hand was ruffed with dummy's last trump, and the rest was easy. A club to the ace allowed Jacoby to draw the missing trumps and claim, taking five more club tricks at the finish.

West was now in a bad temper, but it was entirely his own fault. His greedy redouble had turned a score of plus 1860 into minus 2470.

Jacoby was highly creative away from the table as well as at it. In 1956, in an article in *The Bridge World,* he introduced to the bridge public an idea of crucial importance that is now standard in serious competition.

The idea was the Jacoby Transfer bid. (See below p. 129.) After a one no-trump opening, responses of two diamonds and two hearts are forcing, and show length in the next-higher suit. A Swedish theorist, Olle Willner, had published the same concept in a Swedish magazine two years earlier. It is unlikely that Jacoby knew about this, so this is another example of simultaneous invention, like the calculus. Modern theorists have extended the idea, using it in a wide variety of other situations.

The next generation of American experts changed the face of standard bidding, as established by Culbertson and Goren. First in the field was the dynamic partnership of Alvin Roth and Tobias Stone. Roth was a genius at theory who brought forward, with his partner's help, the idea that a one notrump response to a major opening should be forcing. This makes it possible for two-over-one responses to be game-forcing, or virtually so. For details of the Roth-Stone System, see below p. 130.

Stone was an enfant terrible who created tension wherever he went. When he married Janice Gilbert, an equally dynamic television actress, somebody made book on whether this would last. A would-be investor sought information from the horse's mouth.

"Last?" barked Stone. "Of course it'll last. It'll last for months and months and months and months." It turned out to last for years and years and years and years.

When I met Stone in the mid-sixties, he commented on my appearance.

"You know, Alan, I can't quite make up my mind whether or not you're handsome."

"That's where we're different, Stoney," I responded, "Nobody could have the slightest doubt about you."

In 1957, Roth and Stone teamed with Rapee, Crawford, Becker and Sidney Silodor to win the event that chose the American team for the 1958 world championships. This was one of the deals:

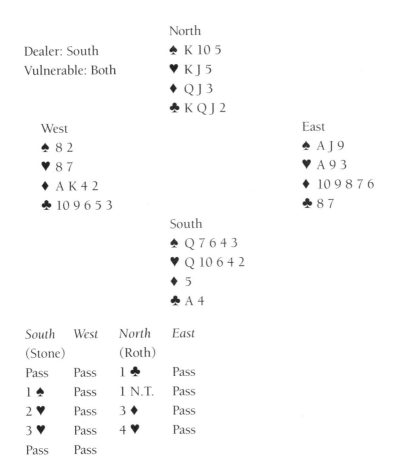

North

Dealer: South   ♠ K 10 5
Vulnerable: Both   ♥ K J 5
                       ♦ Q J 3
                       ♣ K Q J 2

West   East
♠ 8 2   ♠ A J 9
♥ 8 7   ♥ A 9 3
♦ A K 4 2   ♦ 10 9 8 7 6
♣ 10 9 6 5 3   ♣ 8 7

South
♠ Q 7 6 4 3
♥ Q 10 6 4 2
♦ 5
♣ A 4

South (Stone)	West	North (Roth)	East
Pass	Pass	1 ♣	Pass
1 ♠	Pass	1 N.T.	Pass
2 ♥	Pass	3 ♦	Pass
3 ♥	Pass	4 ♥	Pass
Pass	Pass		

One might think that Roth would open the North hand with one notrump, showing 16–18. But a strong hand that lacks aces is not worth its full face value, and he contented himself with one club. When his partner showed both major suits he decided to head for game and temporized with three diamonds. Once he knew that his partner held a five-five hand, he chose to play game in hearts rather than spades. With a choice of suits, the stronger tends to be preferable, and that proved a crucial factor here.

Four spades, as it happens, would have had to lose two trump tricks, a heart and a diamond. That was the result when the opposing team had the North-South cards. Four hearts might appear headed for the same fate, but

Stone read the cards perfectly and found a route home after the lead of the diamond king.

The contract would have failed if West had been inspired to shift to a
spade at the second trick. He led a club, however, and South won with the ace
and played a heart to dummy's jack. East held up his ace, and South continued
with the five. This time East took his ace and returned a trump to dummy's
king.

South ruffed a diamond, a key move, and took two rounds of clubs to
reach this ending:

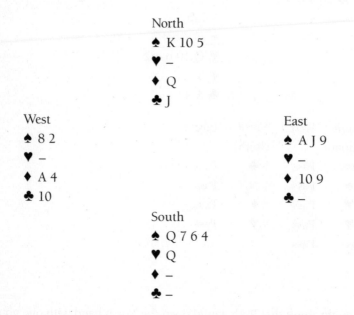

North
♠ K 10 5
♥ –
♦ Q
♣ J

West
♠ 8 2
♥ –
♦ A 4
♣ 10

East
♠ A J 9
♥ –
♦ 10 9
♣ –

South
♠ Q 7 6 4
♥ Q
♦ –
♣ –

On the lead of the club jack East could not spare a spade. He gave up a
"useless" diamond and Stone seized the opportunity. He ruffed the diamond
queen and led a spade to the king. East had to win and lead from his jack, giving South the last two tricks and his game. This was judged the best-played
deal of the tournament.

In 1958 this team played in the world championship in Como, Italy, losing
to the host country by 37 imps, on the old scale. Stone caused considerable
embarrassment by accusing the Italians of cheating. He was the first in a line of
accusers, as will be seen in chapter 12.

The next players to make an impression on the theory of the game were Edgar Kaplan and Alfred Sheinwold. For details of their Kaplan-Sheinwold system see below p. 132.

Sheinwold had been a member of the Culbertson organization, and was a syndicated columnist and author of a popular book. Kaplan was perhaps the most important figure in the world of bridge during the second half of the 20th century. Consider these remarkable qualifications: theorist and system-maker; bridge teacher, co-owner of a school in New York City; player, winner of 25 national titles and twice runner-up in world team championships; owner-editor of *The Bridge World* magazine for 20 years; coach of many American teams; consultant to the World Bridge Federation; chief commentator at many world championships; and world authority on the laws of the game and involved in many revisions of them.

The following deal helped Kaplan win the 1957 Masters Individual title. On his left was another great player, Norman Kay, who was to be Kaplan's partner for more than three decades. One might think that Kay would have opened with a weak two-bid in hearts, but he had a strange partner who may, in those days, have insisted on playing strong two-bids. (See below pages 134–135.)

Dealer: West

Vulnerable: Both

North
♠ A K Q 7 5
♥ A 7
♦ K J 9 4
♣ 9 7

West
♠ J 6 3
♥ Q J 9 6 4 2
♦ Q 8 6
♣ A

East
♠ 9 8 4 2
♥ K
♦ A 10 5 2
♣ 10 6 3 2

South
♠ 10
♥ 10 8 5 3
♦ 7 3
♣ K Q J 8 5 4

West (Kay)	North	East	South (Kaplan)
Pass	1 ♠	Pass	1 N.T.
Pass	2 ♦	Pass	3 ♣
Pass	3 N.T.	Pass	Pass
Pass			

This was Kaplan's description in *The Bridge World:*

As South, I hold no brief for my partner's three notrump bid, although it won the tournament for me. I had done my darndest to scream that my hand was worthless except in clubs. But there I was at three notrump, a foul contract which can make only if an opponent wins the first club trick, either injudiciously or because he has the singleton ace.

West opened the heart queen, which I won in dummy, East's king falling. I led the nine of clubs (not the seven) to my king, and West put on the ace. West shifted to a small diamond, and dummy's jack forced the ace. The diamond return rode to dummy's king. Now I led the club seven from the table, finessed my own eight, and made 10 tricks for a top.

You see, I was lucky enough to have Norman Kay on my left, in the West position. Never in his life has Norman been guilty of so bad a play as winning the first club if he could hold up, so the finesse was marked.

Obviously, the secret of winning individuals is to make sure that your opponents are more expert than your partners.

Kaplan and Kay as a partnership had the ability to win a world title. Why they, and other Americans, failed to do so will be explained in the next two chapters.

The ideas central to Roth-Stone and Kaplan-Sheinwold were established in the fifties. The next major development came from an unlikely source.

In 1963 I was in my first year in the United States, employed by the American Contract Bridge League. While I was struggling against heavy odds to produce the first of the series of Bridge Encyclopedias, I received an unexpected invitation to lunch. It came from a millionaire Chinese-American named Charles Wei whose company owned ships carrying oil and grain in bulk.

During the meal my host showed me a few pages with his outline of a new bidding system and asked me to look at it later. I did so, feeling I owed him something for an excellent lunch.

What he was suggesting was an amalgam of the five-card-major scheme with a strong-club opening and a weak notrump. This was sensible up to a point, but some hands remained unbiddable. I offered some suggestions about curing these problems and thrust the matter aside.

At this time the American Contract Bridge League, for no good reason, required new systems and conventions to be registered. He asked me to attend to this for him, and I did so. The system needed a name, so I gave it a temporary label: "Precision." That became permanent. (See below p. 133.)

I was convinced that the Wei system would go nowhere. Hundreds of inventors of conventions and systems had been at work since the earliest years of the game, but only a handful, all of them famous as players, had attracted a following.

I was, however, quite, quite wrong. Wei was proud of his brainchild, and was entirely willing to use his considerable financial resources to promote it.

First, he subsidized a team of talented young New York experts, two of whom, Peter Weichsel and Alan Sontag, were eventually to become world champions. Seven years later this Precision Team won three major national team titles, upsetting bunches of established stars.

Second, he persuaded the leading players in Taiwan to try Precision, and they did so. This effort paid off quickly. In 1969 the team won silver medals in the Bermuda Bowl; ahead of a strong American team but losing to Italy. In the following year they did equally well, finishing second behind the Americans.

Third, aiming higher, Wei recruited the Italian stars Benito Garozzo and Giorgio Belladonna. Garozzo was, and is, a systems enthusiast, and refined Wei's methods, calling the result Super-Precision. Using this, they won four straight world team titles, in 1972, 1973, 1974 and 1975.

Fourth, Wei subsidized the writing and publication of a series of Precision books.

Fifth, he married a dynamic young Chinese-American woman named Kathie, who knew little about bridge when I first met her. But she learned very quickly and rose to win bunches of national and world titles. She became a friend of Deng Xiaoping, the leader of China after the Cultural Revolution. He adopted Precision, and so did thousands of Chinese players who became enthusiasts with official encouragement.

Charles Wei died in 1987, and his widow, still a contender for major titles, is now Kathie Wei-Sender. His bidding method lives on in all parts of the world. Precision is by far the most popular of nonstandard systems, and is played on all continents. At every world championship today, a number of partnerships will be found playing their own version of Precision.

No. 18 ▸ Stayman

The traditional way of continuing after a Stayman response, still widely used, was this:

1. After a major-suit response, raise to three invitationally or bid game with sufficient values. Similarly, bid two notrump and three notrump naturally. Both imply four cards in the unbid major. (For many modern players, this does not apply to two notrump.)

2. After a two-diamond response, bid two notrump invitationally and three notrump naturally. Bid two hearts and two spades with a five-card suit and an invitational hand. (For many years a group of American experts played these bids as forcing, a treatment now abandoned. A strong modern tendency is to consider two hearts a weak action. It shows an unbalanced hand with no game interest, and typically has some spade length as well as heart length.)

3. Bids of three hearts and three spades are forcing. Bids of three clubs and three diamonds depend on partnership discussion, but are forcing without agreement.

No. 19 ▸ *Transfer Bids*

Transfer bids come in two styles:

1. Traditional Jacoby

After an opening one notrump bid, the responses are:

a. Two diamonds shows at least five hearts.

b. Two hearts shows at least five spades.

And a hand of any strength. Unless he has a maximum with four-card support for partner's suit, opener bids his partner's suit. That may end the bidding, in which case the strong hand is declarer, an advantage.

If the responder next bids a new suit, it is forcing. He may have a very strong hand and be planning to go to game or higher. Almost all other rebids are natural and nonforcing. For example, after one notrump-two diamonds-two hearts, then two notrump (game invitational), three notrump (game values), and four notrump (slam invitational) all show balanced hands with a five-card heart suit.

A direct response of two spades is minor-suit Stayman, showing at least five-four or four-five in the minor suits. Responder usually has slam interest, and will make his intentions clear on the next round.

A similar structure applies after a two-notrump opening, or after two clubs-two diamonds-two notrump.

2. Modern four-suit transfers

After an opening one no-trump bid:

a. Two diamonds shows at least five hearts.

b. Two hearts shows at least five spades.

c. Two spades shows at least five clubs.

d. Two notrump shows at least five diamonds.

The responder who bids two spades or two notrump may have a weak hand with a six-card minor, intending to stop at the three-level, or a strong hand with which he is heading for game or slam (but there are other methods). The corollary is that a direct bid of three clubs or three diamonds should be invitational, since other hands would use a transfer.

No. 20 ▸ *The Roth-Stone System*

Some of the features of the Roth-Stone system are:

1. Five-card-major openings, with a one-notrump response forcing for one round. If the opener has a balanced hand, he is often obliged to bid a three-card minor suit. If the responder is weak, he may pass the rebid, give preference to the opener's major, or make a minimum bid in a six-card suit: one heart-one notrump-two clubs-two diamonds.

With intermediate values in the 10–12 point range, the responder can invite with two notrump or, with three-card support, give jump preference in opener's major (one heart-one notrump-two clubs-three hearts). The corollary is:

2. Two-over-one responses to a major strong, normally 11 points or more, and guaranteeing a rebid. For many modern players these responses are game-forcing, but some make an exception when the responder rebids a minor suit. A modern tendency is for a direct jump in a minor suit (one spade-three diamonds or three clubs) to be invitational, but there are other methods.

This means that the responder can go slowly after responding at the two-level. After one spade-two clubs-two hearts he can bid two spades, two notrump, or three hearts to probe for the best game or a slam without fear of the bidding ending.

3. The negative double. Consider this auction:

West	North	East	South
1 ♣	1 ♠	Dbl.	

Traditionally, this was a penalty double, with the expectation of punishing North. East showed moderate values with long, strong spades. But it rarely came up, and when it did the opponents could often escape into a safer contract.

The Roth-Stone idea was to make this, and other doubles of a suit overcall, a takeout double, which they called "negative." (Since it appeared in the same year as the first Russian satellite, it was sometimes called Sputnik.) It emphasized the unbid major suit and provided for many hands for which there was no convenient bid. In this auction, East shows a hand with at least 6 points and at least four cards in hearts. He denies a hand able to bid two hearts, so he is likely to have exactly four hearts. If he has longer hearts, his hand is not strong, perhaps in the 6–10 point range.

The meaning of the negative double varies slightly with circumstances. If the overcall is one heart, the doubler shows exactly four spades. (A one-spade bid would show five or more.) If the overcall is at the two-level, the doubler should have at least 8 high-card points.

4. The Unusual Notrump. In the early 40's, Roth overcalled one spade with one notrump after passing originally. Stone worked out correctly that this must show both minor suits, since Roth would have doubled with a takeout hand that included heart length. From this developed the idea that notrump bids with no useful natural meaning should show the minor suits.

The commonest use in modern practice is the direct two notrump jump overcall. This shows clubs and diamonds if the opening is in a major suit, but the red suits after a one-club opening, and clubs and hearts after one diamond.

This idea has many applications in competitive auctions, particularly when the bidding seems likely to die at a low level. One of these is shown below on page 159. (Chapter 13.)

These four Roth-Stone ideas were of primary importance, and all have become a part of standard bidding.

Some other ideas proved less popular. For example:

1. Sound opening bids, normally with at least 14 points. Roth-Stone believed in passing borderline hands that other experts would open.

2. Sound free bids. Bids after opponents intervened showed extra values.

3. Constructive major raises. A single raise of one spade or one heart showed the equivalent of a modern limit raise. It usually showed 10–12 points in high cards, and was almost forcing. (Weaker hands responded one notrump.)

4. Opening psychic bids, showing 3–6 points concentrated in the bid suit. As a corollary, a two-notrump response promised 20–21 points and three notrump 22 or more.

5. Weak jump shift responses, with or without an overcall, showing fewer than 6 high-card points. These continue to be played by many modern experts, since the strong jump shift is not an essential weapon.

No. 21 ► *The Kaplan-Sheinwold System*

Kaplan-Sheinwold adopted some of the features of the Roth-Stone System: the forcing one-notrump response; the strong two-over-one response; the negative double; and the unusual notrump. It rejected the Roth-Stone idea of "sound" actions. It used the English style in some areas, with many invitational jump bids.

K-S used the weak notrump, recognizing, as British players had done, that this creates problems for the opponents.

The aim was increased accuracy with strong hands, and preemption with weak ones. "If the opponents continually jam up your auctions while you leave theirs strictly alone," wrote the authors of the system, "you are going to lose." So they designed a system that would put pressure on the opponents, an idea that would be developed later. (See page 189.)

No. 22 ▸ The Precision System

Precision in its basic form consists of:

1. A strong one-club opening promising, in principle, 16 points or more. One diamond is a negative response with fewer than 8 points. Minimum suit responses promise at least 8 points and a five-card suit. Jumps to two hearts and two spades are weak.

2. One diamond is a multipurpose bid, and may be based on a doubleton if no other bid is suitable. A two-diamond response is natural and forcing, in effect a two-over-one.

3. A one heart or one spade opening with at least five cards and 11–15 points. Responses are similar to Roth-Stone and Kaplan-Sheinwold, with the advantage that the opener's hand is limited.

4. A one notrump opening with 13–15 points. (Many modern experts use a 14–16 point range. With 11–13 and balanced, they bid one diamond and rebid one notrump.) Most partnerships use transfer responses.

5. Two clubs shows 11–15 points with a six-card club suit. (Some permit a strong five-card suit.) A two-diamond response is a positive relay asking for further description.

6. Two diamonds is a three-suited hand short in diamonds with 11–15 points. A three-card major suit is possible, with 3-4-1-5 or 4-3-1-5 distribution. A two notrump response is a positive relay asking for more information.

No. 23 ▸ *Strong Opening Bids*

Two clubs, as an artificial opening bid for all hands of great strength, was part of the Official System at the dawn of the game, and was widely used in Europe. It did not spread to the American bridge public until the 1950's, and even then the Culbertson Forcing Two died hard.

Two clubs has many advantages as the strong initial action. It keeps the bidding under control, does not waste four bids to show a rare group of hands, and diminishes the danger that the weak hand will be declarer.

The two-club bidder shows a hand on which he can guarantee, or virtually guarantee, a game. If his partner has moderate values a slam is likely.

Weak hands must respond two diamonds, but that bid is often made with stronger hands that do not have a convenient alternative.

Two clubs commits the partnership to game with one exception: If the bidding starts two clubs-two diamonds-two notrump, the opener shows a balanced hand with 23–24 points. (Some say 22–24.) Responder may then pass with a worthless or virtually worthless hand. (Some allow a second exception. If opener bids and rebids a suit at his second and third turns, responder may pass if very weak.)

No. 24 ► *Weak Two-Bids and Preemptive Bids*

Weak two-bids originated about 1930, and were used by many experts. They did not become popular with the bridge public until the 50's, when the Culbertson influence diminished. They became an integral part of the three systems discussed in this chapter: Roth-Stone, Kaplan-Sheinwold, and Precision.

The classic weak two-bid was based on a strong six-card suit and 6–12 high-card points. This has been diluted with the passage of time; 5–10 is a common range, and a strong suit is not mandatory. Some permit use of the bid with a strong five-card suit, especially in third position. Two hearts and two spades are always weak two-bids. Two diamonds can be used for other purposes. (See page 194 below.)

Responder should raise the opening bid if he can, and keep an eye on the vulnerability. He bids three with three-card support and no interest in game. He bids game with a variety of hands, which may be strong in high cards or have some length in the suit. This puts great pressure on the fourth player.

With a strong hand, and at least game interest, the responder may bid two notrump. This asks opener to describe further, as follows: with a minimum, three of his suit; with a maximum, three of another suit in which a high honor is held; three notrump in the rare case in which the suit is headed by A-K-Q. A popular alternative is Ogust: three clubs shows weak hand, weak suit; three diamonds shows weak hand, strong suit; three hearts shows strong hand, weak suit; and three spades shows strong hand, strong suit.

A new-suit response may be forcing or nonforcing by partnership agreement.

Opening bids of three or more in a suit are *preemptive*. They almost always indicate a hand without the high-card strength to open with a one-bid, so 4–9 high-card points is the usual range. A three-bid typically has a seven-card suit and a four-bid an eight-card suit. Some flexibility is permissible. Be cautious when vulnerable. Be aggressive when not vulnerable against vulnerable opponents. Liberties may be taken when opening in third position.

As with a weak two-bid, responder should raise a three-bid to four when he can. This may mean a good hand, or a bad hand with a few trumps in support.

Similar actions can be taken when the opponents open the bidding. Over one club, two hearts resembles a weak two-bid and three hearts resembles an opening three-bid.

CHAPTER 12

Ethics and Cheating

There is a narrow line, but nevertheless a clear one, between the unethical player and the cheat. Bridge ethics are quite complex. You are permitted to take any advantage you wish, at your own risk, of an opposing hesitation. But you are not allowed to take advantage of your partner's hesitation or other departure from normal behavior. And you are not allowed to hesitate simply in the hope of deceiving an opponent.

Inexperienced players sometimes commit breaches of ethics through ignorance. They bid loudly or softly, conveying information to their partners. They make faces, or otherwise show pleasure or displeasure. (One old lady in England had a habit of turning off her ear trumpet, to make it clear that she did not wish to hear any further bidding from her partner.) In all such cases their partners must ignore the information thus conveyed, and even bend over backward to do so. Nevertheless, some otherwise upright citizens take advantage of such circumstances, perhaps subconsciously, and strongly resent any suggestion that they have committed a breach.

A vast majority of experts are highly ethical in such matters. However, a few Americans, all now dead, used to believe that anything goes. One even taught his students how to give information to partner by hesitating, and how to take advantage from the other side of the table. Almost invariably, such breaches happen without any specific discussion between partners. In a tournament, they may, however, find themselves in front of an appeals committee and perhaps have a score adjusted.

Cheating is another matter altogether, and nearly always involves partnership collaboration. Some cheats, particularly those who are discreet and confine their cheating to rare crucial situations, can get away with it and no doubt do. There are undetected cheats just as there are undetected murderers. Those who cheat in a comprehensive way are usually detected, although the proof may not be sufficient to convince everyone. Evidence may be provided by observers who have seen illegal signals being transmitted, or by analysts who have studied the performance of the players, or both.

In the first half-century of contract bridge, the four European countries that were most successful in international play all had problems with players suspected of cheating. So did one Far East country. We'll consider them in chronological order.

AUSTRIA

Chapter 7 furnished strong evidence that two of the Austrian players who won the world team title in 1937 in Hungary were cheating. One died in a concentration camp, but Karl Schneider was to be heard of after World War II. In 1951 he led an Austrian team in the European Championship in Venice, winning silver medals. He and his partner used methods that were said to be "Culbertson," but observers were baffled. On one deal, the opening bid was one spade and the response was two hearts. The opening bidder passed, and the responder, who had eight points, made exactly eight tricks. This seems to strengthen the idea that Schneider used a signal to show weakness.

In 1954, France had won the European Championship and was due to play against a United States team for the world title. As this was Europe versus America, the French were permitted to add two non-French players, and their choice fell on Schneider. He was asked to play with Jean Besse, a Swiss player who was an outstanding individual performer. Before the match, Schneider told Besse, "You know, we've got to help each other." Besse knew exactly what that meant and refused indignantly.

That may help explain why the Americans won easily—Schneider and Besse were not "helping" each other—and it suggests one way to approach a partner with cheating in mind. (Another way, more delicate, is to discuss in theory how cheating might be done, and then start sending signals without explicitly agreeing to do so.)

In 1957, the European Championships were scheduled in Vienna with the Austrian Federation in the role of host. The anchor pair for the home team consisted of Schneider and Max Reithoffer. They attracted the attention of a young Swiss expert, Jaime Ortiz-Patino, who will feature in the next chapter.

At that time, half of each match was played in an Open Room, where spectators could observe the action. Watching the Austrians, Patino noted a strange habit. After sorting their hands, Schneider and Reithoffer would invariably hold the cards in a block on the table, either vertically or horizontally. Sometimes the left hand was used, and sometimes the right. Sometimes the cards were angled, with a rocking motion.

After taking notes and analyzing them carefully in private, Ortiz-Patino broke the code. The movements were ace-showing, and when he returned to watch he could predict the aces held by either player without being able to see the cards. Such knowledge will occasionally cause a player to make a conspicuously unlikely bid. There was one interesting example from the match between Britain and Austria. The details are not on record, but the bidding, with East-West vulnerable, was this:

South	West	North	East
	(Reithoffer)		(Schneider)
1 ♠	Pass	4 ♠	Dbl.
Pass	Pass	Pass	

Schneider had a balanced aceless 13-point hand, and in normal circumstances the double would be unthinkable. West could have a Yarborough, and the result could easily be a doubled overtrick or a heavy penalty—but . . . Reithoffer had two aces, and the result was down four and 700 (in those days) to Austria. The British South player, Adam Meredith, had psyched with a near-Yarborough.

In the second half of the match, Schneider and Reithoffer played against Terence Reese and Boris Schapiro. The British players were friendly with Ortiz-Patino, who had shared his decoding with them. Schapiro did not trust his memory and had notes on the back of a cigarette box, adding an extra dimension to a tense encounter.

Ortiz-Patino wanted some reliable, discreet witnesses, and I was one of his choices. He showed me the code and I stood in the audience behind Reithoffer. Looking at the hand positions, I could predict accurately which aces the two players held.

Ortiz-Patino had made the correct moves for someone who believes that he has detected cheating, and he reported his conclusions to the authorities. This was highly embarrassing to the officials for an unusual reason: Reithoffer was the president of the Austrian Federation, and in overall charge of the tournament organization and hospitality. An open accusation and condemnation might have resulted in the hosts closing down everything, leaving the European Championships unfinished. Not surprisingly, the politicians decided on diplomatic discretion. There was no inquiry and no verdict, but the players were confronted with the evidence. They agreed never to play again, and did not do so apart from a minor event in London in which they were already entered.

Ortiz-Patino had begun a memorable career in the game that would lead to a virtual end of cheating at the highest levels. I was surprised that I had not been called to testify, but that omission seemed about to be remedied six years later. A brief and guarded account of the affair was included in a book by Victor Mollo, and the Austrians started a legal action against him and his publisher in London. A libel trial was about to begin and I was scheduled as a witness. I was looking forward to a free trip to England, but a phone call stopped me a few hours before I was to board a plane. The case had been settled, on terms that were not announced. Presumably the plaintiffs, the publishers and the insurance company wanted a cheap way out, so, for the second time, truth became a victim of circumstance.

FRANCE

In the 1950's two young Frenchmen, Franck Bodier and Pierre Figeac, rocketed to fame, winning virtually every major competition in which they entered. In 1954 they were members of the French European Championship team in Montreux, Switzerland, that placed second. They were so successful, and their performance so perfect, that suspicion was inevitably aroused. It seemed, for example, that they never misguessed when on lead.

A committee appointed to investigate found some weird items. Against a highly inferior contract of six notrump, one of them was on lead holding the K-Q of one suit and the ace of another. His king was clearly an automatic lead, but he led a third suit in which his partner held the K-Q.

Even more spectacular was the following:

West	North	East	South
			1 ♣
Pass	1 ♥	Pass	1 N.T.
Pass	Pass	Pass	

The normal choice of lead after this bidding is a spade. The last choice, unless holding length and strength, is a club. West chose a club lead with a holding of Q-x-x, and selected the queen. It turned out that his partner's club holding was A-K-x-x-x.

The committee decided that the performance of Bodier and Figeac was too perfect, far beyond the parameters of normality. They were summoned to appear before the committee, but chose to resign from the French Federation and disappeared from the game.

An accusation against another French pair, Claude Delmouly and Gérard Bourchtoff, was vastly more controversial. They were alleged to be using the cleverest illegal signal ever invented. It is called *"l'ascenseur"* in French, "the lift" in English, and "the elevator" in American. The user holds his cards opposite his chest with maximum values, opposite his belt with minimum values, and somewhere in between when they're somewhere in between. The beauty of this is that the user's partner is never induced to do something technically improbable. All that happens is that he uses very good judgment in borderline situations, and the analysts find nothing spectacular to report.

Delmouly and Bourchtoff were members of the winning French team at the first World Team Olympiad in Turin, Italy, in 1960. A few months later, they were accused by Simone Albarran, widow of France's greatest personality, of using *l'ascenseur*.

Unfortunately, the accusation concerned an occasion six months earlier, before the world championship, when several observers said they had seen *l'ascenseur* in action. A committee appointed by the French Federation reported that the trail was cold and that no conclusion could be reached.

French players divided into two camps, for and against the accused players. The Federation, in Gallic fashion, became totally unpopular because it suspended all those directly concerned, the accused and the accusers. This was unrelated to the facts of the case but was a penalty for "the conspiracy of silence." They had all failed in their obligation to tell the Federation about the allegations at the time. Mme. Albarran sued the federation for wrongful suspension, and was eventually awarded damages of one *sou*.

Dr. Pierre Jaïs and Roger Trézel were the top French pair in the fifties. They were an automatic choice for the national team and were highly successful. By winning the World Pairs in Cannes in 1962, the Bermuda Bowl in Paris in 1956, and the first World Team Olympiad in 1960 they became the first partnership to achieve the "triple crown," a feat that has been matched only three times since. (The others are: Bobby Wolff and Bob Hamman of the United States; Jeff Meckstroth and Eric Rodwell of the United States; Gabriel Chagas and Marcelo Branco of Brazil.)

Jaïs and Trézel were unpopular in French tournament circles, and rumors swirled. A sensational hand, which I had good reason to note, occurred in the European Championships in Oslo in 1958. Italy, Britain and France were fighting for the title and the right to play against the Americans for the Bermuda Bowl.

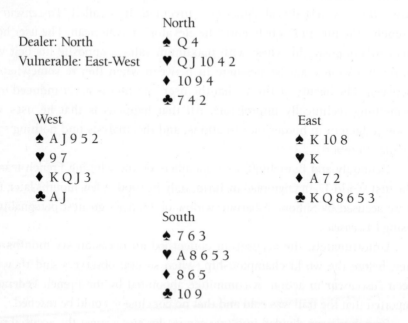

Dealer: North
Vulnerable: East-West

North
♠ Q 4
♥ Q J 10 4 2
♦ 10 9 4
♣ 7 4 2

West
♠ A J 9 5 2
♥ 9 7
♦ K Q J 3
♣ A J

East
♠ K 10 8
♥ K
♦ A 7 2
♣ K Q 8 6 5 3

South
♠ 7 6 3
♥ A 8 6 5 3
♦ 8 6 5
♣ 10 9

It can be seen that six clubs is a laydown for East-West, while six spades depends on a guess for the spade queen. One might expect East-West to have a free run in the bidding since neither North nor South has any reason to bid. However:

West	North	East	South
(J. Sharples)	(Trézel)	(R. Sharples)	(Jaïs)
	Pass	1 ♣	1 ♠
Dbl.	Pass	Pass	IN.T.
2 N.T.	Pass	3 ♣	Pass
3 ♠	Pass	4 ♦	Pass
6 ♦	Pass	6 ♠	Pass
Pass	Pass		

A heart was led, and West later misguessed the spade queen, going down one. At the other table, by a remarkable coincidence:

West	North	East	South
(R. Bacherich)	(Schapiro)	(P. Ehestem)	(Reese)
	Pass	1 ♣	1 ♠
Dbl.	Pass	Pass	2 ♥
3 ♥	Pass	3 ♠	Pass
4 ♠	Pass	Pass	Pass

This was easy to make, and France gained 7 imps, on the imp scale then in use. But if the Sharples brothers (Bob and Jim), who were East-West against Jaïs-Trézel, had reached six clubs, or made the winning guess in six spades, Britain would have won the match and become European champions. I would have played in the Bermuda Bowl later in the year with a good chance to become a world champion. (Instead, Italy won on a split tie and took the world title by defeating the Americans.)

As for the astonishing one-spade overcall, which risks a total disaster if partner has a spade fit, a French magazine put the situation in a bidding competition a few years later. One of the panelists chose to bid one heart over one club but everybody else thought it absurd to consider any action. Trézel, Jaïs and Reese proved to have imperfect memories.

A. Dormer (British player-writer): "Pass—unless I am forced to bid by having a gun stuck in my back."

R. Trézel: "Pass. I don't think my hand will produce a game opposite a partner who has passed!"

P. Jaïs: "Pass or six hearts, or obviously . . . or one heart in the . . . European Championship if one feels like doing something."

T. Reese: "Pass. It would be ridiculous to bid without even raising the level of the auction."

Not so ridiculous, perhaps, if you know that your partner has a five-card heart suit and he knows that you do. Which takes us across the Channel to England.

BRITAIN

For almost two decades, from 1948 to 1965, Terence Reese and Boris Schapiro were acknowledged to be one of the world's best partnerships. They were the anchor pair when Britain won the European Teams title in 1948 and 1949. Reese was also a top writer, producing original books that contributed greatly to the theory of the game. For a short time he organized elite tournaments, and after one event was walking home in the small hours carrying a bag of silver cups that needed to be engraved. When the police were curious, he suggested that they call Schapiro. His sleepy reply was, "Reese? Never heard of him."

At the end of 1949 Reese and Schapiro were invited by the British Bridge League to play in the next British team. Four months later they were disinvited, a bombshell. "We limit ourselves," said the editor of a British magazine, "to the endorsement of the B.B.L.'s view that mere technical superiority is not, and must never be, the sole criterion for national representation."

This was highly confusing to all who read it. Did it mean that their table manners were bad? They were indeed inclined to be arrogant, and rude to the opponents: Irish players had complained bitterly about their behavior the previous summer. Or did it mean something much worse?

Some of the Reese-Schapiro bidding was baffling to observers. They regularly made psychic opening bids with very weak hands, and never suffered the disasters one might expect. They seemed to have a sixth sense—or perhaps had a weakness signal copied from the prewar Austrian stars. On one occasion Schapiro opened one club with a balanced 21-point hand that represented an automatic two-notrump opening. The bidding ended, Reese's dummy was a perfect Yarborough, and Schapiro made exactly seven tricks. Two notrump would have failed.

A year later there were lengthy trials to decide the British representation, with Reese and Schapiro in the lead after three stages. After the first stage there was a brouhaha, however: Harrison Gray, the captain of the winning teams in 1948, 1949 and 1950, withdrew, asking for an inquiry into the performance of Reese and Schapiro, his former teammates. The officials refused this and reprimanded Gray, who was barred for one year from international play.

In the final two stages of the trials, thanks to a format that began with pairs who were then formed into teams, Reese and Schapiro had as teammates a little-known Oxford University partnership: Robert D'Unienville and Alan Truscott. Victory after the fifth stage gave me my first international experience, and we finished third in a strong field in Venice, behind Italy and Austria. One of the Italian winners was a player exactly my age who was soon to be recognized as one of the best of all time: Pietro Forquet.

In 1954 the European Team Championship was in Montreux. The British won, with Reese and Schapiro as the anchor pair, and arrived in New York the following year to play the Americans for the Bermuda Bowl. Rumors about the British pair had crossed the Atlantic, and a young American star, Edgar Kaplan, was designated to keep an eye on their performance. He did not see anything significant, but failed, like everyone else at the time, to find the explanation for the following astonishing deal:

North

Dealer: South   ♠ A 10 9 8 7
Vulnerable: None   ♥ J 7 5 3
                       ♦ K 10 8 3
                       ♣ —

West   East
♠ 5   ♠ K J 6 4 3
♥ K 8 4   ♥ A 9
♦ A 9 5   ♦ J 6 2
♣ A K J 7 6 2   ♣ Q 10 3

South
♠ Q 2
♥ Q 10 6 2
♦ Q 7 4
♣ 9 8 5 4

South	West	North	East
(Schapiro)	(Ellenby)	(Reese)	(Rosen)
1 ♣(!)	Pass	1 ♠	Pass
2 ♣(!!)	Pass	2 ♦	Pass
Pass	3 ♣	Pass	3 N.T.
Pass	Pass	Pass	

For most players, an opening psychic is a risky gamble, and a pass must follow. For any player, to follow a psychic opening with a psychic rebid is absurdly dangerous. It would be unthinkable in the local club, let alone in a world championship, because partner's next bid might be at the game level or even higher.

There was no swing, because the Americans were able to back in to the auction and reach their normal game. The deal remained a mystery, however, for 14 years. In 1969, a Californian enthusiast pointed out to me that the identical deal, spot for spot, was in the match record 96 deals earlier, which is 3 × 32. The first time, against different opponents, Schapiro passed with the South hand. Two days later he remembered the cards and realized that the board had not been redealt. He also remembered that West held good clubs, and thought of a plan that might rob the opponents of their easy game. It did not succeed, but it was certainly creative.

In the same match, Alvin Roth recognized a dummy when defending a one notrump contract. He did what one is supposed to do: He called for the director and proved, in the face of considerable skepticism, that it was a board that had not been redealt and therefore had to be thrown out.

The British team won the world title easily, and Lew Mathe, a feisty member of the American team, pointedly congratulated the other four British players.

In 1957 at the European Championships in Vienna, Reese and Schapiro were involved in the episode described (on page 139) and the accusation against Schneider and Reithoffer. The session of play when these four players were in action was surely the most remarkable in the history of the game: Reese and Schapiro, presumably, had illegal information about *both* pairs of hands.

Nevertheless, the British were unable to repeat their Montreux victory. Italy won and the Austrians were second. Back in London, Reese and Schapiro heard about an accusation against a local partnership that was having notable successes. The players were alleged to have special knowledge about the number of hearts in partner's hand. The deals produced in evidence were inconclusive, and the experts who examined them could not agree. But a seed had been sown and bore fruit in the following year. The Oslo deal shown above (page 142) strongly suggests that the British stars, as well as the French, had improper knowledge about the heart suit.

Reese and Schapiro did not play in the 1959 European Championships in Palermo, Sicily, but were back in action a year later for the first postwar World Team Championship in Turin. This was in effect an Olympics, but that word could not be used. Instead the organizers called it an "Olympiad," which purists complained about. An Olympiad is, strictly speaking, the interval of four years between Olympics.

This tournament had organizational problems. Playing cards, which were attractive to the locals, tended to disappear. The Italian secretary, attempting to protect the gentlemen of the press from intrusion by caddies, locked a door and so prevented the movement of boards between the two playing areas. He was frisked by some angry tournament directors, who unlocked the door and threw the key far into the Mediterranean.

In the qualifying stage Britain had to play a strong Canadian team, whose players were furious and suspicious about the following deal:

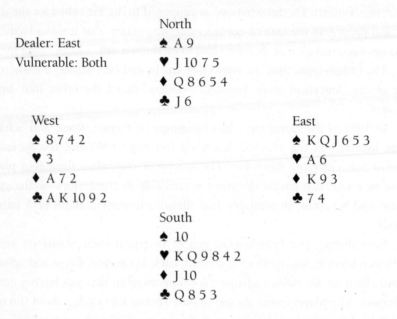

Dealer: East
Vulnerable: Both

North
♠ A 9
♥ J 10 7 5
♦ Q 8 6 5 4
♣ J 6

West
♠ 8 7 4 2
♥ 3
♦ A 7 2
♣ A K 10 9 2

East
♠ K Q J 6 5 3
♥ A 6
♦ K 9 3
♣ 7 4

South
♠ 10
♥ K Q 9 8 4 2
♦ J 10
♣ Q 8 5 3

East-West can make six spades, and the British pair reached it. In the replay the Canadians had little chance because of some remarkable interference.

West (Elliott)	North (Reese)	East (Sheardown)	South (Schapiro)
		1 ♠	1 N.T.
4 ♠	Dbl.	Pass	5 ♥
Pass	Pass	Dbl.	Pass
Pass	Pass		

One no-trump was supposed to be natural, a balanced 16–18 points with a spade stopper. The result was a penalty of 800, which would be a swing of 12 imps on the modern scale. On a bad day, Schapiro might easily find a singleton heart in the dummy and go down 1400 or more. But the partnership never seemed to have a bad day.

Consider this deal in combination with the psychic one-spade overcall shown above on page 142. If two partners know each other's heart lengths, a variety of apparently risky psychic maneuvers are entirely safe. Did they know? And how did they know?

Britain advanced to a six-team round-robin final, a format that has clear disadvantages and has never been used since. France won, with a team including two pairs mentioned above: Jaïs-Trezel and Delmouly-Bourchtoff. The British came close, winning the silver medals, and two trans-Atlantic experts decided to take a close look at Reese and Schapiro.

One was Eric Murray, a young Canadian starting a great international career. He noted several odd deals. On one Reese passed his partner's one no-trump opening that purported to be 16–18 points. Announcing, rather strangely, that he had decided to underbid, he put down an 8-point dummy, running the risk of missing a game if his partner held a maximum. Schapiro's vulnerable opening bid proved to have 13 points.

Murray, a lawyer by profession, is always ready to speak his mind. "It's only fair to tell you," he declared to Reese afterward, "that your opponents are quite convinced they were being cheated." The reply was a snicker.

The other investigator was Don Oakie, a Californian who was a former world champion. His team had been eliminated in the qualifying stage, and he took some paper and sat down to kibitz behind Schapiro. He immediately noticed something weird: On one deal, the British expert held his cards and his pipe in his right hand.

Oakie took notes of three mannerisms. One was the height at which cards were held, which was somewhat subjective. Another was the number of fingers showing behind the cards, which varied regularly. The third, and the one on which he focused, was the hand in which the cards were held.

He established over a large number of deals that cards in the left hand corresponded to below-average strength, and cards in the right hand to above-average strength. Honest players invariably use the same hand. Three extant press photographs, from 1960 and 1965, show Reese using his left hand once and his right hand twice.

Oakie arranged for some American officials to watch, and they completely confirmed his assessment. To his astonishment, the senior officials wanted to avoid embarrassment and asked him to keep quiet. They contented themselves with asking Harold Franklin, the British tournament director, to pass the information to the British Bridge League. Franklin did not do this, and no further action was taken. He did, apparently, tell Reese, a close friend, that there was suspicion. Soon afterward Reese, wishing to avoid the limelight, announced that he would not be a candidate for the next British team. He and Schapiro did not play again until 1964 in New York, where their team lost a close semifinal to Italy.

The bubbling volcano that Reese and Schapiro represented erupted at the Bermuda Bowl in Buenos Aires in 1965. The whole story has been told in two books, but a brief summary is appropriate here.

Dorothy (then Hayden, now Truscott) qualified for the American team in partnership with one of great players of all time, B. Jay Becker. On the first occasion he played the British, he noticed that Reese was holding his cards with two separated fingers showing in a V-formation. He thought this uncomfortable and unnatural. On subsequent deals he saw that both opponents showed varying numbers of fingers.

Later he shared his observation with Dorothy, and they agreed to tell me. I was incredulous, but was convinced when I watched at the next opportunity. I was reporting for *The New York Times,* and had more time than they did to consider the problem. When Dorothy and Becker were sitting out they watched Reese and Schapiro in play in a grandstand area and took notes. After a day of unsuccessful effort by me, Dorothy had a crucial decoding thought. The finger positions, we discovered, corresponded with complete accuracy to the number of hearts a player held.

Becker told the story to the American nonplaying captain, John Gerber, and he advised officials. Some of them watched, together with the British nonplaying captain, Ralph Swimer, and all were convinced. Swimer spoke privately to Schapiro, who confessed to him; a confession he later denied having made. Swimer testified about this to the later inquiry in London.

The World Bridge Federation (W.B.F.) Executive held hearings, and asked the witnesses to keep quiet temporarily. This put me in a difficult position, with a conflict between my duty as a witness and my responsibilities as a reporter. As a result, I suffered the indignity of having a news agency story, with limited factual basis, appearing on the front page of my newspaper, *The New York Times.*

The W.B.F. delivered a guilty verdict, and its announcement made frontpage news around the world. But the executive made a tactical error. It could have announced that the players were permanently suspended from international play, but instead referred the matter to the British Bridge League.

The expectation was that the league would decide on an appropriate penalty, but friends of the accused players rallied round. The league announced that it was setting up a quasi-judicial inquiry. It would be headed by Sir John Foster, Q.C., and General Lord Bourne. Both were social bridge players with no knowledge of the tournament scene and its players, and admitted they were "in the 18th rank."

I traveled to London to give evidence, together with Dorothy and Becker. Other Americans who had made observations did not make the trip, and their evidence, including an affidavit from Waldemar von Zedtwitz, was disregarded.

The evidence of finger mannerisms, together with correspondence to the heart suit, was overwhelming, certainly enough to satisfy any knowledgeable expert. But there was much argument about the deals. Did they or did they not indicate cheating? This was an extraordinary example:

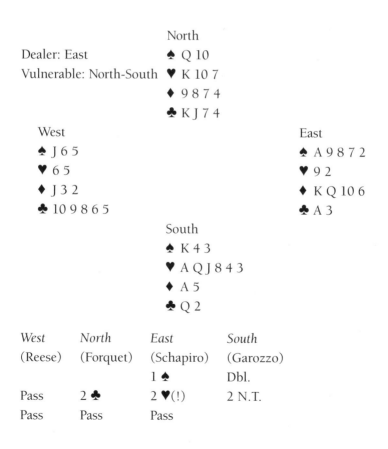

	North	
Dealer: East	♠ Q 10	
Vulnerable: North-South	♥ K 10 7	
	♦ 9 8 7 4	
	♣ K J 7 4	

West		East
♠ J 6 5		♠ A 9 8 7 2
♥ 6 5		♥ 9 2
♦ J 3 2		♦ K Q 10 6
♣ 10 9 8 6 5		♣ A 3

	South
	♠ K 4 3
	♥ A Q J 8 4 3
	♦ A 5
	♣ Q 2

West	North	East	South
(Reese)	(Forquet)	(Schapiro)	(Garozzo)
		1 ♠	Dbl.
Pass	2 ♣	2 ♥(!)	2 N.T.
Pass	Pass	Pass	

The psychic bid of two hearts by Schapiro may be unique in the literature of the game. It offers no safety whatever. West has not raised spades and is quite likely to have heart length. In that case he might raise hearts with catastrophic consequences.

In the replay the British North-South pair had no trouble bidding and making four hearts for a gain of 10 imps. For the next two days Forquet showed the hand to everyone he met. "How can they bid like this?" he demanded. Nobody had an answer for him, but now there is one.

If two partners have knowledge of each other's heart length, it offers possibilities for tricky maneuvers: The psychic shown here, when the opponents are known to have a good heart fit, and the psychic in Oslo shown above, when the psychic bidder and his partner know that they have a heart fit.

Evidence from deals is rarely conclusive in a cheating case, although it may be suggestive. If players are observed to be passing illegal information, that should be enough to satisfy any expert bridge committee, with or without a decoding of the signals.

To the astonishment and indignation of many, including all the Americans, Sir John and his colleague found the case against Reese and Schapiro not proven. They said that the evidence of the deals created "reasonable doubt" in spite of "the direct evidence as to the exchange of finger signals, strong as it is." Some called the verdict a whitewash.

This created a strange situation. The two players were guilty in the eyes of the World Bridge Federation but innocent in Britain. Three years later, after furious arguments behind the scenes, they were permitted to return to play. But they were virtually retired from that point, and never played together again in an international event. (Late in life, at 89, Schapiro won a World Senior Pairs title with Irving Gordon, an age record for victory in any international arena.)

When the verdict was announced, Reese immediately produced a book, entitled *Story of an Accusation*. It omitted all the details of the observations made by witnesses. This provoked me to write a book entitled *The Great Bridge Scandal* and Reese did not sue me. "I would not get justice in America," he told his friends.

In preparing for my book, I found press photographs from 1960 and 1965 showing the two players with varying finger positions. I also found, with difficulty, the records of the deals observed by Oakie in 1960. The fingers he noted exactly matched the heart code established five years later.

INDONESIA

Indonesia won three consecutive Far East Championships in the period 1972–74. Australian opponents found the performance of the brothers F. E. and M. F. Manoppo quite astonishing and asked for an investigation. Their leads were incredible:

West	East
♠ A 10 9	♠ J
♥ A Q 8 5	♥ 9 6 4 3 2
♦ K Q 2	♦ 10 8 7 5 3
♣ A 7 3	♣ K 9

West	North	East	South
(M.F. Manoppo)		(F.E. Manoppo)	
	Pass	Pass	1 ♠
1 N.T.	3 ♠	4 ♥	4 ♠
Pass	Pass	Dbl.	Pass
Pass	Pass		

Any good player would lead the diamond king from the West hand, expecting to establish a fourth trick. M.F. Manoppo led the club seven, a remarkable choice that produced a club ruff for the defense.

The Manoppo problem was referred to a W.B.F. expert committee, which examined 600 deals. On 75 of them one of the brothers led from an ace or a king, and each time his partner held the other top honor. The verdict was that this was not possible without improper information, and the players were suspended for a long period. They were barred permanently from playing with each other.

The next scandal to break on the world bridge scene needs a chapter to itself.

CHAPTER 13

Curing the Problem

The various scandals involving European players, particularly the one concerning Terence Reese and Boris Schapiro, provoked officials to consider ways in which cheating could be inhibited, if not totally prevented. The leader in this effort was young, energetic, and determined. His name was, and is, Jaime Ortiz-Patino. He was one of the heirs to a vast business empire: His grandfather, Simon Patino, had been a poverty-stricken miner in Bolivia when he struck a rich vein of tin and from it built one of the world's biggest fortunes.

Today Ortiz-Patino lives in Valderrama, Spain, where he presides over one of the world's greatest golf courses. Many top international events, including the Ryder Cup, have been played there. But in the fifties and sixties he lived in Switzerland and represented that country internationally. One of his favorite deals is the following:

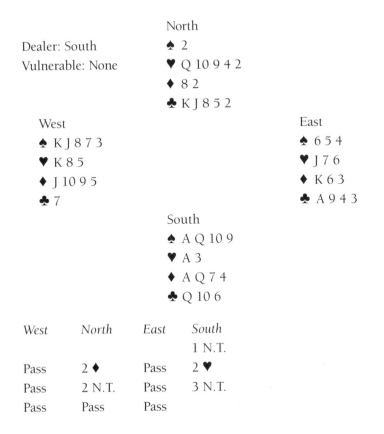

Dealer: South
Vulnerable: None

North
♠ 2
♥ Q 10 9 4 2
♦ 8 2
♣ K J 8 5 2

West
♠ K J 8 7 3
♥ K 8 5
♦ J 10 9 5
♣ 7

East
♠ 6 5 4
♥ J 7 6
♦ K 6 3
♣ A 9 4 3

South
♠ A Q 10 9
♥ A 3
♦ A Q 7 4
♣ Q 10 6

West	North	East	South
			1 N.T.
Pass	2 ♦	Pass	2 ♥
Pass	2 N.T.	Pass	3 N.T.
Pass	Pass	Pass	

Ortiz-Patino was South, playing in a Men's Pair Championship in Bermuda in 1982. His partner was Edgar Kaplan, an American who did great service to the game as a writer, commentator and lawmaker. He came close to a world title on several occasions, and might indeed have won one if the screens described below had been introduced earlier.

The two-diamond response was a transfer (see above p. 129), and the bidding might well have ended in two hearts. However, North bid an aggressive two notrump at his second turn and South naturally continued.

A routine spade lead would have given away an important trick, and West made a good decision by leading the safe diamond jack. South allowed East's king to win the first trick, won the next diamond lead with the ace, and was at a crossroads.

The obvious move was to play the strong club suit, but the contract would be virtually hopeless if the defense proved able to hold up the ace until the third round. Even if the club ace proved to be a singleton or a doubleton there would be only eight sure tricks.

South therefore decided to attack hearts, on the surface a less promising suit. After playing the ace and another, with a smooth duck from West, he made the right percentage play by putting up dummy's queen. This was due to establish the suit against a doubleton or tripleton jack on the right, whereas the ten would gain only against a tripleton king.

It was still not clear that the hearts were divided favorably, but another lead brought the missing honors to the table. Another diamond lead was won with the queen, and South led the club queen, overtaking with dummy's king. He could not then be prevented from making nine tricks, and with defensive help made an unimportant overtrick. The deal helped the international partnership to win the event.

In the previous chapter, Ortiz-Patino's brilliant decoding of the signals used by an Austrian pair was described. A year later he was present when the World Bridge Federation was founded in Oslo, and began a rise to the top of the bureaucracy of the game.

Italy had experimented with what was called a Franco Board. This was placed on the card table in a way that prevented a player from seeing his partner. From this Ortiz-Patino developed the screens that are used today in all major competitions. They consist of two uprights standing diagonally opposite each other, with a horizontal connecting section. From the crosspiece hangs a movable screen, which is totally closed during the bidding. It is then raised just enough to permit the declarer and the defenders to see the dummy. At all times a player can see one opponent, but cannot see his partner or the other opponent. The effect is to prevent most forms of cheating, although noises and electronic devices are not ruled out.

There were two other important elements. One was the bidding box, a device developed in Sweden and adopted for international play in 1974. Instead of announcing a bid verbally, a player places face up on the table a card from his box with a printed bid, anything from "one club" to "seven notrump," or else "pass," "double" or "redouble."

At first, official monitors were needed to repeat aloud the bids that the players showed silently. This was unsatisfactory, and the monitors were soon replaced by a sliding tray. This carries the bidding-box cards backward and forward under the screen.

Ortiz-Patino completed the tests of the screens just in time for use in the 1975 Bermuda Bowl, with results that are described below.

ITALY

The Italian team that won the European Championship in Venice in 1951, pushing the British team of which I was a member into third place, lost heavily to an American team in the subsequent World Championship playoff. Italy then worked hard to develop a better team, under the leadership of Carl Alberto Perroux, a prominent trial lawyer. He was a tough man who insisted on total discipline. During a championship his players were expected to concentrate entirely on the business at hand. Wives and girlfriends were expected to stay away, which sometimes provoked rebellion.

An obvious step was to develop better systems, and four soon emerged. The most original was Marmic, a name derived from the first names of the inventors, Mario Franco and Michele Giovine. (See below p. 170.) They represented Italy in one European Championship, earning silver medals. They soon resigned from competitive play, for reasons never clearly explained. One suggestion was that they were not willing to go along with their teammates by "helping each other."

The second system was Neapolitan, developed by Eugenio Chiaradia, Pietro Forquet and Guglielmo Siniscalco. (See below p. 171.) When Benito Garozzo replaced Siniscalco as Forquet's partner in 1962 he enlarged the theory of the system and it became known as the Blue Team Club.

The third system was Roman, used by Giorgio Belladonna and Walter Avarelli. (See below p. 172.) The fourth was Little Roman, played by Camillo Pabis-Ticci and Massimo D'Alelio. (See below p. 173.)

From 1957 to 1975, the Blue Team had an almost unbroken run of success in world championships, regularly beating their American opponents. Their only major failure was in 1960, when they finished well behind France and Britain in the first Team Olympiad. They also sat out the 1970 and 1971 championships, and the Americans took those two titles.

Any successful team or partnership may find itself suspected of "helping each other." In their two decades of dominance, the Italians were regularly targets of suspicion. At the 1958 Bermuda Bowl they were accused of improprieties by some of the American players, but the officials were not impressed by the evidence put forward.

The nonplaying captain is usually a minor figure, but in 1963 the American John Gerber, filling that role, made two highly controversial decisions. Early in the Bermuda Bowl competition in St. Vincent, Italy, he received a mysterious letter. On opening it, he discovered that the writer was proposing to explain in detail how the Italian team was cheating. What a captain should do in such circumstances is certainly debatable. Should he read the letter and tell his players? Should he enlist the help of some reliable, discreet observers, as was done earlier in Vienna and later in Buenos Aires? Should he pass the information to officials, with the distinct possibility of leakage to the Italian players? Should he tear it up?

What Gerber did was decidedly quixotic. Without reading further, he handed the letter to the Italian captain. This must have been a great disappointment to the letter writer, who surely became persona non grata with the Italian players and officials.

Gerber seemed to want a victory that he could claim as his own personal effort. When his team was well placed during the American match against Italy, he broke up two of his regular partnerships to field an improvised one: Howard Schenken with Bobby Nail. His team immediately lost 45 imps in one session, 26 more than the margin by which Italy eventually won the title.

The following deal came in for considerable attention.

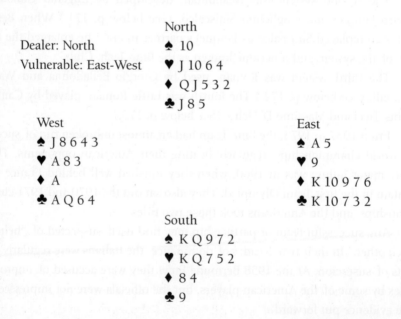

```
                              North
Dealer: North                 ♠ 10
Vulnerable: East-West          ♥ J 10 6 4
                               ♦ Q J 5 3 2
                               ♣ J 8 5
        West                                      East
        ♠ J 8 6 4 3                               ♠ A 5
        ♥ A 8 3                                   ♥ 9
        ♦ A                                       ♦ K 10 9 7 6
        ♣ A Q 6 4                                 ♣ K 10 7 3 2
                              South
                              ♠ K Q 9 7 2
                              ♥ K Q 7 5 2
                              ♦ 8 4
                              ♣ 9
```

When Italy was North-South, the bidding went like this:

West	North	East	South
(Nail)	(Forquet)	(Schenken)	(Garozzo)
	Pass	Pass	1 ♠
Pass	1 N.T.	2 ♦	2 ♥
Pass	3 ♥	Pass	Pass
Pass			

Three hearts went down one, which was a disaster for the Americans. In the replay Italy reached five clubs, making a safe game and gaining 11 imps. American critics blamed Nail for his decision to pass throughout, although they could not agree about what he should have done. It is understandable that he chose to be passive, with both opponents bidding and his partner, who had passed originally, having, apparently, nothing but diamonds. The majority of the critics thought that Nail should have bid three hearts over two hearts, although that cue bid might seem to imply a fit for diamonds.

Nobody pointed out that Schenken could have saved the day by bidding two notrump over one notrump, showing length in both minor suits. Most modern experts would make that bid routinely, although the "unusual notrump" was a relatively new idea at that time.

And if Schenken had been permitted to play with his regular partner, Peter Leventritt, he would probably have opened the bidding: They used a strong club system, and were therefore able to open the bidding with slightly weaker hands than standard bidders. A one-diamond opening would surely have uncovered the club fit eventually, and perhaps led to six clubs. The slam could have been made, which would have been enough to win the world title.

In the replay the bidding began the same way, but the Italian East, Belladonna, overcalled with two clubs, a decidedly odd decision. Two diamonds allows for the possibility of introducing clubs later. Two clubs may have been a lucky guess, but it fitted West's hand. The Italians had a habit of making lucky guesses.

A decade later the Blue Team was undergoing some changes. Avarelli, D'Alelio and Pabis-Ticci retired after the 1972 Championships, and a year later Italy had a new look. Belladonna had now started playing with Garozzo, using their version of the Precision System. (See above p. 133.)

Forquet improvised a partnership with Benito Bianchi, and together with Belladonna-Garozzo defeated strong American teams in 1973 in Brazil and in 1974 in Venice. Forquet and Bianchi were particularly impressive, given that they had never played together in Europe or anywhere else and were playing a version of Precision that was new to both of them.

Which brings us to the watershed year of 1975. The Bermuda Bowl was to be played in the small Atlantic island where the modern series of world championships had been founded 25 years before. Coincidentally, it was the 50th anniversary of Harold Vanderbilt's cruise through the Panama Canal, when he introduced three friends to contract bridge.

The World Bridge Federation, prompted by Jaime Ortiz-Patino, was ready with screens. These would presumably prevent any cheating or accusations of cheating. There were, however, two problems.

The sliding tray, carrying the bidding cards under the screen, was still two years in the future, so each table needed two monitors who would announce the bids as they were made. This was labor-intensive and a great strain on the organizers. It also produced occasional erroneous announcements by the monitors, which created difficulties. But the presence of monitors turned out to have a positive value for a surprising reason.

Another problem seemed quite minor. Somebody pointed out that the screens were only above the table, and should perhaps be extended below it. Everyone else laughed heartily, and the tournament began.

Before play started, the Italians had been angry about the appointment of Alfred Sheinwold as the American nonplaying captain. They refused to speak to him, threatened him physically, and wanted him barred from the playing rooms. The reason was something he had written a few months earlier about the Italian victory in the 1974 Championships.

"Oh well, they did it to us again, but next year we'll have the screens. I've been saying for years that any good team can beat them on even terms. It will be interesting to see whether or not the screens make a difference next year in Bermuda. I'll be there ready to eat my words if the Blue Team can still play as if they can read each other's minds."

The Blue Team had a new look. Belladonna and Garozzo were still the anchor pair. Vito Pittala, who had been a winner two years earlier, was back with a brilliant young partner, Arturo Franco. Finally, there was an entirely new pair, Gianfranco Facchini and Sergio Zucchelli. They had been achieving astonishing results, some thought beyond the parameters of normality, in pairs tournaments in Europe. Their playing skills seemed to be short of world class.

In the first session of play the audience watching in the Vugraph theater saw a deal in which Zucchelli had to lead against four hearts with the following:

♠ 10 9 4 3
♥ 4 2
♦ Q 6 4
♣ Q J 9 7

The declarer had opened one notrump and there was a transfer response. The club queen was an automatic lead, but Zucchelli chose the spade ten. His partner held the ace-king of spades, but nothing in clubs, and knowledgeable observers immediately concluded that this Italian partnership was cheating.

Late the same night the American players were told the news. While serving as a monitor, an American journalist, Bruce Keidan, had observed the Italians foot-tapping. Zucchelli's large feet were anchored under the table, well into the middle of the floor area. At crucial moments, including the one mentioned above when Zucchelli had to lead, Facchini's foot would reach out and tap once or twice on his partner's foot, either right or left. Later, other movements were noted.

Other observers were briefed, including members of the World Bridge Federation executive. They all saw the foot-tapping, and one Australian, who had been pro-Italian, left the room and threw up.

The president of the World Bridge Federation was an elderly American named Julius Rosenblum. Rather curiously, he asked Keidan what should be done. Would he be satisfied if screens were placed under the table to prevent further cheating? The reply was an unhesitating "No." The other teams involved, France and Brazil, had already been cheated.

The officials were as unprepared for this type of problem as they had been a decade earlier in Buenos Aires. They were now concerned to avoid bad publicity for the game, and the real possibility that strong action would wreck the tournament: It was likely that the Italians would walk out, and they were accompanied by 300 raucous, partisan fans.

So the officials crafted a compromise that infuriated all the Americans in the know, including Keidan. A committee statement read:

"It was resolved that Gianfranco Facchini and Sergio Zucchelli . . . be severely reprimanded for improper conduct with respect to Mr. Facchini moving his feet unnaturally and touching his partner's feet during the auction and before the opening lead."

This appeared to be saying: We know you were cheating, but we choose not to do anything about it. The American players threatened to walk out if Facchini and Zucchelli were permitted to play any further. American officials predictably ordered them to play, and they obeyed.

At the midpoint of the match, with 48 deals remaining, the Americans were leading by 73 imps. But Italy then benched Facchini-Zucchelli and surged back to win by 25.

The Italians had one large slice of luck in the final session. The Belladonna-Garozzo bidding for once went off the rails and reached a terrible grand slam.

```
                              North
Dealer: East                  ♠ Q J 8
Vulnerable: North-South        ♥ A J 9 6 5
                              ♦ K 8 2
                              ♣ A Q
         West                                      East
         ♠ 7 6 5 2                                 ♠ 4 3
         ♥ K 4 3 2                                 ♥ Q 10 8 7
         ♦ J 5 3                                   ♦ Q 10 6 4
         ♣ K 10                                    ♣ 7 5 4
                              South
                              ♠ A K 10 9
                              ♥ ——
                              ♦ A 9 7
                              ♣ J 9 8 6 3 2
```

West	North	East	South
(Kantar)	(Garozzo)	(Eisenberg)	(Belladonna)
		Pass	2 ♣
Pass	2 ♦	Pass	2 ♠
Pass	3 ♥	Pass	3 N.T.
Pass	4 ♣	Pass	4 ♦
Pass	4 N.T.	Pass	5 ♦
Pass	5 ♥	Dbl.	Redbl.
Pass	5 ♠	Pass	5 N.T.
Pass	7 ♣	Pass	Pass
Pass			

Perhaps Belladonna's last bid should have been six clubs, since his suit was so weak. The grand slam had only a 13 percent chance of success, but it came home. South ruffed the opening heart lead, finessed the club queen successfully, and cashed the ace to collect the king. After mentally thanking the gods of the game, he crossed to his hand, drew the missing trump, and claimed the grand slam.

The American North-South were also in the wrong contract. Instead of six clubs, they reached six no-trump, which would have been in jeopardy after a heart lead. Italy gained 12 imps.

Soon after, in an article in *The Bridge World*, the great Swiss veteran Jean Besse pointed out that Kantar would probably have defeated the contract, and won the world title, if he had been inspired to play the club king smoothly when Belladonna led the first trump.

That would have given the Italian star plenty to think about. Taking the king at face value, he would probably have planned this play: Cash the ace of hearts, discarding a diamond; ruff another heart; cash three spade winners and the ace-king of diamonds. After another heart ruff, he would expect to reach this ending:

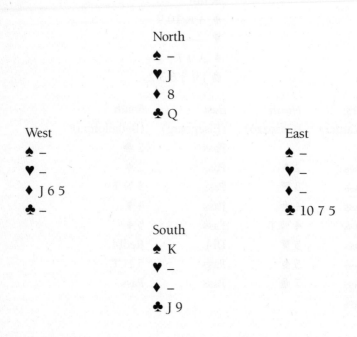

North
- ♠ –
- ♥ J
- ♦ 8
- ♣ Q

West
- ♠ –
- ♥ –
- ♦ J 6 5
- ♣ –

East
- ♠ –
- ♥ –
- ♦ –
- ♣ 10 7 5

South
- ♠ K
- ♥ –
- ♦ –
- ♣ J 9

Ruffing the spade king would bring home the grand slam, for East's trumps would be trapped.

In real life this attempt would have failed, for East would have ruffed the third round of spades. The play of the club king would have deceived one of the world's greatest players and decided the issue.

Italy completed a remarkable recovery and won the match by 25 imps. They would have lost by 4 if the grand slam had failed. If the clubs had been placed less favorably for North-South, the world title would then have hinged on the Italian lead against the American six notrump contract.

There were three ironies in all this.

First, the Americans' demand that Facchini-Zucchelli be barred from playing went against their own interests. While that pair played their 32 deals in the final, Italy lost 36 imps.

Second, Sheinwold was proved to be both right and wrong. He was right that some Italians might be cheating. He was wrong, but only just, in predicting that any good American team would win with screens in use.

Third, the presence of monitors proved unexpectedly useful. If the W.B.F. had thought of using the sliding tray, introduced by Henny Dorsman of Aruba two years later, Keidan would not have been involved and the foot-tapping would presumably have gone on, and on, and on.

Having swept the foot-tapping scandal under the table, the W.B.F. and the Italian Federation thought they could relax. They were wrong. On February 20 1976, a leading Italian player, Leandro Burgay, walked into the office of Prof. Luigi Firpo, the president of the Italian Federation, and gave him a "smoking gun." Like the more famous "smoking gun" that forced the resignation of President Richard Nixon, it took the form of an audiotape.

Burgay was collecting materials for a book, and it was generally known that he taped his telephone conversations for this reason. The one he gave Firpo, made one day earlier, was with Bianchi, who in it explained the illegal signals that he had used with Forquet, and that Belladonna had used with another partner, Renato Mondolfo. They involved the use of cigarettes and head positions. The cigarette could point up or down, left or right, to indicate an honor card or a suit. (Belladonna pointed out that for many years he had smoked cigars, not cigarettes.)

The reaction of the Italian authorities was to shoot the messenger. Burgay was accused of attempting to blackmail Firpo to be selected for the national team. Since the team had already been selected, and Firpo had no say in it, this made no sense and Firpo eventually admitted that this was just his inference. Another Burgay offence was speaking privately to Jaime Ortiz-Patino, the W.B.F. president-elect.

Bianchi was at this time on bad terms with his former teammates. He admitted the phone conversation, but denied some of the statements by him in it and claimed that the tape was a doctored collage. The federation's judges suspended Burgay for six years. Bianchi was suspended for six months. His offence was not that he cheated. It was declaring *without proof* that he had made illegal signs to Forquet, and that he had declared that Forquet and others had used such methods. Both players appealed.

The accusation, if accepted, would cast a shadow on two decades of Italian success at world level. On April 23 the designated expert, Signor Bacicchi, reported to the federation that the tape was authentic and had not been doctored. On the same day, all concerned were officially summoned to a hearing.

One day later, the Blue Team, which had been selected to play in the world championships beginning in Monte Carlo in May, threatened to refuse to play. One day later still, the Managing Board announced officially that the players selected for the World Championships (who included Forquet and Belladonna) "turned out not to be involved." The investigation was remarkably brief.

"The decision . . . by which the players Belladonna-Forquet-Mondolfo were acquitted of any charges, was reached that not only was there a complete lack of concrete proof of any incorrectness, but also of the profound 20-year conviction of the absolute correctness of the above-mentioned players. The decision was also political in the sense that the federation had the duty to protect the honor of our world champions abroad."

On May 2, in Monte Carlo, Firpo promised the W.B.F. that there would be serious inquiries. (That seemed unlikely, since there had already been a "political" decision.) He said, "Should the inquiry determine that the tape was authentic and furthermore that the declaration by Bianchi of his cheating with Forquet was confirmed, then the Italian Bridge Federation would renounce all European and World titles won with either Bianchi or Forquet on the team." Note that this was nine days after the report from the designated expert that the tape was authentic.

A few days later, play began in Monte Carlo. The Blue Team barely qualified for the final against a strong American squad. Going into the final session, the Italians trailed by 19 imps. Would they surge back to take the title as they had done a year earlier in Bermuda?

One of the American players was Ira Rubin, now a member of the American Contract Bridge League's Hall of Fame. As he began play in the Open Room, he noticed an odd circumstance. Belladonna, the cigar smoker, was on the same side of the screen and had a cigarette in his mouth. On the table in front of him was a lighter which he would click occasionally during the bidding. Rubin did not have a lighter, but he had a pen, and joined in with occasional clicks of his own. Coincidentally, the monitor recording the bidding and play was joining in with pen clicks.

This barrage of clicks may have had an impact on the second deal:

North

Dealer: East
Vulnerable: North-South

♠ K 4
♥ 10 9 7
♦ A J 9 7
♣ A K 8 6

West

♠ A J 10 7 3
♥ 6
♦ K 5 2
♣ 10 9 5 2

East

♠ 8 6 5
♥ K J 8 5 3
♦ Q 4 3
♣ J 4

South

♠ Q 9 2
♥ A Q 4 2
♦ 10 8 6
♣ Q 7 3

West (Soloway)	North (Belladonna)	East (Rubin)	South (Forquet)
		Pass	Pass
2 ♥	Dbl.	2 ♠	3 ♥
Pass	4 ♥	Dbl.	Pass
Pass	Pass		

The two-heart opening was a multimeaning action, but usually based on a weak two-bid in spades. The commentator in the book of the championships said, ". . . the Italians' bidding does not seem to have harmonized. Was Belladonna's four hearts an overbid with a hand that had already been fully expressed on the previous round, and where there was no guarantee of a 5-3 fit? Or did he assume that South must hold appreciable length in hearts because he would have doubled responsively instead of bidding three hearts with fair values and a balanced hand?"

The singleton heart was led, and covered with the ten, king and ace. The diamond eight was ducked to the queen, and the spade eight was returned. This was ducked to dummy's king, and South crossed to the club queen. He led the diamond ten, but rejected the finesse. Instead he played dummy's ace and surrendered a diamond to the king.

Soloway cashed the spade ace and continued the suit. Expecting a ruff on his right, South ruffed with the heart nine in dummy and led the heart seven. This was covered by the jack and queen, and a club was led to the ace.

This left a three-card ending in which South held the 4-2 of hearts and a club. He should have led the last diamond from dummy, promoting the heart four as a trick. He erred, however, by attempting to cash a club winner, and Rubin, with 8-5-3 was able to ruff low and take the last two tricks for down three and a penalty of 800. In the replay North-South failed by one trick in three notrump, and the Americans gained 12 imps.

Rubin says that when the session ended, Belladonna and Forquet appeared irritated. The Americans increased their lead, winning the Bermuda Bowl by 34 imps.

The next Italian hearing, in February 1977, relied heavily on an alleged statement by Bianchi on the tape, "I did not do those things with Piero (Forquet)." Whether that is accurate is doubtful: Burgay denies that such a statement was made on the tape. The judges refused to check this by looking at a complete version of the tape. Bianchi's sentence was reduced from a six-month suspension to a censure. The other three players mentioned denied vigorously that they had done anything improper, and the court accepted these self-serving denials without testing them.

Burgay's suspension, for being a nuisance and for telling Ortiz-Patino that the tape had not been doctored, thus contradicting Firpo, was reduced from six years to one year. Six months had already been served. But the Italian establishment was so hostile to Burgay that he gave up the game for 15 years. In the past decade he has resumed play, winning a world transnational team title and a silver medal in the European Team Championship. His Big Diamond System has been used by some top Italian players, and his structure for responding to one notrump, replacing Stayman, has some theoretical advantages.

The final Italian verdict did not satisfy the World Bridge Federation. Ortiz-Patino sent a letter in July demanding that the Italians improve their investigative procedures. In October the W.B.F. threatened to suspend the Italian

Federation from membership and eventually carried out the threat. The Italians were suspended for six months, which excluded them from the 1977 Bermuda Bowl in Manila.

Ortiz-Patino then announced a procedure by which world championships would be by invitation only. (They still are. Names have to be submitted in advance, and in rare situations a player may be barred.) He told the Italian secretary that certain of his players would not be invited. Bianchi and Forquet were never again selected to represent Italy, together or separately.

An obvious method of inquiry that the Italian Federation never considered was to examine the deals played by Bianchi and Forquet in the 1973 and 1974 World Championships, the last before screens were introduced. A quarter of a century later, analysis offers a wealth of evidence that the Italians were "helping each other": They were almost 100 precent in choosing the bids and leads that fitted partner's hand.

Looking back over the past 64 years of world championships, the impact of screens is clear. Of the 26 teams that won world titles up to and including 1975, all but five are strongly tainted by indications of cheating. Since 1976, with screens in use, there are no such taints, although it is possible that something has happened without detection.

The possibility of using noises to defeat the screen barrier is mentioned above. Another attempt, though not at the international level, allegedly occurred in Houston in 1977. During a trial to select the North American team for the Bermuda Bowl, accusations were made by officials of the American Contract Bridge League (A.C.B.L.) against Dr. Richard Katz and Lawrence Cohen. (Not to be confused with Larry N. Cohen, whose work is discussed below on page 189.) Observers said that during the bidding they had noted a pattern of sniffs and coughs which would be audible on the other side of the screen. Rather than face a hearing to rule on these charges, Katz and Cohen immediately chose to resign from the league. Soon afterward they began a lawsuit, which was eventually settled five years later. The players were readmitted to the A.C.B.L., but undertook never to play with each other again.

So Ortiz-Patino and the World Bridge Federation deserve full credit for cleaning up the game. Screens are not only used in world events, they are regularly used in the late stages of major championships in North America and many other places. What is more, they are popular with the experts. Behind a screen, the honest player can relax; smiling, frowning and fiddling with his

pencil without fear of conveying illicit but unwanted information to his partner, or even perhaps raising a suspicion of cheating. The small hesitations that
create controversy are largely absorbed behind a screen.

No. 25 ▸ *The Marmic System*

Marmic introduced a bizarre idea that was later to bear fruit
in other parts of the world. With a strong balanced hand containing 16–19 points, a player was required to pass in first or second seat, or when an opponent opened the bidding in a suit. This
was the "strong pass," and the passer's partner was required to
reopen with quite modest values.

I encountered the inventors of the system, Franco and
Giovine, at a tournament in Belgium in 1952. In third position I
felt an urge to bid with a Yarborough and the auction began:

West	North	East	South
(D'Unienville)	(Franco)	(Truscott)	(Giovine)
Pass	Pass	1 ♠	Pass
2 ♠	2 N.T.	Pass	

This was before the days when questions had to be asked
only when due to bid. West, surprised, asked what two notrump
meant. He was even more surprised by the answer. Translated
from the original French, it was, "He has 16-19 points. Your partner is completely psychic. Six notrump."

Both my opponents had passed on the first round with about
17 points, and had now reached a normal contract by an abnormal route. Never before or since has my partner been told by an
opponent that I was completely psychic.

Marmic was not totally efficient, but the idea of the strong
pass was later taken up, mainly in New Zealand, Australia and
Poland. Usually the user was required to pass in first or second
seat with any hand with 16 points or more. The corollary was
that one bid, known as a "fert," indicated any weak hand. This
was usually one diamond.

The strong-pass systems proved extraordinarily difficult to defend against, some thought unfairly difficult. Normal constructive auctions became rather rare for the unfortunate opponents, and their indignation caused the authorities to take action. Strong-pass systems were barred in most competitions, and nearly all the users gave up. Using methods that could only be used in a few top events did not permit much practice.

There was a strange development when two strong-pass pairs faced each other in a European tournament. The dealer and his left-hand opponent both held 20 points and their opponents each had a Yarborough. The bidding went:

West	North	East	South
Pass(1)	Pass(2)	Pass(3)	Pass(4)

1. I have a strong hand, partner. Please bid.

2. I have a strong hand, partner. Please bid.

3. Since North is strong, I choose not to open with my Yarborough.

4. Since West is strong, I choose not to open with my Yarborough.

And West and North were both totally furious.

No. 26 ▶ *The Neapolitan and Blue Team Club Systems*

It will be recalled that the first bridge system was the Vanderbilt Club, introduced by the man who codified contract bridge in 1925. His game flourished, but his system, which called for an artificial opening one-club bid with strong hands, did not.

The idea surfaced again in Italy two decades later, but whether the inventor knew about Vanderbilt is doubtful. His name was Eugenio Chiaradia, known as "the Professor." In private life he really was a professor of philosophy. His Neapolitan System was adopted by several young stars, notably Pietro Forquet, Guglielmo Siniscalco, and eventually Benito Garozzo. In the sixties Garozzo was responsible for refining the system, and giving it a new name: Blue Team Club.

One club was the opening bid with nearly all hands of 17 points or more, with slight flexibility. The responses showed controls, starting with one spade showing an ace and a king or three kings. One diamond was a true negative, and one heart showed 6 or more points lacking three controls. Two hearts and two spades were weak jump shifts.

One notrump was usually 15–17 points, but could be 13–15 with 3-3-2-5 or 3-3-3-4. Other one-bids were natural, showing a four-card suit with roughly 12–16 points.

In opening the bidding and in responding, the system made much use of the canapé principle, bidding a short suit with a longer one in reserve.

A two-club opening bid was natural, with a strong suit of at least five cards. A two-diamond response was a strong relay, asking for further information.

Weak two-bids were used, but Garozzo eventually added a two-diamond opening to show a very strong three-suited hand with 17–24 points. Such hands are difficult to bid in almost all systems.

No. 27 ► The Roman System

Roman was devised by Giorgio Manca, and then developed by Giorgio Belladonna and Walter Avarelli. It had one highly original feature: all opening bids of one of a suit were forcing.

One club was usually a balanced 12–16 points, but could be a standard two notrump opening, or a game-going unbalanced hand, or a strong two-suiter with clubs and a side-suit of five cards or more. One diamond was a negative response, suggesting fewer than nine points. Minimum suit responses were semi-positive with 8–11 points.

One diamond, one heart and one spade were in principle natural, but could be made on a three-card suit. In a two-suiter, the shorter suit was bid first on the canapé principle unless the shorter suit was clubs. A single raise and a minimum response were both negative.

One notrump was 17–20 balanced. Two clubs (12–16) and two diamonds (17–20) showed three-suiters. Two hearts and two spades showed 12–16 with at least 5–4 in the suit bid and clubs.

Another feature of the system offered a glimpse of the future. In response to four notrump, the system called for a five-club response with three aces or none, and a five-diamond response with four aces or one.

No. 28 ▸ *The Little Roman System*

Little Roman, also called Arno, was played by Camillo Pabis-Ticci and Massimo D'Alelio. It was a version of the Roman System in which a 17–20 point balanced hand was shown by opening one diamond and rebidding one notrump. The one notrump opening was very strong and forcing, either 21–24 balanced, or distributional and game-forcing.

CHAPTER 14

Aces, Kings and One Queen

♠ ♥
♦ ♣ In the past 30 years professional arrangements have become more and more common, at all levels of the game. In a local club, an inexperienced player may play a session with an expert, and pay for the privilege. In effect, it is a playing lesson, and the professional will explain the nuances that have escaped the notice of his, or her, partner.

This happens also in tournament play, in which it is common to hire a partner for several days. Wealthy players often hire a team and, perhaps, win major titles by doing so. (Usually, there are six players and the sponsor plays half the time.) Most of the top teams in the Vanderbilt, Spingold and Reisinger Championships are sponsored in this way. Since 1978, seven of the 11 United States teams to win major world championships included playing sponsors. (The other titles were won by France, five times; Italy, twice; and Poland, Brazil, Germany, Iceland and the Netherlands, once each.)

Only once in the history of bridge has there been a full-time professional team, dedicated to success in the manner of the Yankees on the baseball diamond or the Chicago Bulls on the basketball court.

The promoter and financier was Ira Corn Jr. of Dallas, a multimillionaire who had started as an assistant professor in a business school and built up a major conglomerate called Michigan General. In 1964 he watched in New York as the American team lost the world championship final to Italy. He decided that he would bring the title back across the Atlantic. It was then 10 years since the Americans had won. (Some of the reasons for the drought were discussed in chapters 12 and 13.)

His first move was to talk to Bobby Wolff, one of the top-ranked players in Texas. By 1967 they had a team. Wolff would play with Jim Jacoby, son of the great Oswald. They would each play occasionally with Corn himself. The rest of the team would be a threesome. One was Billy Eisenberg, an effervescent playboy from New York City with a great deal of talent but a tendency to make overimaginative leads. Another was Mike Lawrence, a shy Californian who was to become one of the all-time great bridge writers. The third was Bob Goldman of Philadelphia, who was good at tennis as well as bridge.

This formation did not work well, and they soon made two effective moves. Corn conceded that he should stay on the sidelines, and they recruited Bob Hamman, another brilliant Californian. Hamman was still in a bad temper because he was a member of the 1964 team that lost to Italy, and he and his equally young partner had been benched for the entire final by a captain who chose to rely on his Old Guard. Hamman now formed a partnership with Lawrence, leaving Eisenberg happily paired with Goldman.

The choice of players was extremely successful. All six would eventually win major world titles: Wolff nine, Jacoby three, Hamman ten, Lawrence three, Eisenberg five, and Goldman three.

The next move was to hire a coach, and the man chosen was Joe Musemeci, a retired Air Force lieutenant colonel. He was a believer in discipline, and forced a group of prima donnas who just wanted to enjoy life to buckle down to work. For a short time they even had to do physical workouts, on the theory that a healthy player would have more stamina at the table. Most of them objected strongly.

Each of the players would practice and then spend hours on "performance review," discussing what had gone wrong. Most of them were happy to criticize others but resented anything fired in their own direction. At times five players would scream at a sixth, attempting to convince him that some action was stupid, sloppy or crazy. The exception was Goldman, an ardent seeker after truth who was quite willing to be criticized. He used a computer to produce practice deals, testing different areas of bidding.

The effect was dramatic. Within a year, Eisenberg-Goldman headed a pairs trial for the American team. However, Italy won again. The Aces won the next two titles, with Oswald Jacoby in the role of nonplaying captain, but the victories, in Stockholm and Taipei, although satisfying, were slightly hollow, since the Italian Blue Team was in temporary retirement.

In Taipei, Wolff made a remarkable play on the following deal against a strong French team:

		North	
Dealer: East		♠ K 9 4	
Vulnerable: None		♥ K 10 3	
		♦ K Q J 10 6	
		♣ J 3	

West			East
♠ A J 8 5			♠ 10 7 2
♥ Q 9 5 2			♥ 6
♦ 4 3			♦ 9 8 7 5 2
♣ K 7 5			♣ A 10 8 4

		South	
		♠ Q 6 3	
		♥ A J 8 7 4	
		♦ A	
		♣ Q 9 6 2	

West (Szwarc)	North (Jacoby)	East (Boulenger)	South (Wolff)
		Pass	1 ♥
Pass	2 ♦	Pass	2 ♥
Pass	4 ♥	Pass	Pass
Pass			

South has three top losers in the side suits, so he must avoid a trump loser. In the replay, the French declarer, Jean-Marc Roudinesco, made the standard play of taking the king and leading the ten. This would have allowed him to pick up Q-9-x-x of trumps on his right.

But Wolff had a subtle clue. The defense began with a club to the ace, a spade to the ace, and the club king. The West player, Henri Szwarc, owns three world titles and has been one of Europe's best for more than 40 years. He won the second and third tricks with no hesitation and appeared quite relaxed. That strongly suggested that he believed he was going to make a trump trick.

So Wolff proceeded on the assumption that Szwarc held not just Q-x-x, which would look like a possible trick, but Q-9-x-x, a highly probable trick. After winning a spade lead in his hand at the fourth trick, Wolff backed his judgment by leading the heart jack. This was covered by the queen, which confirmed his estimate of the situation: West would not cover with Q-x or Q-x-x.

A diamond to the ace allowed Wolff to lead the heart seven for a finesse. Then another trump was led to the ten, and closed hand was re-entered with a diamond ruff. The last trump was drawn with the ace, and dummy made the remaining tricks.

This seemed like wizardry. Could Wolff see through the backs of the cards? No. He had used brilliant psychology.

The same championship in Taipei produced the most bizarre episode in the history of international competition.

	North	
Dealer: South	♠ K J 4 3	
Vulnerable: None	♥ 10 9 7 2	
	♦ J 9 7 6 2	
	♣ –	

West		East
♠ 8 6 2		♠ A 10 9 7 5
♥ A 5 4		♥ 6
♦ A 10 5		♦ K 8 4 3
♣ A 5 4 2		♣ 8 7 6

	South	
	♠ Q	
	♥ K Q J 8 3	
	♦ Q	
	♣ K Q J 10 9 3	

West	North	East	South
	(Stoppa)		(Trézel)
			1 ♣
Pass	1 ♦	Pass	1 ♥
Pass	3 ♥	Pass	4 N.T.
Pass	5 ♣	Pass	7 ♥
Dbl.	Pass	Pass	Pass

How could two world-class players bid a grand slam missing four aces? Stoppa assumed that his jump to three hearts was invitational. Even at that, it was a considerable overbid. Trézel came from an older tradition and thought that three hearts was forcing. When his Blackwood received a five-club response, showing no aces or four, he could not conceive that his partner was aceless. West was happy to double seven hearts, and it failed by three tricks. South had to find West with the club ace to escape with a 500 penalty.

The explanation is that this came at the end of a qualifying competition and the French had a score that would guarantee them a place in the final. Their nonplaying captain, with nothing at stake, fielded an experimental partnership. He would not, of course, have tried it if the score was going to be significant. The only captain to do such a thing when it mattered was the American John Gerber. (See above page 158.)

The Aces had to face more serious tests in the next three years. In 1972, 1973, 1974 and 1975 they lost to the Blue Team. As described in the previous chapter, some observers claimed that the Italians could play as if they could see through the backs of the cards.

Some members of the Blue Team retired, and the Aces, too, were starting to disintegrate. Eisenberg, Lawrence, Jacoby and Goldman dropped off the team in turn. Hamman played briefly with Paul Soloway, but then began a highly successful partnership with Wolff that was to last a quarter of a century.

The 1977 Bermuda Bowl in Manila was different. The Italians were not present for reasons mentioned above (page 169), and there were two American teams in the final. (This happened because at that time the defending champions played by right, and each continental zone was represented. The rules have changed, and that cannot happen again. If two American teams reach the semifinal, which has happened, they are required to play each other.) One was the Aces team that had suffered in Bermuda two years earlier, and one was approximately the American team that had won the previous year in Monte Carlo.

The Aces were in a deep hole, trailing by 43 with 32 deals remaining. But they surged back to win by 30, thanks in part to Hamman's play on this deal:

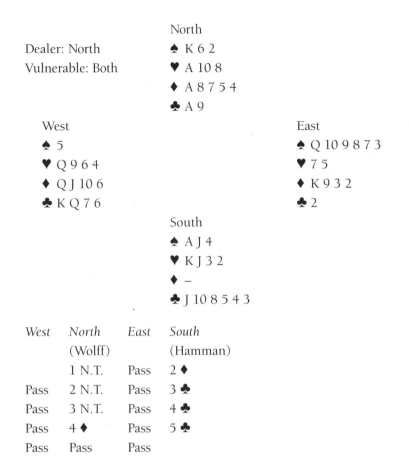

Dealer: North
Vulnerable: Both

North
♠ K 6 2
♥ A 10 8
♦ A 8 7 5 4
♣ A 9

West
♠ 5
♥ Q 9 6 4
♦ Q J 10 6
♣ K Q 7 6

East
♠ Q 10 9 8 7 3
♥ 7 5
♦ K 9 3 2
♣ 2

South
♠ A J 4
♥ K J 3 2
♦ –
♣ J 10 8 5 4 3

West	North	East	South
	(Wolff)		(Hamman)
	1 N.T.	Pass	2 ♦
Pass	2 N.T.	Pass	3 ♣
Pass	3 N.T.	Pass	4 ♣
Pass	4 ♦	Pass	5 ♣
Pass	Pass	Pass	

Wolff and Hamman were one of the few top pairs who did not use transfer bids. Two diamonds was Forcing Stayman, an artificial bid guaranteeing game. Wolff might well have made three notrump. He could have won an opening spade lead with the jack and led a club. If West played low the nine would win and North could play on hearts. If West put up an honor the clubs would be established.

But Hamman feared a diamond weakness in a notrump contract, and staggered on to five clubs. He ruffed the opening diamond lead in his hand and led a trump, winning with the nine when West played low. He cashed the ace and was disappointed to find that West had two sure trump tricks.

Nevertheless, Hamman came home with his 11 tricks without any guessing in the major suits. He ruffed a second diamond and cashed the ace and king

of spades. West discarded a diamond. Now the diamond ace was cashed, for a
spade discard. The position was this:

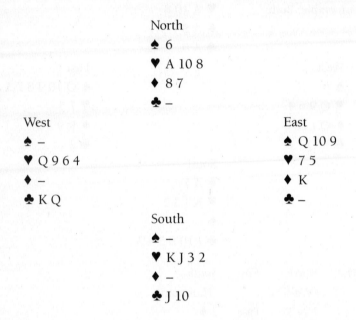

North
♠ 6
♥ A 10 8
♦ 8 7
♣ —

West
♠ —
♥ Q 9 6 4
♦ —
♣ K Q

East
♠ Q 10 9
♥ 7 5
♦ K
♣ —

South
♠ —
♥ K J 3 2
♦ —
♣ J 10

Yet another diamond was ruffed, and West refused to overruff since he
would then have to break the heart suit. That did him no good, however, for
Hamman led to the heart ace and threw a heart on the last diamond.

That was the end for West. If he ruffed, he would have to lead a heart at the
finish. And if he refused to ruff, South would take the heart king and grace-
fully concede the last two tricks. That was a gain of 10 imps, for the opposition
stopped cautiously in three clubs.

In the next decade United States teams won all five Bermuda Bowls,
although they were desperately close to elimination in three of them. In 1979
a team including three Aces—Eisenberg, Goldman and Soloway—won by just
5 imps against a modified Italian Blue Team.

In 1983, Wolff and Hamman, with four young stars from the New York
area, won by the identical margin against a similar Italian team. But it took an
Italian blunder to bring it about.

With three deals remaining in the marathon final match of 176 deals, the
Americans led by 2 imps. The next deal was a borderline slam. The Italians bid

and made it, while the Americans did not. The last two deals did not seem likely to change anything. The Italians watching in the Vugraph theater thought that they had won, and the Americans thought they had lost.

But on the penultimate deal an astonishing thing happened. Hamman and Wolff, trying for slam, reached a precarious five-spade contract and survived. Belladonna and Garozzo had the father and mother of bidding misunderstandings and bid a slam off two aces. So the Americans won after all. Winning with Hamman and Wolff were Peter Weichsel, Alan Sontag, Ron Rubin and Michael Becker. That was the end of the Blue Team: Belladonna retired, and Garozzo became an American resident soon afterward.

In 1985 politics intruded into bridge. The Bermuda Bowl was supposed to be in India, but the government of that country refused to provide the required guarantee that all contending teams would be admitted. The obvious deduction was that the Israeli team, which had qualified to play, would be barred, so the championships were moved at the last minute to Sao Paulo, Brazil.

This was not the first time politics had affected a bridge tournament. In 1976 teams entered for the Team Olympiad in Monte Carlo were required to promise that they would play all the teams they were scheduled to meet. Some arrived who were under government orders: They were not allowed to play against South Africa, or Israel, or perhaps Taiwan, so they manufactured excuses when the time came.

When Thailand was due to play South Africa, at 10 P.M., the nonplaying captain arrived triumphantly waving medical certificates. Two of his players, he told the director, were sick. "But you have two other players," the director pointed out, "and they must play." The captain thought quickly, and declared, with little plausibility, "They're out buying rice."

In the 1985 Bermuda Bowl in Brazil, Hamman and Wolff were in action again with different teammates: Hugh Ross, Peter Pender, Lew Stansby and Chip Martel. The crisis came in the semifinal, when they played the host country. With one deal remaining the scores were exactly tied, a unique event.

North

Dealer: North

Vulnerable: North-South

♠ 10 9 7 6 4
♥ A K 4
♦ J 10
♣ A K Q

West

♠ A 8 5
♥ 8 6 3
♦ K 8 6 5
♣ 7 6 2

East

♠ K J 3 2
♥ Q 9 7 2
♦ Q 7 2
♣ 5 3

South

♠ Q
♥ J 10 5
♦ A 9 4 3
♣ J 10 9 8 4

West	North	East	South
(Stansby)	(Cintra)	(Martel)	(Barbosa)
	1 ♣	Pass	1 ♦
Pass	1 ♠	Pass	2 N.T.
Pass	3 N.T.	Pass	Pass
Pass			

The score was not known to the players, but it was known to an audience of over 300, nearly all Brazilians, watching tensely in the Vugraph theater. Everyone understood that a gain for either side, even an overtrick, would decide the match, and if the score was still tied extra deals would be played.

The deal was first played in the Closed Room, and Hamman opened the North hand with one notrump. This concealed his five-card major suit, and his partner, Bobby Wolff, chose to pass. The opening showed 15–17 high-card points, and it seemed unlikely that there would be a good play for game.

After the opening lead of a heart, Hamman had an easy nine tricks, and with a little help emerged with 10. This overtrick might have been crucial. He unblocked the clubs, and the diamond ace was available as an entry to the dummy. It was not clear whether or not this was a good result.

When the deal appeared in the Vugraph theater, the audience was told that the American North-South had scored 180 in one no-trump. Could the host country bid and make a game? The Brazilian North, Gabino Cintra, opened one club, as shown in the diagram. This was strong and forcing. He might have rebid one no-trump after the negative one-diamond response, in which case his partner would probably have continued. If they had reached three no-trump Martel would probably have led a major suit from the East hand. If he had picked a heart, Brazil would have won the match. If he had selected a spade, the contract would have failed and the Americans would have won.

But Cintra chose to show his five-card spade suit, and three no-trump was reached from the South position. Now Stansby had to lead from the West hand, with little clue. A hush fell over the audience. The gods of the game had given Stansby a four-card diamond suit. After much thought he produced the diamond five, which allowed the defense to remove the vital entry from the declarer's hand.

The groan that erupted from the Brazilian audience could be heard all over Sao Paulo. Three notrump failed by two tricks and the Americans won the match by 9 imps. However, the groan came too late: It should have come when South became declarer. From that side of the table, three notrump was unmakable, even with a passive club lead.

The Americans went on to defeat Austria, very easily, in the final, and the Brazilians had to wait four more years for their first victory in the Bermuda Bowl. And what a victory it was! Playing in Perth, Australia, Brazil reached the final in which they faced Martel, Stansby, Ross, Peter Pender, Lawrence and Kit Woolsey. To the astonishment of the pundits, Brazil won by the remarkable margin of 104 imps.

The spearhead of the Brazilian team for a quarter of a century, and still going strong, has been the superb partnership of Gabriel Chagas and Marcelo Branco. Chagas has a creative imagination that permits him to defeat contracts that would succeed easily against anyone else. The following, which helped them win a major Brazilian event, is perhaps the cream of a large crop:

North

Dealer: South   ♠ K Q 5 4
Vulnerable: Both   ♥ A J 3
                         ♦ Q 4
                         ♣ K 10 7 5

West   East
♠ 8 6 2   ♠ 9 7
♥ Q 5   ♥ 10 9 6 2
♦ 10 8 7 6 3   ♦ K 9 5 2
♣ 9 4 2   ♣ A Q J

                         South
                         ♠ A J 10 3
                         ♥ K 8 7 4
                         ♦ A J
                         ♣ 8 6 3

South	West	North	East
	(Branco)		(Chagas)
1 N.T.	Pass	2 ♣	Pass
2 ♥	Pass	3 N.T.	Pass
4 ♠	Pass	Pass	Pass

South's one notrump opening was the weak variety, promising 13–15 points. His partner's use of Stayman followed by a jump to three notrump implied a four-card spade suit, so South could select the right game.

East-West were using traditional fourth-best leads, which was just as well. (See Sidebar 29.) The club two was led, and Chagas won with the jack and thought it over. To justify his opening bid, South had to have two aces and the heart king. If he also had the heart queen, his contract must be a laydown.

Looking at all four hands there seems no hope for the defense, but Chagas did something weird: He cashed the club ace and shifted to the diamond nine. South was sure that he knew the position. He could not afford to finesse for fear of a club ruff, so he grabbed the diamond ace and drew trump, ending in his hand. Then he confidently finessed the club ten, and Chagas produced the club queen and the diamond king to defeat an "unbeatable" game. Notice that if the defenders had been using modern third-and-fifth leads, South would have known that West did not have four clubs and that something fishy was going on.

That is my nomination for the best defensive play of all time.

The Brazilian victory was their first, and only, Bermuda Bowl title. In 1976 they had won the World Team Olympiad in Monte Carlo in weird circumstances: They finished just ahead of the Italians without playing a single deal against them. The title was decided by a round robin with no playoffs, an unsatisfactory format that has never been used since. When Brazil played Italy, they were seated wrongly, although the tournament director had been asked to verify the seating. The match should have been replayed but was not, a clear case of organizational incompetence.

This type of accident was not infrequent. While returning across the Atlantic, I thought of a way to prevent it. Since then, in virtually all major events, and some minor ones, the players use a "Truscott card." This carries the names and positions of the players, and travels with the boards when they are exchanged. If this reveals a seating error, or the boards have been taken to the wrong table, it is easy to correct the problem.

Chagas and Branco are one of four pairs who have won the Triple Crown, meaning that they have won the big three world titles: the Bermuda Bowl, the Olympiad Teams and the World Pairs. The other three are Jaïs-Trézel, Hamman-Wolff, and Jeff Meckstroth-Eric Rodwell.

Meckstroth and Rodwell made their mark in 1981 by winning the Bermuda Bowl at the age of 25. This would have made them the youngest-ever Americans to win but for the fact that one of their teammates, Bobby Levin, was a year younger.

Another surprise in that year was that the silver medallists, losing to the Americans in the final, were not Brazil, or Italy or any of the strong European teams, but Pakistan. The key to the Pakistan success was 34-year-old Zia Mahmood, a charismatic personality who was soon recognized as one of the world's great players.

He is based in New York and London, but travels the world to compete. In two decades he has played in more countries, and won with more partners, than anyone else. He is remarkably adaptable, able to adjust to any partner and almost any system. His favorite partner is Michael Rosenberg, a Scotsman living in New York. Together they have a remarkable record of success in national championships.

In January 2001, Zia was in The Hague, the Netherlands, competing in an elite field in the Cap Gemini World Top Pairs. He was defending the title with an Englishman, Andrew Robson, and they snatched a second victory thanks to the following deal. Almost at the finish, they faced Krzystof Jassem and Pyotr Tuszynski, two Polish experts who had won silver medals in the World Team Olympiad four months earlier.

Dealer: East
Vulnerable: East-West

```
                              North
                              ♠ A 3 2
                              ♥ A K 10 8 5 2
                              ♦ Q 4
                              ♣ J 7

        West                                     East
        ♠ J 9                                    ♠ 7 6 4
        ♥ Q 6                                    ♥ 7 4 3
        ♦ 10 8 5                                 ♦ J 7 3
        ♣ A K 9 6 5 3                            ♣ Q 10 8 2

                              South
                              ♠ K Q 10 8 5
                              ♥ J 9
                              ♦ A K 9 6 2
                              ♣ 4
```

West	North	East	South
(Zia)	(Jassem)	(Robson)	(Tuszynski)
		Pass	1 ♠
Pass	2 ♥	Pass	2 ♠
Pass	4 ♣	Pass	5 ♣
Pass	5 ♥	Pass	6 ♠
Pass	Pass	Pass	

The slam is a good proposition, but only three pairs out of eight hit the target. It is not clear how South should proceed after two top clubs are led, but everything will work. All the key suits break evenly, and the heart queen is well placed.

On the face of it, Zia and Robson were due to lose heavily. The experts present were astonished to be told that the slam had failed, and some suspected a revoke.

One Swedish expert, Anders Wirgren, correctly worked out what had happened. On the second trick South led the spade king and Zia produced the jack instead of playing the nine. This surprising falsecard could in theory have been fatal if East held the spade queen, but it worked like a charm.

After much thought, declarer decided to accept the jack at face value. Assuming a singleton, he led to the diamond queen and returned to the ace. He then ruffed a diamond and finessed the spade eight. That would have been fine if the jack had been singleton, but the diabolical Zia produced the nine to defeat the slam.

Zia has never won a world title, largely because for many years he chose to represent Pakistan. He now plays for the United States, and is likely to be successful at some future time.

In the same category of players with the world championship credentials but no title are three pairs from North America. One consists of Edgar Kaplan and Norman Kay, and another is Eric Murray and Sami Kehela of Canada. Both pairs reached world championship finals three times, losing each time to the Italian Blue Team. (The Italians had special weapons. See above chapter 13.)

The third pair, still active and hoping for the top honors, consists of David Berkowitz and Larry N. Cohen, who just missed winning the world pairs title in 1998.

In 2001, Berkowitz won the International Bridge Press Association's Digital Fountain award for Hand of the Year for the following. See if you can identify the vital spot card.

			North
Dealer: South			♠ –
Vulnerable: Both			♥ K 7 4
			♦ A K 8 6 2
			♣ K Q J 5 3

West			East
♠ 7			♠ Q J 10 6 5 4 3 2
♥ Q 10 9 8 5 2			♥ J
♦ 5 4			♦ Q J 10 7
♣ 9 7 4 2			♣ –

		South	
		♠ A K 9 8	
		♥ A 6 3	
		♦ 9 3	
		♣ A 10 8 6	

South	*West*	*North*	*East*
(Berkowitz)		(Cohen)	
1 N.T.	Pass	2 ♠	4 ♠
5 ♣	Pass	5 ♦	Pass
5 ♥	Pass	7 ♣	Pass
Pass	Pass		

Playing at the 2000 Fall Nationals, the partnership reached seven clubs. Two spades was a transfer to clubs, and East's jump to four spades suggested an eight-card suit. A double would probably have collected 800, although 1100 is possible with double-dummy defense that includes two diamond ruffs.

South's five-club bid was based on good reasoning. His partner's failure to use Stayman suggested that he did not have four hearts, so there were most unlikely to be any major-suit losers. A hand with as little as six clubs headed by the king would probably offer a play for game. Two cue-bids followed (the modern term is control bids) and the grand slam was reached.

South won the spade lead in his hand, throwing a heart from the dummy. He did not make the mistake of cashing the club ace, but led to dummy's jack, uncovering the bad break. He then played diamonds, ruffing the third round with the club ten.

South continued by leading his remaining spade winner. If West had ruffed, it would have been easy to overruff and establish dummy's last diamond with another high ruff. So West discarded a heart and dummy a diamond. A spade was ruffed and the heart king was cashed.

Dummy's last diamond was ruffed with the club ace, and this position was reached:

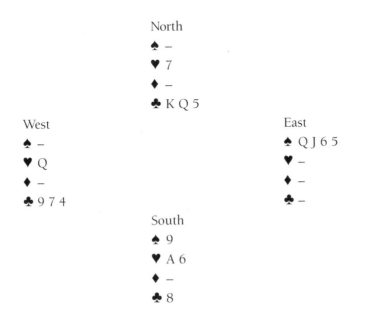

```
                        North
                        ♠ —
                        ♥ 7
                        ♦ —
                        ♣ K Q 5
    West                                    East
    ♠ —                                     ♠ Q J 6 5
    ♥ Q                                     ♥ —
    ♦ —                                     ♦ —
    ♣ 9 7 4                                 ♣ —
                        South
                        ♠ 9
                        ♥ A 6
                        ♦ —
                        ♣ 8
```

The club eight was led and covered by the nine and queen. A heart to the ace left West trapped in a coup position. Dummy's K-5 was poised over West's 7-4. Did you see that North's club five was the vital card?

Larry N. Cohen has been responsible for the most important development in bidding theory in two decades. It is called the Law of Total Tricks, and in two books he built on a pioneering thought by a Frenchman, Jean-René Vernes, in the 50's.

The object is to allow players to judge how high to bid in competitive auctions. A simple version is this: Bid to the level equal to the number of trumps in the combined hands. So, with an eight-card trump fit bid to the two-level, a nine-card trump fit to the three-level, and so one. If the contract fails, it will usually be true that the opponent would have made a plus score in their contract.

If both sides have a nine-card fit, the total number of trumps is 18. This approximately equals the number of tricks available, which may be nine for each, or 10 for one and eight for the other, or any other division. The same is true for other numbers. Add the number of trumps available for each side in its best fit, and the total should be the total number of tricks available.

Other factors that have to be taken into account are extreme distribution, possession of queens and jacks in the opponents' suits, and double fits.

The 80's ended with the surprising Brazilian win in the Bermuda Bowl. The next decade had some more surprises. The French won three times, which was not a shock since France has a group of world-class players, including Paul Chemla, Christian Mari and Michel Perron. But there were also victories for three long-shot teams, Germany, the Netherlands and Iceland. And the Italians, matching the glory days of the Blue Team, won twice.

There were four American victories. The first, in 1994, was in Salsomaggiore, Italy, and the winners were Martel and Stansby, Michael Rosenberg, Roger Bates and Gaylor Kasle, with Seymon Deutsch as sponsor-captain.

The second was in Beijing in 1995. The team was captained and financed by Nick Nickell, who played with Dick Freeman and two of the world's top pairs: Hamman-Wolff and Meckstroth-Rodwell.

This was, understandably, Meckstroth's favorite deal.

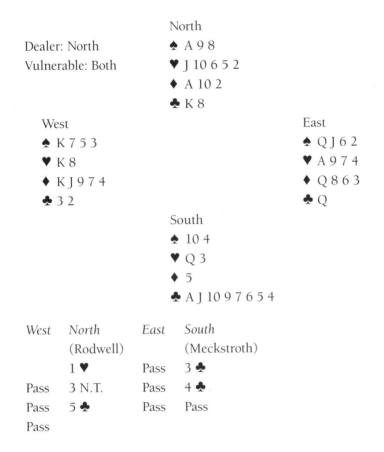

Dealer: North

Vulnerable: Both

North
♠ A 9 8
♥ J 10 6 5 2
♦ A 10 2
♣ K 8

West
♠ K 7 5 3
♥ K 8
♦ K J 9 7 4
♣ 3 2

East
♠ Q J 6 2
♥ A 9 7 4
♦ Q 8 6 3
♣ Q

South
♠ 10 4
♥ Q 3
♦ 5
♣ A J 10 9 7 6 5 4

West	North	East	South
	(Rodwell)		(Meckstroth)
	1 ♥	Pass	3 ♣
Pass	3 N.T.	Pass	4 ♣
Pass	5 ♣	Pass	Pass
Pass			

The response of three clubs to one heart was natural and invitational in the partnership style. If Meckstroth had passed his partner's three no-trump rebid all would have been well, but he continued with four clubs and his partner went on to game.

The contract would have been hopeless after a spade lead, but West led a diamond. On the face of it, South has no chance. But Meckstroth made a brilliant move: without any revealing hesitation, he played the diamond ten from dummy.

East was one of the world's greatest players, but after winning with the queen he did not see the danger. Instead of leading a heart, and defeating the contract immediately, or shifting to a decisive spade, he returned a diamond.

Now Meckstroth felt happier. He won with dummy's diamond ace, throwing a heart from his hand. When he then led a heart from the dummy, the contract proved to be unbeatable.

If East had taken his ace, South would have ruffed a heart later, removing the king and establishing his 11th trick. In practice, East played low and West won with the king. West shifted to a spade, but it was too late. South won with the ace in dummy and led the heart jack. He ruffed out East's ace, drew trumps ending in dummy, and cashed the heart ten to discard his spade loser and make the game.

Meckstroth's remarkable first-trick play did not gain imps, for in the replay the opposing North-South reached the unbeatable three no-trump contract. But it averted a heavy loss.

The Nickell team won again in the 1999 Bermuda Bowl, with Soloway replacing Wolff. The first championship of the new century was played accidentally in Paris in 2001. The planned venue was Bali, Indonesia, but the terrorist attacks of September 11 in New York City and Washington changed everything. Many players did not wish to go to a Moslem country, and World Bridge Federation President José Damiani performed an astonishing feat by relocating the championship within two weeks.

The result of the Bermuda Bowl was memorable. For the first time in the history of the game, a woman won a major open world title. Rose Meltzer sponsored and led a team that included Kyle Larsen and two well-established partnerships. One was Peter Weichsel and Alan Sontag, reviving a pairing that had been successful 18 years earlier. The other was Martel and Stansby, who were winning their fifth major world title. This raises them to a pantheon of American pairs with at least that number of wins. The others in this select category are Hamman and Wolff, and Meckstroth and Rodwell.

In the period described in this chapter, a large number of bidding conventions became popular, other than those described in earlier chapters. The most important of these are listed below, p. 193.

No. 29 ▸ Opening Leads
The traditional leads are:

1. Top of all honor sequences.

2. Fourth-highest from long suits.

3. Top from three or four low cards.

The modern leads, preferred by most experts, are:

1. Third-highest from interior sequences such as king-jack-ten. (This is usually expressed by saying that a lead of a jack, ten or nine promises zero or two higher cards.)

2. Third-highest from three or four cards, the fifth-highest from longer suits. This is called "third and fifth."

3. Second-highest from four or more low cards.

When fourth-highest leads are used, the Rule of Eleven applies. This means that the leader's partner or the declarer can calculate the number of cards above that led in the other three hands by the following procedure: Subtract from 11 the pips on the card led.

If third-highest leads are used, the Rule of Twelve applies similarly. However, this is seldom useful. More important is to consider the spot cards below the one led. A fourth-highest lead cannot be from five if there are no smaller cards missing. If one is missing, watch for its subsequent appearance.

Similarly, if a third-best lead is clearly the lowest card, it cannot be from a four-card suit: It must be from three cards or five.

No. 30 ▸ *Conventions*

A multiplicity of bidding conventions have become popular in the past half century. A summary of the commonest follows.

1. Michaels Cue-bid

When an opponent opens one heart or one spade, a bid of two of opener's suit shows at least five cards in the other major and least five cards in a minor. A two notrump reply—nowadays called an advance—asks the cue-bidder to show his minor suit. If the opening bid is a minor, the cue-bid shows length in both majors. The bid suggests opening values, but may be weaker if not vulnerable against vulnerable opponents. (Many experts play Michaels as weak or strong, but not in-between.)

This is the commonest example of a low-level cue-bid in the opponent's suit, which comes in many guises. It may be an advance to an overcall or a takeout double, or it may come on a later round of the bidding. In general, the cue-bid means, "I think we have a game partner, but I don't know where." Frequently it is an invitation to three notrump if partner has a stopper in an opponent's suit.

A special case occurs after an overcall. Then the cue-bid (one club-one spade-two spades) shows three-card support with invitational values or better. Four cards are needed or longer if opener has bid a minor suit. The direct jump raise is weak.

2. Flannery Two Diamonds

This shows, by agreement, opening values with roughly 11–15 points, exactly four spades and exactly five hearts.

3. Multi Two Diamonds

This is popular in Europe and shows a weak two-bid in hearts or spades. (Some partnerships allow certain strong hands also.) It is sometimes combined with a two-heart or two-spade opening showing five cards in that suit and length in an unspecified minor suit.

4. Lebensohl

A two notrump bid that requires partner to bid three clubs. It can apply when an opening one notrump bid is overcalled, in which case the two notrump bidder may be planning to sign off in a suit. Or it can be used similarly by the partner of a player who has doubled an opening weak two-bid.

5. New Minor Forcing

If the opening bidder rebids one notrump or two notrump after a one-level response, a cheap minor-suit bid can be an artificial exploring move with at least game interest. Opener shows three-card support for partner's major if he can.

6. Jacoby Two Notrump

Oswald Jacoby, the inventor of the transfer bid, introduced another idea that is very popular in tournament play. A two notrump response to an opening bid of one heart or one spade traditionally showed a balanced hand with 13–15 points and stoppers in the unbid suits. This hand-type can be bid in other ways. The Jacoby idea is to use it to show opening values, or better, and at least four-card support for opener. This may lead to a slam exploration. The opener bids a singleton or a void, if he has one, at the three-level. With no short suit, he bids: game in his suit with a minimum; three notrump with some extra values; and three of the anchor suit with a maximum. A jump to the four-level shows a strong side five-card suit.

7. Drury

If one heart or one spade is the opening in third position, two clubs can be used to show a strong raise, with roughly 9–11 high-card points. If the opener has subminimum values, he signs off in two of his major suit. A two-diamond rebid can be used to show a minimum opening.

8. Inverted minors

A single raise of a minor suit (one club-two clubs, or one diamond-two diamonds) can be used to show a strong hand with at least invitational values. The bidding may end in two notrump or three of the opener's suit. A direct raise to the three-level is weak.

For more details about these and other conventions see *The Official Encyclopedia of Bridge* published by the American Contract Bridge League. (Telephone 901-332-5586.)

CHAPTER 15

Some Strange Situations

 In 60 years of bridge, we have encountered some strange situations. They will be presented in quiz format, with answers at the end of this chapter. If you, the reader, can get one right you are doing well. You can solve three of them if you have read the earlier chapters carefully.

STRANGE SITUATIONS QUESTIONS

1. What is the worst ruling ever given at the bridge table?
2. What is the worst hand anyone has ever had in fourth position after three initial passes?
3. In what circumstances is it not only correct but desirable deliberately to fill in a wrong score in a duplicate game?
4. What is the penalty for accidentally looking at an opponent's hand on purpose?
5. In what circumstances can a player with the worst possible hand (four twos, four threes, four fours and one five) take a trick in notrump?
6. What is the record for the number of different situations a director has been asked about in the course of one deal?
7. When and why was the final of an international championship not played after the semifinals had been concluded?
8. When and why did the winners of a world team title never play a board against the runners-up?
9. When and why was an international match aborted with a few deals remaining to be played? (Two answers.)

10. In world mixed-pair events, why are the men required to sit North and East and the women South and West?

11. A declarer has four low cards opposite a doubleton king. He leads a low card, plays low from the dummy, and the ace appears on his right. What is the name of this play?

STRANGE SITUATIONS ANSWERS

1. I claim the record here. (Dorothy's situation described on page 238 does not qualify, because there was not a ruling at the table.)

I played in a London tournament in 1948, and the bidding went like this:

West	North	East	South
	(Alan)		
1 ♥	No	3 ♥	No
No	No		

In England the word "pass" is not used. "No bid" is standard, and is often contracted to "No."

West, a large and aggressive woman, won 11 tricks and wrote 450. She then claimed that her "No" was actually "Four." I wrote down 200, as did my partner and the dummy.

The director announced that when there was a dispute about the facts it was his duty to award an average. He did this despite three significant facts:

a. There were three votes for 200 and only one for 450.

b. If she was correct the bidding had not ended.

c. The other results were all 480. So 450 would have given us a top score. In those days I had never heard of an appeal of a ruling.

2. I used to think I held the record. I passed with four jacks, after each of the other three players had passed with 12 points. One had three bare aces, one four kings, and one four queens and an ace. However, the right answer arose with strong-pass bidding. See above page 171.

3. I have done this. It was the last deal of a duplicate game scored manually with traveling slips. I played in an obvious three notrump contract, making nine tricks, vulnerable, and was about to enter 600. All the previous North-South pairs had done the same. But the first declarer had misread the vulnerability and written 400. The others had done the same, and I was looking at a string of wrong scores. So I entered 400 also, knowing that entering a correct 600 would confuse things and perhaps create error.

4. It was the last deal of a duplicate game, and three of the players had a train to catch. I was waiting for my partner to lead, and I decided to save a little time. As dummy's cards were face down on the table, I picked them up, and held them so that the declarer and I could see them. We could start planning.

   Unfortunately I had mistaken the bidding. I had picked up the declarer's hand and looked at it. What the director would have said about a situation not covered in the Laws Book will never be known. Rather than call the director, waste time while he brooded, and thus miss the train, we gave the declarer back his cards and played.

5. This is theoretical, and has never happened. One player accidentally plays two cards to one trick. He wins the 12th trick but has nothing to lead. The Law says that the lead passes in rotation, and the "hopeless" hand makes a trick with the last card of his four-card suit.

6. I once had three, which is probably the record. I was defending one notrump. After the second trick, with all the cards turned, the declarer led to the third trick. He then reached over and turned over my partner's previous card, to verify his recollection.

   "You're not allowed to do that," I told him gently.

   "I am," he retorted firmly.

   "I don't think you are."

   "I am, I know I am, I'll bet you $20 I am."

   There is a regulation, little known and seldom observed, against betting on the results of a tournament, but there is no law against betting on the Laws. Luckily, I had $20 and produced it.

   The tournament director ruled in my favor, and said I should call him at the end if I felt injured.

   Half a minute later, we needed the director again. I had won the third trick and was about to make a key shift, holding the declarer to one notrump and scoring a top. A spade contract would have made nine tricks. Unfortunately, my partner had dropped the wrong card on the third trick. He corrected the impending revoke, but there was an exposed card and I was barred from making the play I wanted to make.

The director stayed, fortunately.

After five tricks the declarer claimed nine tricks, saying he would concede one at the finish. Ten seconds later he noted that he had an extra winner in the dummy, and changed his claim to ten tricks.

"I'll leave it to the director to say how many tricks you've made," I said cleverly.

The director turned pale, but decided that the declarer could not adjust his claim and concession once made.

I did not claim that I had been injured by the first misdemeanor. I did not feel injured, because I had a profit of $20.

"I was quite sure I was right," grumbled the declarer. "I would have bet $100."

So I now think that I lost $80.

7. At the 1999 Africa and Middle East zonal championships in Sri Lanka, Pakistan and South Africa qualified for the final. One of the Pakistan players, Asrar Umar, dropped dead of a heart attack, and the final was canceled as a mark of respect.

8. In 1976 Brazil and Italy, the winners of the gold and silver medals, did not play an effective board against each other. See page 185.

9. The *plafond* match between Culbertson and France was aborted near the end and declared a draw. See page 64.

In 1965, the last 16 deals in the match between the United States and Britain began with officials aware that Britain was about to default because of the Reese-Schapiro situation. After a few deals it was discovered that the players were seated wrongly, and play was canceled.

10. Players in first and second position are more likely to be declarer than those in third and fourth positions. When Tobias Stone was a moving player, he switched from East to West and back with this in mind. He had worked out which positions would put him in first and second seat most often and improve his chance to be declarer. Finally, the authorities put a stop to it. Today, for the same reason, players are not allowed to change positions in any event without official approval.

11. A Peeking Duck.

CHAPTER 16

Alan's Bridge Memories

When I was 15, and at school 10 miles south of London, I instructed three of my friends to read a book, and told them we would play our first game of bridge the following Thursday. On the first deal my partner bid one spade and I bid three clubs, with a monster hand. He passed, I made 12 tricks, and was furious. He had failed to read far enough in the book. But 12 years later he had represented England and I had played for Britain in the European Championship.

It was the summer of 1940 and the Battle of Britain was in progress. German planes flew overhead aiming for London. I frequently felt vulnerable during the many hours we spent in the air-raid shelter, but not because of the bombs. We were playing bridge, and soon advanced to duplicate. We had no boards, so the cards were rubber-banded together and placed in envelopes. One night we ventured on to the school roof and played bridge by moonlight. I doubled a bad player in a slam because I did not think he could see, but I was proved wrong.

I read every book about the game I could find, then and later while in the Royal Navy. Still in my uniform as a sublieutenant, I ventured to a tournament in Yorkshire, met Terence Reese, and played a session with Dr. Paul Stern, the nonplaying captain and guru of the prewar Austrian team. (See above, page 71.) He had one remarkable ability: He could write beautifully upside down. In contrast, I could write quite badly right way up.

I was reasonably expert when I arrived at Oxford University in 1947. There I played many hours of bridge, many hours of chess, and did just enough work to earn a history degree. A few days after arriving there, another student spotted me reading a bridge magazine and started a conversation. His name was Robert D'Unienville, he came from the beautiful island of Mauritius, and he became a great player.

Three years later, just for the experience, we entered the trials to choose the British team for the European Championships in Venice the following year. To our considerable surprise, we qualified for the team together with Terence Reese and Boris Schapiro. At 26 and 24 we were the youngest pair to represent Britain, before or since. (Nobody represents Britain today. England, Scotland and Wales compete separately on the international scene.) In Venice, the team finished third, behind Italy and Austria. Soon after, to my great regret, D'Unienville returned to his tropical island.

For seven years after leaving Oxford, I struggled with the demands of a nine-to-five job and a family. I gave up chess, my first love, but managed plenty of bridge. I wrote my first magazine article and pioneered, with the Dutch expert Herman Filarski, something that has been standard ever since. At the 1955 European Championships in Amsterdam we wrote the first Daily Bulletins. Because of ___ the players could read each morning the results and a selection of deals from the previous day.

Playing for an English team touring Belgium, I had this playing problem:

North
♠ J 10 9
♥ 8
♦ J 10 8 7 6 3
♣ Q J 6

South
♠ K 7 3
♥ A Q 6 5 3
♦ A K Q
♣ A 4

South	*North*
2 ♣	2 ♦
2 N.T.	3 N.T.
Pass	

The spade five was led, and dummy's nine won the first trick. How would you play?

There would be no entry to dummy after unblocking diamonds, and I expected to go down. But there was a ray of hope. It seemed very likely that West held five spades headed by the ace-queen, and I saw that I could succeed if he also held a small doubleton heart. He did, and the complete deal was:

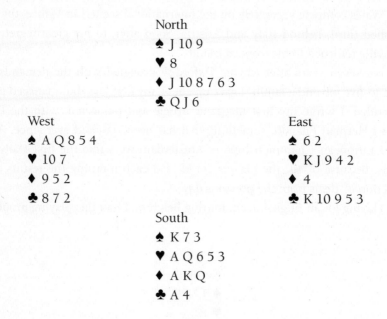

North
♠ J 10 9
♥ 8
♦ J 10 8 7 6 3
♣ Q J 6

West
♠ A Q 8 5 4
♥ 10 7
♦ 9 5 2
♣ 8 7 2

East
♠ 6 2
♥ K J 9 4 2
♦ 4
♣ K 10 9 5 3

South
♠ K 7 3
♥ A Q 6 5 3
♦ A K Q
♣ A 4

With this distribution in mind, I finessed the heart queen at the second trick. I then cashed four red-suit winners and led the spade king. West was welcome to take four spade tricks but had to lead a club at the 11th trick. Wherever the club king was, I could reach the dummy and score one diamond trick together with two clubs, making the game.

Other foreign trips included European Championships in Montreux, Switzerland, and in Vienna. But these were in backroom capacities. My attempts to qualify again for the British team were frustrated, usually by Reese and Schapiro. My life changed in 1958, when three things happened. First, to my relief, I was downsized from my dull nine-to-five job in London. Next, I spent two weeks in a country cottage writing my first bridge book. It is still in print 40 years later, after numerous updates. Third, I qualified for the British team due to play for the European title in Oslo.

I had the great pleasure of playing for a year with Harrison Gray, who had led three British teams to victory a decade earlier. Our teammates were the twin brothers Bob and Jim Sharples. All three of them believed that Reese and Schapiro regularly cheated. I was not convinced. It was therefore somewhat embarrassing when the British Bridge League added Reese and Schapiro to complete the required six-man squad. That meant three who were not speaking to two, and I was the neutral in the middle.

I had one deal that was highly satisfying:

North
Dealer: North ♠ 7 6 4 3
Vulnerable: Both ♥ Q 8
♦ Q 9 7 2
♣ A J 8

West
♠ K
♥ 9 6 5 3
♦ J 10 8 5
♣ K 10 9 4

East
♠ 9 8 5 2
♥ K J
♦ K 6 4 3
♣ 5 3 2

South
♠ A Q J 10
♥ A 10 7 4 2
♦ A
♣ Q 7 6

West	North	East	South
	Pass	Pass	1 ♥
Pass	1 N.T.	Pass	2 ♠
Pass	4 ♠	Pass	Pass
Pass			

The diamond jack was led and rode to my ace. It seemed likely the king was on my right. I led a heart to the queen, and East won with the king and shifted to a trump. A finesse lost to the king, and a heart was returned to the jack and ace.

I drew a round of trump, uncovering the bad split, and ruffed a heart. East overruffed and returned a trump to my ace. I won, finessed the club jack successfully, and reached this position:

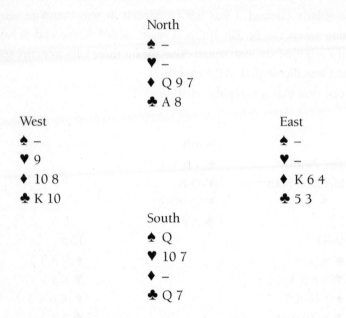

I led the diamond queen, and ruffed East's king. Then I played two heart winners, ruining West and making the game. A transfer squeeze does not happen every day, and this was a major occasion.

The championships proved to be a close battle between Britain, Italy and France. One key deal from the match against France has been given above. (Pages 142–143.) Another, from the match against Italy, has been giving me nightmares ever since:

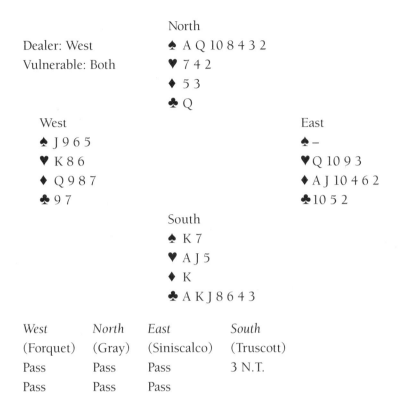

Dealer: West
Vulnerable: Both

North
♠ A Q 10 8 4 3 2
♥ 7 4 2
♦ 5 3
♣ Q

West
♠ J 9 6 5
♥ K 8 6
♦ Q 9 8 7
♣ 9 7

East
♠ –
♥ Q 10 9 3
♦ A J 10 4 6 2
♣ 10 5 2

South
♠ K 7
♥ A J 5
♦ K
♣ A K J 8 6 4 3

West	North	East	South
(Forquet)	*(Gray)*	*(Siniscalco)*	*(Truscott)*
Pass	Pass	Pass	3 N.T.
Pass	Pass	Pass	

West led a diamond and the defense took the first six tricks.

I got the blame for my opening bid. I certainly would not do it today, but the hand was a close fit for the Acol three notrump opening: long, very strong minor suit with at least two side suits stopped.

Nobody said a word about Gray's extraordinary decision to pass at his first turn, and then fail to bid his spades at his second turn. I never had the courage to ask him for an explanation.

Since I had promised a minor suit, it would have been normal for West to lead a major. Forquet led a diamond, which might have been my suit. At the time, I thought he made a lucky choice. Now, with the hindsight of years, I do not think it was luck. He and his partners hardly ever made the wrong lead. (See chapter 13 above.)

In the replay, the Italian North-South bid to the excellent spade slam, which failed unluckily when two rounds of diamonds were led to force a ruff and establish a trump trick for the defense.

We lost the title on a split tie with Italy. France finished one victory point back. Improve our results on either of the crucial deals, the one against Italy or the one against France, and we would have been European champions. I would probably have become a world champion, since the American team the following year was relatively weak and was in practice crushed by the Italians. A sadness.

I went to the first World Team Olympiad in 1960, and noted enviously that my partner, Tony Priday, had a dinner date with one of the members of the American women's team. She was a rare item of youth and beauty in a women's field that had little of either. It did not occur to me that she would one day be my wife.

I had undertaken a bunch of journalistic chores, and toiled all day in the press room. My industry was noted by a senior American writer, who proceeded to change my life. His name was Richard Frey, one of the original group of 10 life masters named when that rank was instituted by the Americans in 1936. He invited me out to dinner, along with his charming wife, Mabel, and followed with an offer.

Would I care to serve as a ghost for his syndicated column? I would, and I did. I was struggling to make a living out of bridge, and all work was welcome. So I began the process, still not quite complete 42 years later, of mastering American English and American bridge idiom.

One of my roles at this time was secretary of the British Bridge League, a post that carried a small honorarium. I was asked to start planning the 1961 European Championships in Torquay, a coastal town in the southwest of England. This took a great deal of my time, and I eventually had to fight for a fair financial reward for my efforts.

At the same time, I was, as usual, trying to be a member of the British team. Reese had announced that he would not be a candidate, because he wished to be the chief commentator. (But see above, pages 149–150.) Priday and I won the trials, so I had to play in Torquay. I manfully resisted the temptation to look around to see if my organization was working as intended, and we won the title.

There was one comedy in the match against Italy:

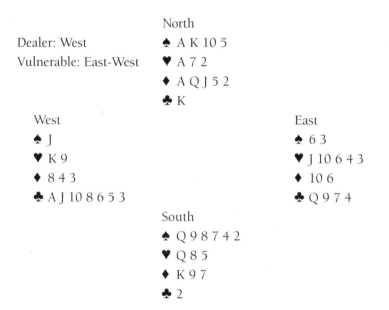

Dealer: West
Vulnerable: East-West

North
♠ A K 10 5
♥ A 7 2
♦ A Q J 5 2
♣ K

West
♠ J
♥ K 9
♦ 8 4 3
♣ A J 10 8 6 5 3

East
♠ 6 3
♥ J 10 6 4 3
♦ 10 6
♣ Q 9 7 4

South
♠ Q 9 8 7 4 2
♥ Q 8 5
♦ K 9 7
♣ 2

Six spades is clearly easy for North-South, but my teammates, with a free run, came to rest timidly in four spades. At my table:

West	North	East	South
(Priday)	(Mascheroni)	(Truscott)	(Cremoncini)
3 ♣	Dbl.	Pass	4 ♠
Pass	5 ♣	Pass	7 ♠
Pass	Pass	Pass	

The spectacular jump to seven spades, almost inconceivable for a player who was willing to play in game on the previous round, fooled Priday. He assumed that one of his opponents must have a club void, and instead of leading the club ace he produced the "safe" spade jack. South drew trumps, ran diamonds, and then played his remaining trumps. Poor Priday was squeezed in clubs and hearts, so the grand slam succeeded.

Italy had a second-level formation because the Blue Team, as defending champions, was already qualified for the Bermuda Bowl. Cremoncini had to bid in English, and, in the heat of battle, his limited command of the language deserted him. He meant to bid *six* spades and accidentally bid seven.

We therefore lost 14 imps when we could have gained 11. It mattered not, however, because we slaughtered the opposition on the remaining deals and took all the available victory points.

The following was my high point, from a match against Belgium. We were playing on Bridgerama, a giant electronic board that was a forerunner of the modern Vugraph. The four players were confined in a soundproof room with one-way glass: The audience could see us, but we could not see them.

North
♠ Q 5 4
♥ 5 2
♦ 8 7 3
♣ K 8 7 6 3

Dealer: West
Vulnerable: North-South

West
♠ K J 10 9 8 6 3 2
♥ Q 7
♦ Q 6
♣ 5

East
♠ 7
♥ A 8 6 3
♦ K 9 4 2
♣ J 10 9 4

South
♠ A
♥ K J 10 9 4
♦ A J 10 5
♣ A Q 2

West	North (Priday)	East	South (Truscott)
2 ♠	Pass	Pass	Dbl.
3 ♠	Pass	Pass	4 ♥
Pass	Pass	Pass	

Nobody today would consider making a weak two-bid with the West hand, and four spades would be the normal choice. In any event, I was in four hearts and the singleton club was led. Ominous.

Looking at all four hands, the contract seems hopeless. I needed a smidgen of help, and got it. The six, nine and ace were played on the first trick, and I continued with the heart king. East won with the ace and returned the club jack; the four would have been better. I played the queen, and as I expected West ruffed.

A spade was led, and I won and drew trumps. The position was:

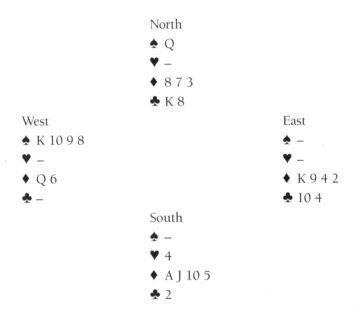

North
♠ Q
♥ –
♦ 8 7 3
♣ K 8

West
♠ K 10 9 8
♥ –
♦ Q 6
♣ –

East
♠ –
♥ –
♦ K 9 4 2
♣ 10 4

South
♠ –
♥ 4
♦ A J 10 5
♣ 2

I led the diamond jack, hoping for a doubleton honor on my left. I was considerably encouraged when West hesitated and then played low. If he had won and played the spade king he would have squeezed his partner.

East won with the king and returned a diamond. I knew what to do: I put up the ace, collected the queen, and played the last trump. This squeezed East in the minor suits. I had 10 tricks, and I could hear a faint roaring sound, like the ocean beating on the beach. I realized later that it was the sound of several hundred pairs of hands in action. The soundproofing was not quite as advertised, and it was very satisfying.

There were several reasons to feel happy. My preliminary organization had worked fine. We had won the title easily, with victory certain before the last round. Tony and I were judged the best pair on the winning team. We were also about to go to New York and perhaps win a world title.

Looking back four decades later, there is another reason for satisfaction.

Reese and Schapiro were not our teammates, so our victory was not tainted. It was probably the first postwar European Championship in which everyone was playing honestly.

Priday and I prepared carefully to play in the Bermuda Bowl, but were handicapped because details of the opposing systems were not provided. We spent several hours discussing how to defend against the Roman two notrump opening bid, only to be told when we arrived that Belladonna and Avarelli had abandoned that device.

The play was at the Barbizon Plaza, near Central Park, and we were sometimes placed in an open room. It was too open: Spectators were clustered on top of us, which would not be permitted today. At one point, the director claimed that I had returned only 12 cards to a board. After much research, the missing item was discovered under a pocketbook placed on the table by a lady kibitzer.

It was rather better when we were playing on Bridgerama, but even then there were problems. I discovered much later that on one deal the commentators had alleged that I had taken advantage of my partner's hesitation and subsequent pass. I had indeed led a doubleton king, hitting his suit. What the pundits did not know was that in the middle of the bidding a waitress had arrived delivering coffee.

Tony and I had a bidding triumph on the following deal:

```
                        North
Dealer: East            ♠ K Q 9
Vulnerable: Both        ♥ J
                        ♦ J 10 9 7
                        ♣ Q 10 6 4 2
West                                        East
♠ 7 5 3                                     ♠ J 2
♥ K 8 7 6 2                                 ♥ 10 9 5 4 3
♦ 8 5 4 2                                   ♦ K 6 3
♣ 3                                         ♣ 9 8 7
                        South
                        ♠ A 10 8 6 4
                        ♥ A Q
                        ♦ A Q
                        ♣ A K J 5
```

West	North (Priday)	East	South (Truscott)
		Pass	2 ♣
Pass	2 ♦	Pass	2 ♠
Pass	3 ♠	Pass	3 N.T.
Pass	4 ♣	Pass	6 ♣
Pass	7 ♠	Pass	Pass
Pass			

My partner could visualize my hand exactly, and his final bid was brilliant. He was sure that I had 5-2-2-4 with all the aces plus the club king. He could therefore count 13 tricks including a heart ruff. Seven spades needed only a 3-2 trump split, while seven clubs would have needed a winning guess in the red suits. It is seldom that a 5-3 fit is clearly superior to a 5-4 fit. Take away both red queens from the South hand and the grand slam is still an excellent contract.

Our American opponents did not come close. They bid briskly to six notrump without locating either black-suit fit.

We played well against the Americans, but our teammates were shaky and we lost narrowly. We played less well against the Italian Blue Team, losing easily, but so did everyone else in those days partly because they were good players and partly for reasons discussed above in chapter 13.

From my point of view, the result of the championships was less important than the sequel. Dick Frey invited me to stay at his house on Long Island and made me another offer, far more important than the first one.

He was the director of public relations for the American Contract Bridge League, and he wanted me to work for him. I would be deputy editor of the league's *Bulletin*, but my main task would be to write an *Encyclopedia of Bridge*. He flattered me by stating that there was nobody in America capable of doing it.

I went home and consulted my wife. I had been scratching out a living in England, from bridge writing, teaching and organizing. This was a chance for regular employment doing work I wanted to do. Nine months later I was on my way, enjoying the comforts of Britain's luxury liner, the *Queen Mary*. (My family followed three months later.) I arrived just in time to go to the 1962 Fall Nationals in Phoenix working in the press room. Among my other duties there, I prepared the first analysis sheets, predicting the probable course of bidding and play for the post-mortem entertainment of the players. These have been standard ever since on special occasions such as charity games.

In Phoenix, I asked all the New York players where I should make a home for my family. The most helpful reply came from Dorothy Hayden, the American player I had noticed in Turin two years earlier. She told me that the schools were very good in her home of Hastings-on-Hudson, 18 miles north of Manhattan. I took a look, liked it, and bought a small house there. So Dorothy and I were neighbors for the next seven years.

Writing and family now occupied all my time, and I had few opportunities to play. A tournament director bet me that the encyclopedia would never be finished. I did it in 18 months, with some clerical help that was almost entirely useless, but forgot to collect on the bet. Fairly quickly, I realized what Frey meant when he said that no American could do the work: No American would have considered doing the job for the tiny salary that he was paying me.

When the work was half complete, word spread that Albert Morehead was giving up his position as bridge columnist of *The New York Times*. I ignored this, believing that the newspaper of record would not want someone fresh off the boat. Luckily, Dorothy insisted that I apply. There were about 50 applicants, but I was one of only two with substantial writing experience. The other was Edgar Kaplan.

I had a bunch of interviews with some formidable characters. One was with the managing editor, Turner Catledge. Another was with Abe Rosenthal, the future managing editor. A third was with Clifton Daniel, who was married to Harry Truman's daughter, Margaret. A fourth was with the czar of the Sunday Department, Lester Markel, who scared everyone. None of them knew anything about bridge, but that did not stop Markel from summoning me to his office a year later to tell me I was not writing the daily column—which was none of his business—in the way he had ordered. I said I understood, and went on as before.

The most pleasant interview was a lunch with Abby Catledge, Turner's wife, who was a tournament bridge player. She was a lovely woman and must have given a good report. Two weeks later I was hired, and I am still not sure why I was favored ahead of Kaplan. One theory is that Sam Stayman was feuding with Kaplan and had the ear of the Sulzbergers, the proprietors of *The New York Times*. Another is that the editors thought I wanted the job more and would stick with it. They were right about that: I am still at it nearly 40 years later.

I have had very good editors, but I can recall three problems. One week-end, for example, I delivered a column for Monday and a column for Tuesday. Monday's paper printed the first half of the Monday column together with the second half of the Tuesday column. Which left an interesting problem in damage control. What should appear on Tuesday?

The printers occasionally created a disaster. One column appeared without a South hand in the diagram, which was not fatal, because the intelligent reader could construct the full diagram by subtraction. But an alert editor spotted the error and told the printer to add the South hand in the second edition. He did, but in doing so he eliminated the clubs from the East-West hands. The reader was now totally helpless.

By far the worst editing was contributed some 30 years ago by a man whose name I never discovered. Let's call him Jones. My column featured a player who recognized that his opponent was from Montreal and was French-speaking. As a gesture of good will, he made his final bid in French. Instead of saying three notrump, he announced *"trois sans atout."*

It seemed to me that some of my readers would know a little bridge French, and those who did not could consult the diagram. But Jones believed that everything must be explained to the reader, who should not be credited with any education or common sense. Unfortunately, Jones was totally ignorant about both French and bridge. He went to the dictionary and looked up the three words separately. *"Atout"* was defined as "a master or higher card" and next morning's column read like this: *trois sans atout* (three without higher cards)

I spent the day hitting my head against a wall, crying and laughing. For the first half of 1964 I was doing two jobs. In my A.C.B.L. capacity I wrote a long memorandum about things that needed to be done to prepare for the upcoming World Team Olympiad in New York. I had my Torquay experience behind me, and the American officials knew nothing whatever about the problems involved. Nobody paid any attention, and when play started the officials were running around frantically doing the things I had told them about six months before.

The exposure of Reese and Schapiro in Buenos Aires the following year left me feeling aggrieved. Although I had been their teammate twice, without winning, I had missed several chances for international honors because they were cheating against me. I now weep for the many players in Austria, France and Italy, as well as Britain, who were deprived of similar opportunities. In most countries the honest players suffered in silence, usually unaware of what was happening. The exception was Leandro Burgay in Italy (see pages 165–168 above) who ran into defensive stonewalling by his national organization. Also deserving condolences are the honest players in other countries, who might have won European or world titles if they had not had to put up with the players from Austria, Britain, France and Italy.

I was already collecting material for my book, *The Great Bridge Scandal*. There were press photographs, which accidentally revealed cheating. And there was plenty of past history. The story of Oakie (see page 149 above) was particularly significant, but the Foster Inquiry did not wish to hear about it.

My international career, I soon realized, was effectively over. I would travel to all the national and world championships but I could not expect to play at the highest level while worrying about the writing I had to do. I could not play a session of serious bridge and make calls to an editor who wanted to know why the deal included two spade deuces. Still, the work was fun.

Some of the correspondence I received was remarkable. One man from New Jersey used to write to me regularly, enclosing a clipped column. At the top he would scrawl, perhaps, "Wouldn't South have made five clubs?" It was a ridiculous question. South wouldn't, and nobody in their right mind would think of such a contract.

Fed up with him, I did not always reply. Then I received a long letter from him, saying that he could understand my problem. Since I did not always answer him, he concluded that I was a manic-depressive and should consult a good psychologist. So I stopped answering altogether, and he stopped writing.

Even more curious was a rather illiterate lady from Detroit. She was convinced that the cards in my diagrams included the winning numbers in the New York lottery. She demanded that I explain this to her, otherwise she would expose me to the authorities. Failing in this, she became plaintive. She badly needed the money. I considered reporting this in my column, with the idea of increasing readership, but received an editorial veto.

I was of course reporting in Deauville, where the British players were patriotically not speaking to me. Most of them thawed when *The Great Bridge Scandal* appeared and they had a chance to read it. One holdout was Rixi Markus, the dynamic British star who was violently on the side of Reese and Schapiro. She spotted Priday playing two deals with me in a demonstration of somebody's product, and poured a glass of water on his head for consorting with the enemy.

Rixi was a constant nuisance to Dick Frey, the chief commentator. She regularly invited herself on to the commentary panel, so he tried to get rid of her: He arranged for her to be the announcer in the Bridgerama playing room, calling the cards for the benefit of the audience. At one point, she was sure that East was about to play the eight of hearts and announced it prematurely. East played something else, and the director then had to deal with a unique problem, not covered in the laws, of a card exposed by an announcer.

Since my journalistic duties meant that I had little hope of playing in international tournaments officially, I decided to do so unofficially. Early in 1970 I arranged for a top team to visit Australia and New Zealand. (In later years we made two further tours Down Under, both highly successful.) Dorothy and I went with Bob Jordan and Arthur Robinson, who had played frequently in world championships in the sixties, just missing the top honors. Our fifth player was Bill Root, long a top teacher as well as a member of the American team on two occasions.

I thought we would have a good chance to win all our matches, but we were defeated by the top Australian team. This was partly because they had one of the all-time great players, Tim Seres. I knew him well. Five years earlier I had gone on a cruise to Australia and he had shown me the following:

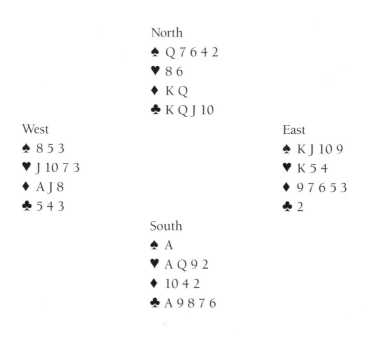

North
♠ Q 7 6 4 2
♥ 8 6
♦ K Q
♣ K Q J 10

West
♠ 8 5 3
♥ J 10 7 3
♦ A J 8
♣ 5 4 3

East
♠ K J 10 9
♥ K 5 4
♦ 9 7 6 5 3
♣ 2

South
♠ A
♥ A Q 9 2
♦ 10 4 2
♣ A 9 8 7 6

Seres played in six clubs as South, and received a trump lead. He won in dummy, finessed the heart queen successfully, and cashed the spade ace. A diamond lead was won by West, who led a second trump. This was also won in dummy, and South ruffed a spade, crossed to the diamond king, and ruffed another spade. The ace of hearts and a heart ruff led to this remarkable ending:

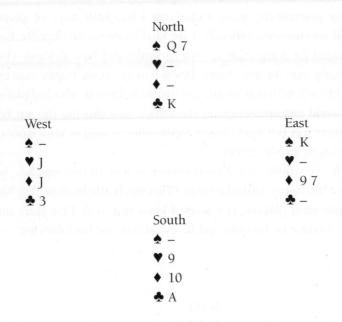

The spade seven was led and ruffed, catching West in a strange triple squeeze. If he "discarded" his losing trump, dummy would take two tricks. And if he discarded a jack, South would have a winner to lead with the same result.

This position was new to theory at the time, and is known as the Seres Squeeze. Today it would be considered a variety of the backwash squeeze.

The Australians, with Seres as the star, had strong teams at this time. They came close to winning medals in Deauville, but just missed out because Seres's partner, Dick Cummings, fell ill at a crucial moment. They would surely have contended for medals on other ocasions were it not for the fact that some of the opponents they faced were "helping each other."

Later that year, 1970, my life changed abruptly. My wife and I separated, and later divorced. Soon after, she returned to England with our children.

I now made a plan for a longer tour. C. C. Wei, the originator of the Precision System, wanted to showcase his methods. He and his wife, Kathie, asked me to work out a world tour for 1971. It was to begin in Taipei, Taiwan, after the world championships. We would be a group of eight, with two stars of the Italian Blue Team, Benito Garozzo and Giorgio Belladonna, as the playing spearhead.

Getting to the starting point was not straightforward. I had a one-night stopover in Tokyo, and chose to dine in my hotel's Chinese restaurant. There was only one occupied table, with four men at it. Looking carefully, I identified my wife's lawyer, with whom I had been discussing a marriage settlement two days before, half a world away in Manhattan. He was friendly, and gave me a tour of the city the following morning.

Later I boarded a virtually empty jumbo jet for Taipei. The seat lights nearly all flashed on and off like lighthouses, and when I arrived Northwest Airlines had sent my checked bag to Hong Kong. They called me in the middle of the night to tell me I would have to come to the airport to retrieve it at noon the next day, and then kept me waiting for an hour while they found a customs officer.

I had planned the logistics carefully, and all went well. In each country we were the guests of the local bridge organization. The first stops were in Hong Kong and Manila, where we won our matches easily. The third was Bangkok, where we beat the Thailand team on the last board. I was enjoying myself greatly, and it was about to get even better.

I thought that while we were in India everyone would want to see the Taj Mahal, but I was wrong. Five members of the group were not interested in sightseeing, so I arrived in Agra accompanied by Dorothy and an English World Champion, Dimmie Fleming.

Dorothy and I wanted to see the Taj at dawn, and Dimmie did not care to get up early. That suited my plans perfectly. With this most beautiful backdrop, I asked Dorothy to marry me, pointing out that she would never have another opportunity to get engaged in front of the Taj. To my great delight, she said yes. For the rest of the tour, which took us to Bombay, Mauritius, Johannesburg, Tel Aviv and Rome, I was in a daze of delight. In spite of that, we only lost one match. Nine months later we were married, and lived happily ever after.

No. 31 ▸ *Relays*

Relay bidding is an advanced modern idea that breaks away from traditional methods. It is for serious partnerships aiming at tournament success. The general idea is that one player takes control and makes a series of minimum, or relay, steps. The second player describes his hand in a prearranged way. Eventually, the first player knows enough about his partner's hand to make a final decision. The second player knows virtually nothing.

There are several relay languages, and the users cannot communicate with others. The one we use is a development of a New Zealand idea known as Symmetric, and the bidding starts on Precision Club lines.

After a strong club opening and a positive response, the opening bidder makes relays to find out his partner's distribution, number of controls, and high-card location. Similarly, after an opening bid of one of a suit, a one notrump response asks for information, with more relays to come. Different relays apply after other opening bids.

CHAPTER 17

Dorothy's Bridge Memories

I was introduced to bridge at the age of 7. My parents played, as did my grandmother and most of their friends. After dinner there were often two tables of bridge in play, and I would sit behind my mother and watch. I was not really interested in the game but if I sat there quietly enough, Mother would usually forget about my bedtime. I already knew how to play some bridge-related games such as euchre and honeymoon bridge so I understood vaguely what was going on.

The high point of the evening for me came when my father went to mix drinks for the company. I was conscripted to sort his cards, bid his hand, and sometimes play it as well. (By the way, Grandmother did not permit stakes higher than one-twentieth of a cent a point, so it was not as though financial ruin threatened if I goofed.) Then, when I was about 7, a guest was very late in arriving. I played for one full hour and was hooked for life.

Was I any good? No, I was terrible. So were the others, but it would be years before I realized it.

At school my fellow students were not interested in bridge so I concentrated on basketball, tennis and softball. At 17 I entered Smith College, where there was a bridge game starting after lunch. The problem was that I had a Russian class from 2 to 4. I was good at math and sports, but otherwise a mediocre student. And, you guessed it, I never did learn Russian.

I was married when I was 20, and soon had three wonderful children. This left little time for bridge, but I did read just about everything I could get my hands on, which included *The Bridge World* from cover to cover. I even played Autobridge in the bathtub. (This is trickier than it sounds.) Ironically, as things turned out, my favorite book was *Reese on Play*. It still is.

219

About this time I became convinced that the only way forward was to play with people who were better than I. Not so easy to do in the pleasant, sunny town that was Kalamazoo half a century ago. Anyhow, I hired a baby-sitter and joined a group of women who met every Thursday afternoon and were reputed to be the best in town. And this is where I met Penelope. (A pseudonym to protect the innocent.)

The other girls were actually decent players. Penelope, however, was a lovely girl, but the worst bridge player I had ever seen. I was certain that she was the worst bridge player in the United States.

Then one day I ran into Penelope in the market.

"Dorothy, Have you met our new neighbor? Her name is Betty." (Again, a pseudonym to protect the even more innocent.)

When I confessed that I had not met Betty, Penelope confided in me that Betty was "the worst bridge player in the world and she personally was never going to play in Betty's game ever again."

This sounded promising. "What did she do?" I inquired cautiously.

"Well, when she was my partner I opened the bidding with one spade and she passed me out holding five spades including the ace-king and an outside ace."

"Don't you ever raise your partner, Betty?" asked Penelope.

"Oh, Penelope! I didn't know I was *your* partner!" was the marvelous reply.

Things progressed faster in 1952 when we moved to Park Forest, Illinois, a suburb of Chicago. One afternoon a week I would hire a sitter and take the train into Chicago, where for the first time I played in a real bridge club. In those days, there was virtually no duplicate. It was all rubber bridge for stakes. Where I played there were three stakes available: I started at the lowest but soon worked my way up to the highest. When you can't afford to lose you learn quickly.

I soon discovered that I had a secret weapon: I was pleasant to my partners, even when they goofed. Most of the so-called experts felt it their duty to humiliate their partner by pointing out every mistake. Naturally their partners then played worse and mine played better.

In 1956 my marriage ended in divorce. The children and I moved to New York, where I went to work for New York Life as an actuarial student. They had a bridge team, and I was delighted when they asked me to join. We played in the Commercial League and cleaned up. On the way home from work I played rubber bridge in the high-stake game at the Cavendish Club, where the men were a bit suspicious of a woman at first. They soon either forgave me or forgot about the matter. It was here, playing with and against the best rubber bridge players in New York, that I finally began to learn how to play the game.

In 1957 the Summer Nationals were in Pittsburgh. I was asked to play on a mixed team with Ozzie Jacoby and Sally Johnson in one room. I was to alternate with Sam Fry and Ira Rubin in the other room. There were over a hundred teams competing. When Ira and I came to play at the table where Charlie Goren and Helen Sobel were North-South, the place was completely surrounded by noisy kibitzers eager to watch the world's most famous mixed pair.

The chief director, Al Sobel, announced loudly, "No standing kibitzers! If you don't have a chair, get out."

Of course I paid no attention. In the first place I was not a kibitzer. In the second place I was too busy trying to break through the barrier of occupied chairs to reach the East seat where I belonged.

"No standing kibitzers, young lady," he repeated, as I vaulted over the last barricade into my seat.

"She's my partner, Al," said Ira.

"Well, I'll be a monkey's uncle!" was the expurgated reply.

I'm not sure if this was a compliment or not, but it does show that I was virtually unknown at the time. When we finished second overall, rumor had it that Jacoby-Johnson must be a hell of a pair to do this with a beginner in the other room.

In 1958 New York Life sent a team (Jay Wendt, Dave Strasberg, Nick Zampino and me) to the Spring Nationals for the four-session Commercial Board-a-Match Teams. We won by a mile.

In 1959 I had an extraordinary piece of luck. The American Contract Bridge League decided to send a women's team to the first World Olympiad, which was to be held in Turin, Italy, in 1960. The board of directors would select the six players from among any women to finish first or second in a national event in 1959. I was not even a Life Master at the time and knew nothing about this, but I happened to win the National Women's Pairs (with Betty Goldberg) and the National Mixed Pairs (with Johnny Crawford) that year. I had never played a session of bridge with either of them beforehand, but it didn't matter because almost everyone in those days played Blackwood and Stayman, *period.*

There are a lot of politics in board selections, and I would never have been chosen but for the fact that I was the only candidate to have won two events—

so they could not refuse to pick me. It was a little unsettling to realize that I would be playing for the U.S. with five women, none of whom I had ever played with before. Looking back, it might be the worst selection method ever devised.

On the plane to Turin I was seated just in front of three famous names: B. Jay Becker, Sidney Silodor and Norman Kay, all members of one of the U.S. Open Teams. When they invited me to go sightseeing with them I was quick to accept.

My teammates in Turin included two excellent players, Agnes Gordon and Helen Portugal, and three relatively inexperienced players. We finished fifth. The sad thing is that we could have won the gold medal if our captain, Charlie Solomon, had not insisted on rotating the players equally to avoid complaints from those sitting out.

I did meet President Eisenhower, at the Summer Nationals in Washington. He had come to watch a few hands of bridge, escorted by General Gruenther, Charlie Solomon and a brigade of Secret Servicemen. As they paraded across the hotel lobby, the general saw me.

"Ike, I'd like you to meet Dorothy Hayden."

We shook hands, and I told him that Jim Hayden was my father-in-law. That started him on a long discussion of the good times that he and Jim used to have when they were stationed together at West Point.

Then I suddenly realized that the whole lobby was blocked up waiting for the president to move on, and I quickly said my goodbye. Later, when he was in the hospital, I sent him my first book, and he sent me a lovely letter in reply.

One good thing to result from Turin was my partnership with Helen Portugal. She lived on the West Coast so we only got together at Nationals but we had an excellent record. We qualified easily as one of the U.S. pairs to be sent to Cannes, France, in 1962, for the World Women's Pairs, and were thrilled to take home the bronze medal.

An even better result from Turin was my partnership with B. Jay Becker. And he lived conveniently in New York. He was always known as "Mister Becker" for an interesting reason. At the start of his career he played with P. Hal Sims, a fiery and intolerant partner. When something went wrong he would scream, "Becker, you idiot, you nincompoop, you dunderhead . . ."

Eventually Becker took him, aside and told him, "Mr. Sims, if we are going to have a successful partnership you'll have to treat me with more respect."

Sims thought about this, and after the next disaster he chose his words carefully, "Mr. Becker, you idiot, you nincompoop, you dunderhead . . ."

And Mr. Becker he became from that moment. The first time we played together was in a mixed pair event and the following came up:

		North	
Dealer: South		♠ 10 8 7 3	
Vulnerable: Both		♥ A 6 5 2	
		♦ A 5	
		♣ 8 6 5	

West			East
♠ A K 9 6 2			♠ Q J 4
♥ Q 7 4			♥ 10 9 8
♦ J 9 6 3			♦ 10 8 7 4
♣ 4			♣ Q J 2

		South	
		♠ 5	
		♥ K J 3	
		♦ K Q 2	
		♣ A K 10 9 7 3	

South	West	North	East
(Dorothy)		(Becker)	
1 ♣	1 ♠	Pass	Pass
Dbl.	Pass	2 ♥	Pass
3 ♣	Pass	4 ♣	Pass
4 ♥	Pass	5 ♣	Pass
Pass	Pass		

West led the spade king, and while he was thinking about what to do next I made my plan. How could I avoid losing two more tricks if the trumps did not split evenly and West, as was likely in view of the vulnerable overcall, held the heart queen?

West shifted to a diamond, and I won with dummy's ace and ruffed a spade. I cashed the top trumps, finding that East had a trick there, and took the diamond king. Then I ruffed the diamond queen. This was a winner, but I needed an extra entry to the dummy. I ruffed one more spade, and gave East his club winner. The position was then:

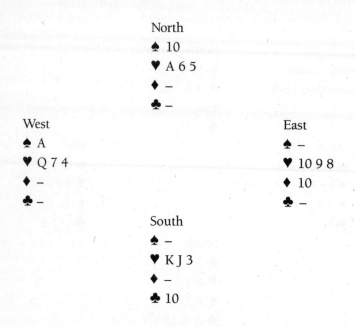

North
♠ 10
♥ A 6 5
♦ –
♣ –

West
♠ A
♥ Q 7 4
♦ –
♣ –

East
♠ –
♥ 10 9 8
♦ 10
♣ –

South
♠ –
♥ K J 3
♦ –
♣ 10

If East had returned a diamond, West would have been squeezed in the major suits when I ruffed. Instead, East shifted to the heart ten, which simply postponed the issue. I won with the king, led my trump, and West had to surrender.

Becker was impressed by the speed with which I played this contract. (I did not tell him that I had done my thinking while waiting for West to play at trick two.)

"Next time we'll play in the open pair," he said.

When we did, we experimented with a device suggested by Alan, who was now my neighbor. It was the void-showing bid: an unusual jump to show a void, a good fit and slam interest. I persuaded Becker, and other partners, to use it for a singleton as well as a void, which meant it came up seven times as often. And so was born the splinter bid. It quickly became popular and is now standard in most parts of the bridge world. (See below, p. 239.)

In Phoenix in 1962, Becker and I won the National Open Pairs, our first title. He always kept track of mistakes (his own as well as partner's) with little black dots on his convention card. He claimed that this was the only time he had ever played in a major four-session pair event without assigning a single little black dot to his partner. How I wish I could play that well today for even one session in a row. In the next five years we won the Blue Ribbon Pairs and the Life Master Pairs and we were second twice in the Spingold and once in the Vanderbilt.

For the 1964 Team Olympiad, to be held in New York, there was to be a pairs trials to select the U.S. Open team and another to select the U.S. Women's team. I was qualified for both, with Portugal for the women's and Becker for the open. Unfortunately the trials were to be held simultaneously and I had to make up my mind.

I can't tell you how many people advised me to play in the women's.

"Your chance of qualifying for the women's team is 90 percent and for the open it is 1 percent. Don't be an idiot!"

Ask an addicted mountain climber whether he would prefer to climb Mount Everest with a 1 percent chance of success, or Mount Marcy with a 90 percent chance. I played in the Open trials.

Here is an incredible feat of legerdemain by Becker in those trials.

North

Dealer: South
Vulnerable: None

♠ Q 8
♥ 10 6 3
♦ A Q J 9 6
♣ A Q 4

West

♠ 5 4 3
♥ A 8 5
♦ K 5 3 2
♣ 10 5 2

East

♠ J 10 7 2
♥ K Q 7 4
♦ 10 8 7
♣ 7 6

South

♠ A K 9 6
♥ J 9 2
♦ 4
♣ K J 9 8 3

South (Becker)	West (Stayman)	North (Dorothy)	East (Mitchell)
1 ♣	Pass	1 ♦	Pass
1 ♠	Pass	3 ♣	Pass
4 ♣	Pass	4 ♠	Pass
6 ♣	Pass	Pass	Pass

The bidding needs a little explanation. Becker and I played virtually no conventions, not even Stayman. We did play Blackwood and over notrump we played Gerber. Just before this session we agreed to play Gerber over minor suits as well. When my partner bid four clubs I was happy to bid four spades showing two aces.

Becker, however, had forgotten all about Gerber. He thought I was showing 3-1-5-4 shape and a very good hand, so he jumped to six clubs. Stayman had heard this strong bidding and decided to attack with a diamond lead. Believe it or not, the hand could no longer be defeated thanks to my *six* of hearts. Interchange my six with Stayman's five and the contract cannot be made.

My dummy horrified Becker, but he maintained his usual poker face and calmly finessed the diamond jack. He then cashed the diamond ace, throwing a heart, and ruffed a diamond. He crossed to the club ace and ruffed another diamond, establishing dummy's queen. He cashed the king and queen of clubs, and the lead was in dummy in this position:

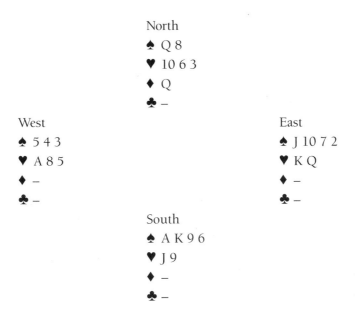

North
♠ Q 8
♥ 10 6 3
♦ Q
♣ –

West
♠ 5 4 3
♥ A 8 5
♦ –
♣ –

East
♠ J 10 7 2
♥ K Q
♦ –
♣ –

South
♠ A K 9 6
♥ J 9
♦ –
♣ –

When the diamond queen was played from dummy, Mitchell had to give up a heart honor to maintain his spade guard. Becker threw the nine of hearts and Stayman parted with a spade.

Now the spade queen was cashed and the eight led. Mitchell had to play an honor to prevent the nine being finessed, and the king won. Now Becker administered the coup de grace by leading the heart jack. If Stayman played low, the spades in the closed hand would take the last two tricks. And if he won with the ace, he would have to lead from the eight-five, giving dummy's ten-six two tricks.

The slam was made, and the defenders were in shock.

"He couldn't have made it without the six of hearts," muttered Mitchell.

"Without the six of hearts," stated Becker placidly, "we wouldn't have bid so much!"

I wish I could say that Becker and I made the team. We finished tied for fourth out of sixteen with only the top three pairs to be selected. No, I never regretted my choice.

We did better two years later. Playing in Dallas in November 1964, we finished third in the trials for the world championship. This qualified us for the U.S. team to play in Buenos Aires for the Bermuda Bowl against Argentina, Britain and Italy.

The most famous hand was perhaps this from our match against Italy. Becker and I were pitted against the great Italian pair, Garozzo and Forquet. Before play began Gerber, our nonplaying captain, jokingly asked Garozzo "not to make the young lady cry"!

North and South were vulnerable. As South, I held:

    ♠ K
    ♥ A 10
    ♦ A K 8 7 5 4 3
    ♣ K 6 5

South	West	North	East
(Dorothy)	(Garozzo)	(Becker)	(Forquet)
1 ♦	1 ♠	Pass	Pass
2 ♦	Pass	Pass	2 ♠
Pass	Pass	3 ♦	Pass
3 N.T.	Pass	Pass	Pass

When Becker showed some diamond support I was sure I could make three notrump if I could survive the opening lead, but this was no time to think. I bid three notrump confidently and Garozzo led the spade queen from a holding of A-Q-10-9-x. We scored 630 against a part score in diamonds in the other room.

After the session, Gerber asked Garozzo if he had made the young lady cry?

"She make cry me," was the reply in broken English.

People often ask if being a mathematician helps me at the bridge table. The answer is practically never. Here is a deal from our match against Argentina which will show you what I mean.

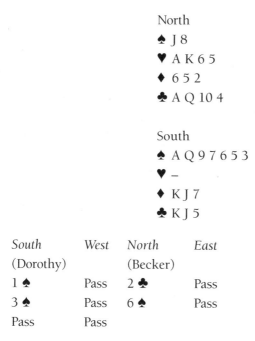

North
♠ J 8
♥ A K 6 5
♦ 6 5 2
♣ A Q 10 4

South
♠ A Q 9 7 6 5 3
♥ –
♦ K J 7
♣ K J 5

South (Dorothy)	West	North (Becker)	East
1 ♠	Pass	2 ♣	Pass
3 ♠	Pass	6 ♠	Pass
Pass	Pass		

West led the diamond ace and shifted to a club. How should I play the trump suit?

There are three possibilities. The worst, in theory, is to lead the spade jack from dummy and play East for K-10-x. Slightly better is to lead the spade jack from dummy, and if this is covered, win with the ace and cash the queen. Best, by a clear margin, is to lead the eight from the dummy planning to finesse the queen. This allows you to handle a singleton king with East.

I deliberately made the worst play by winning in dummy and leading the spade jack. When this was covered with the king, I went back to dummy, threw my diamond loser on the heart ace and finessed East for the spade ten. Why did I play it this way? Because East looked too alert. According to my calculations, East should have been in a hopeless frame of mind after his partner cashed the diamond ace. Yet he didn't look like a man who knew the jig was up. The only explanation for his continued confidence in life was that his trump holding was K-10-x or K-10-x-x. He actually held K-10-x, so I made the slam.

Moral: One twitch of an opponent's eyebrow is worth two degrees in mathematics.

In 1965 my first book was published. It was entitled *Bid Better, Play Better,* was very popular, and still is after two updates. My second book, *Winning Declarer Play,* followed three years later and also continues to sell well.

In 1966 there was a world pairs championship in Amsterdam, and Becker and I had qualified to represent the United States. After innumerable sessions of qualifying we had made it to the four-session finals. We finished third and took home the bronze medal. If I had played half as well as my partner we would have won the whole thing. At the time I did not realize that third place was very good: Never before or since has a woman finished in the top ten.

The winners of the title, in a blanket finish, were two talented Dutchmen, Bob Slavenburg and Hans Kreijns. Slavenburg told me the following remarkable story. He had, he said, been playing on an earlier occasion in a match between the Netherlands and France. He picked up:

♠ 6 2
♥ 9 5
♦ 4 3
♣ A Q J 7 6 5 2

With both sides vulnerable, he had ventured a psychic overcall of one spade when his right-hand opponent opened one heart. When this was doubled for penalties—before the days of negative doubles—he retreated to one notrump. He intended to beat a second retreat into clubs after a further double, but his partner got in the way by bidding two spades. Slavenburg assumed that this indicated great length and strength in spades and stood his ground.

The complete deal was this:

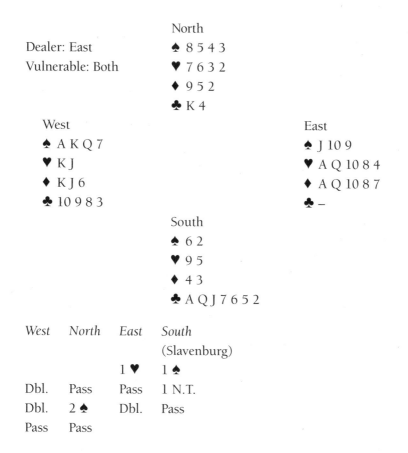

Dealer: East

Vulnerable: Both

North
- ♠ 8 5 4 3
- ♥ 7 6 3 2
- ♦ 9 5 2
- ♣ K 4

West
- ♠ A K Q 7
- ♥ K J
- ♦ K J 6
- ♣ 10 9 8 3

East
- ♠ J 10 9
- ♥ A Q 10 8 4
- ♦ A Q 10 8 7
- ♣ –

South
- ♠ 6 2
- ♥ 9 5
- ♦ 4 3
- ♣ A Q J 7 6 5 2

West	North	East	South
			(Slavenburg)
		1 ♥	1 ♠
Dbl.	Pass	Pass	1 N.T.
Dbl.	2 ♠	Dbl.	Pass
Pass	Pass		

It is easy to see that two spades doubled was not an ideal contract. The defenders could have taken all the tricks with something to spare, scoring 2,300. That is, however, very little more than the value of the grand slam they were entitled to in spades, hearts or diamonds. But something went wrong with the defense.

A French expert sitting West led the spade ace, and East dropped the jack. West continued with the king, not stopping to think that his partner must have the ten: A double of two spades with a singleton would be inconceivable. East should now have played the nine, making it clear that he held the ten, but he erred in his turn by playing the ten. West continued by cashing the queen, completing the ruin of the defenders' trumps.

A shift to a red suit at this point would have enabled the defense to take 11 tricks for a penalty of 1700, but West's feet were still set firmly on the road to disaster and he led a club. Slavenburg gratefully won with dummy's king, drew the missing trump with the eight over the seven, and claimed his contract. Seven club tricks and one trump trick were enough for a score of 670.

In the replay the Dutch East-West played in six spades, making an overtrick, and felt guilty about their failure to bid seven. "Did the French pair reach the grand on Board 13?" they demanded urgently when the team assembled at the end of the session.

"We made a game in spades," reported Slavenburg modestly.

"That's a different board," said his teammates impatiently. "On Board 13 East-West are cold for seven spades."

"We made game in spades," Slavenburg persisted, and it took half an hour to dissipate the others' incredulity.

Some have expressed skepticism about this, but if the story is fiction it indicates remarkable creative imagination.

In the next few years, Becker and I qualified regularly for the Team Trials, until they ended in 1969.

On the women's side, I developed a good partnership with Emma Jean Hawes of Fort Worth. We won the first event that we entered, the national women's pairs, and went on to win eight other national titles over the next fourteen years: Our international record was even better: four bronze medals and four gold medals.

Here is a famous deal from the 1967 National Women's Team Championship, which in those days was board-a-match. Emma Jean and I, together with Margaret Wagar, were playing with Agnes Gordon, who was dying of cancer. This was to be her last tournament and we were determined to win it.

Of course we did not know it at the time, but first and second place were virtually tied going into the final round. All depended on this one last deal. In the other room North-South had already scored 450 in an obvious four hearts. If we scored better than 450 we would be the winners. If we scored less than 450 we would finish second, and if we scored exactly 450 it would be a dead tie.

You may think something is missing in the bidding (Blackwood, for example), but this was the actual auction:

North
♠ K Q 6 4
♥ Q 7 6
♦ 5 2
♣ K Q 6 3

West
♠ A 8 3 2
♥ 5 4
♦ J 10 9 7 6
♣ 7 2

East
♠ 10 9 7 5
♥ 10 3
♦ 8 4 3
♣ A J 10 5

South
♠ J
♥ A K J 9 8 2
♦ A K Q
♣ 9 8 4

South	*West*	*North*	*East*
(Dorothy)		(Emma Jean)	
1 ♥	Pass	1 ♠	Pass
3 ♥	Pass	5 ♥	Pass
6 ♥	Pass	Pass	Pass

Both of us were slightly pushy, and the result was a hopeless slam.

I won the opening diamond lead with the ace, crossed to the heart queen, and led a low spade toward the jack. I was hoping to steal a trick if East held the ace, but unfortunately West won. Fortunately she returned a heart, not a club, but I still had absolutely no play for 12 tricks.

I decided to abandon the good spades in dummy and ran all but one of my red-suit winners coming down to this position:

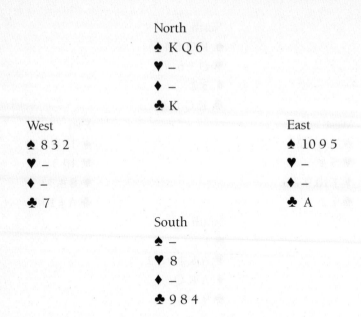

North
♠ K Q 6
♥ —
♦ —
♣ K

West
♠ 8 3 2
♥ —
♦ —
♣ 7

East
♠ 10 9 5
♥ —
♦ —
♣ A

South
♠ —
♥ 8
♦ —
♣ 9 8 4

I led the last trump and threw the club king from the dummy. East could not conceive that I had abandoned two spade winners in the dummy, so she clung to her spade guard and threw the club ace. I won the remaining three tricks with the 9-8-4 of clubs—and Agnes Gordon had won her last championship.

One of the best deals I had with Emma Jean was the following:

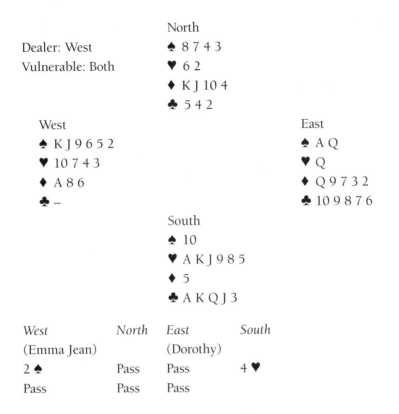

Dealer: West
Vulnerable: Both

North
♠ 8 7 4 3
♥ 6 2
♦ K J 10 4
♣ 5 4 2

West
♠ K J 9 6 5 2
♥ 10 7 4 3
♦ A 8 6
♣ –

East
♠ A Q
♥ Q
♦ Q 9 7 3 2
♣ 10 9 8 7 6

South
♠ 10
♥ A K J 9 8 5
♦ 5
♣ A K Q J 3

West (Emma Jean)	North	East (Dorothy)	South
2 ♠	Pass	Pass	4 ♥
Pass	Pass	Pass	

After a weak two-bid from Emma Jean, South jumped to four hearts. I won the opening spade lead and shifted to the club ten. West ruffed the club ace and led the spade king. Declarer ruffed this and drew trumps. I knew that South held a singleton diamond and would try to steal a trick in that suit. It was important that Emma Jean take her diamond ace when the suit was led, so I removed the temptation to duck by discarding my diamond queen at the first opportunity.

When the singleton diamond was led Emma Jean knew what to do. She grabbed the ace and led a spade winner, leaving no escape for the declarer. He had to lose a club at the finish for down one.

I had a unique problem later in 1968, when I played with Emma Jean in the Life Master Women's pairs in Coronado, Calif. The computer ran amok and produced 28 deals that had been used in the International Team Trials six weeks before in Atlantic City. As the only woman to have played in the '68 trials I became involved in a brouhaha that seems funny today but felt like a nightmare at the time.

It wasn't until the third round that I suspected something was wrong. I picked up:

♠ J 10 6 4 3
♥ 4 3
♦ 9 8 6 5
♣ K J

Emma Jean opened the bidding with one club, then doubled the opponents for penalties in three hearts. I was about to lead the king of clubs when it passed through my mind that I had had a similar hand six weeks before in the trials. My partner had opened one club and eventually doubled the opponents in four hearts. I had led the king of clubs, which turned out to be a disaster. Dummy's clubs were 10-x-x-x-x opposite declarer's A-Q-x, and the lead had given declarer five club tricks.

"Lightning does not strike twice in the same place," I told myself and led the club king. To my horror, dummy showed up with 10-x-x-x-x and declarer soon proved to have A-Q-x. I had been victimized twice on the same board.

When the deal was over I left to report this. Did you ever try to tell some directors that you have already played a deal six weeks before and 3,000 miles away? Believe me, they don't take kindly to this information.

First, I was informed that the hand records for this event had been in sealed envelopes until a few minutes before game time; second, the hand records were a new type only in use for the last two weeks; and third, the A.C.B.L. had switched computer companies since the trials. All in all it was totally impossible that I had ever seen that deal before and I should go back to my table and forget about it.

So I went back to the table and concentrated on the next deal, a nothing board that did not ring any bells. Then I picked up this beauty:

♠ A K 9 7 6 5 4
♥ K J 3
♦ –
♣ A K 2

A hard hand to forget. It had been the dummy when I saw it before. I decided to bid the hand before wasting any time trying to reconstruct it. However I took the precaution of writing on my scorecard, "If LHO is void in spades I am calling the director."

The Bidding:

Dorothy	Emma Jean
2 ♣	2 ♥
5 N.T.	7 ♥
All Pass	

Why did LHO fail to double for a spade lead? Was she just comatose or could I be wrong about the board?

By now I had reconstructed the hand. Yes, West was comatose.

Emma Jean did not like any tension at the table and her hands were shaking as she played the dummy. I left to look for a director again. I think they were all hiding.

In the directors' office I found the whole staff in chaos. It seems they really had believed me the first time and had been doing some frantic checking in the meantime, including telephoning A.C.B.L. headquarters for instructions. They were dreading my return like the plague. With four rounds already completed, there was no way to adjust the movement and it was much too late to restart the session.

By now poor Emma Jean was practically in tears. She refused to play with a substitute. This proved immaterial because there were no substitutes to be found. Finally, as the only possible solution, I volunteered to play the rest of the boards as honestly as possible, which I did. Afterward I discovered that there was a committee meeting in progress to determine how much of a penalty to assess against us in order to be fair to the field. When it turned out that we had scored only 158 on a 156 average they all laughed and voted to allow us to keep the whole 158.

The best joke about the mix-up was by the chief director, Jerry Machlin. He brought me a large package just before game time the next day. He explained with a straight face that these were the hand records for the session we were about to play and the women had gotten up a petition that I be allowed to study them thoroughly before the game.

The year 1974 was a big one for Emma Jean and me. We won bronze medals in the World Women's Pairs in Las Palmas, in the Canary Islands, and would have had silver but for an extraordinary condition of contest. The officials wanted to discourage scoring corrections, which caused them a lot of trouble. They therefore announced that there would be a fine of 100 match points for any pair asking for a correction. In general such pairs had made an error and there was some justice in penalizing them.

At one table we were moving as East-West, and at the end of a slow round a director told us to move, promising to verify the score. He failed. It was entered as four spades by North, down one, 50 to North-South. This was clearly impossible as we were vulnerable. It should have been 50 to East-West. The correction would have been worth 100 match points to us, and we would have lost the same amount in a penalty. So we did nothing. In retrospect, we should have appealed.

From Las Palmas we went to Venice, and competed in the first Venice Cup. This was a challenge match, something like the Ryder Cup in golf, between the American champions and the European champions. With Alan as our non-playing captain, we played Italy, and won easily.

As it turned out, I had won my first world title without knowing it. We won again in 1976, and yet again in 1978, at which time the Venice Cup became a world championship, with all continental zones competing. The earlier events were recognized retroactively, so Emma Jean and I suddenly found that we had three world titles.

In Valkenberg, the Netherlands, in 1980, we won our fourth title. But this was the World Women's Teams, with all countries competing individually. The U.S. team was Gail Greenberg, Jacqui Mitchell, Mary Jane Farell, Marilyn Johnson, Emma Jean Hawes and myself. I am now semi-retired.

As to the top women players, I can tell you one thing: There are a lot more of them today than when I started out. It makes me happy to think that I paved the way for some of them. Many experts, both men and women, have told me that *Winning Declarer Play* was the book that got them on the road to good card play.

I am often asked why men play better than women, and I do not know the answer. Perhaps it is because women have too much common sense to devote so much time to a game.

Another question I have had to deal with is: How do Alan and I manage to play bridge together without killing each other? Most married couples prefer to find other partners, but we have had no trouble because we respect each other's ability.

My theory is this: When one spouse is clearly better than the other, he or she should avoid criticizing and should shoulder as much of the blame as possible when something goes wrong. When both partners are relatively equal, as Alan and I are, things become more delicate. Now gender does matter. Men have a certain macho instinct that prohibits them from admitting a mistake, just as it prohibits them from asking directions when they are lost. The sooner a wife realizes this the better. It is much easier for a woman to say "Sorry, partner."

No. 32 ▶ *The Splinter Bid*

The splinter is an unusual jump guaranteeing a fit for partner's last-named suit. It shows a singleton or void in the suit in which the jump is made, and suggests slam possibilities.

For example:

West	East
1 ♠	4 ♣

East has opening values. He shows a forcing raise that includes a club shortage. (However, the modern tendency is to weaken the direct splinter slightly, with a probable range of 9–12 points. Stronger hands use the Jacoby two notrump. See page 195.)

West	East
1 ♣	1 ♠
4 ♦	

Here West shows a powerful opening bid (willing to play in four spades opposite what may be only 6 points) with four-card support and diamond shortage.

Splinter bids suggest slam, but on the basis of fit and distribution rather than high cards. Over a one-spade opening, responder would try four clubs on as little as:

♠ Q J 7 4 2
♥ A 8 4
♦ A 10 5 2
♣ 8

Even if opener has a minimum hand, slam may have a good chance if he has no wasted strength in clubs, e.g.:

♠ A 10 8 5 3
♥ K Q 2
♦ K 4
♣ 9 5 2

Most experts also use splinters in the majors:

West	East
1 ♠	4 ♥

or

West	East
1 ♥	3 ♠

There are many opportunities for splinters on later rounds of the bidding. For example:

West	East
1 ♥	1 ♠
2 ♥	4 ♣

This time East is showing only three trumps.

Splinters are very useful over a minor-suit opening bid.

West	East
1 ♦	3 ♥

East denies a four-card major, but shows excellent diamond support (usually five cards), opening bid values and heart shortage.

CHAPTER 18

The Future of
Bridge Life

♠ ♥
♦ ♣
Computers have changed the lives of bridge players in an assortment of ways. For me, as a journalist, the effect has been dramatic. I can write at home, and send my articles by modem to *The New York Times*. If I am on the road, perhaps halfway around the world, I know an accurate version of my story will reach my editor instantaneously. At a national championship I can go to bed on time and work the next morning. Before I had a computer I had to stay up waiting for results, hammer out a story on a typewriter, and then go out into the cold, dark night looking for Western Union. On a good day my editor would have the story, slightly garbled, in the afternoon.

The first impact of computers on the players came in the 50's, with the introduction of computer deals. Computers have the advantage of making it possible for hundreds of players to have similar possibilities. Everyone enjoys the subsequent post-mortems, sharing sad stories with players who were in a different section, or even room, but facing identical deals. There have indeed been glitches. Badly managed computers have been known to serve up deals that one or more players have encountered before. (See above, pages 235–38.)

Even more important was the use of computers for scoring. It took time to get it right. The first world-championship effort was in Cannes in 1962, and the players had to wait 12 hours for scores. They would have preferred the old-fashioned pencil-and-paper approach, which usually took an hour with much mental effort by the directors. Nowadays the scores are entered into the computer as the boards are played, and results are posted three minutes after the last result is available.

The ultimate in this direction arrived with the new century. The World

Bridge Federation introduced a World Wide Bridge Contest in which players around the world not only played the same deals but had their scores compared. In 2001, there were 5,389 pairs playing at 259 clubs in 40 countries. Remarkable software to make this possible was produced by Anna Gudge and Mark Newton of England.

One brilliant computer program has proved a mixed blessing. William Bailey's Deep Finesse (www.deepfinesse.com) is an instant hand analyzer. Given a full diagram, or a partial diagram, it will report within a few seconds whether a particular play will succeed or not. This is a boon to people like me. I can confidently write in my column statements such as, "Any lead except a club would have defeated the slam." Equally, readers can verify whether I am right, with a chance of sending me gotcha letters.

The downside is that Deep Finesse has ended a significant bridge sideline. The double-dummy problem has tested the brains of composers and solvers for more than a century, but is of little interest if a computer can deal with it instantaneously. The world expert in this area, Hugh Darwen of England, has had to abandon his monthly column in *Bridge Magazine*.

A great many teaching devices are now available as computer programs. There are even programs that will bid, play and defend, either against human beings or each other, and there is an annual competition for them. The best is probably Matt Ginsberg's GIB, which has proved that it can play on even terms with good human players. They are not yet as good as the best chess programs, for they cannot beat the world champions. But their time is coming.

The most interesting development of the past decade has been the introduction of online bridge. Players can play in their own homes, with partners, and perhaps teammates, at distant locations. They can watch the experts play in short challenge matches.

This is of great advantage to those who have physical handicaps, or work strange hours, or live a long way from a bridge club. The chief networks providing this service are OKbridge (okbridge.com) and Ebridge (e-bridgemaster.com). OKbridge has staged world championships in which all the play is online, and there will be more such developments in the future.

Few of those born in the first quarter of the 20th century have made a smooth adjustment to the computer age. As a result, the very old rarely take full advantage of the opportunity to play online. But that will change, and the opportunity of using bridge as a gateway to an even longer, fuller life will improve.

If you analyze the life-spans of the great American players of the past, the result is interesting: The average is 76. (And it would be 79 if the two women on the list were excluded.) This is an extraordinarily high number. Could it be that bridge keeps its devotees alive?

An Englishwoman named Julia Chadwick played tournament bridge regularly when she was over the age of 100. The great Oswald Jacoby won the Reisinger Teams, perhaps the toughest event in the calendar, at the age of 81 when he knew he was mortally ill. The equally great Waldemar von Zedtwitz won the World Mixed Pairs when he was 74.

Among the living, Jessel Rothfield of Australia represented his country in the Bermuda Bowl at the age of 82. Dr. George Rosenkranz of Mexico City, who changed the world by synthesizing the birth control pill in 1951, was a runner-up in the prestigious Vanderbilt Teams half a century later at the age of 85. (At the other end of the spectrum is Shivam Shah of England, who learned to play at the age of 5 and was an expert at the age of 8.)

Among active United States players, mention should be made of 71-year-old Sidney Lazard, who is playing as well as ever after half a century of tournament activity. In 1998 his team came close to a world title, losing a semifinal match by a hair to the Italians who eventually took the title. One of his favorite deals, played in 1986, is the following:

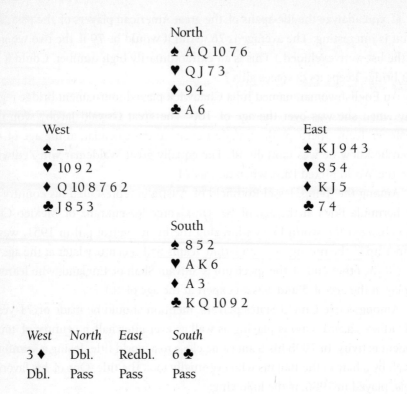

North
♠ A Q 10 7 6
♥ Q J 7 3
♦ 9 4
♣ A 6

West
♠ —
♥ 10 9 2
♦ Q 10 8 7 6 2
♣ J 8 5 3

East
♠ K J 9 4 3
♥ 8 5 4
♦ K J 5
♣ 7 4

South
♠ 8 5 2
♥ A K 6
♦ A 3
♣ K Q 10 9 2

West	North	East	South
3 ♦	Dbl.	Redbl.	6 ♣
Dbl.	Pass	Pass	Pass

West's eccentric pre-empt and East's strange redouble talked North-South out of their 5-3 spade fit. West doubled six clubs to prevent a save by his partner and led the heart ten.

Lazard, South, won with the ace and decided to believe West's double. He led the club ten for a winning finesse and crossed to the club ace. He came to his hand with a diamond to the ace and drew trumps. Two heart leads left him in dummy in this position:

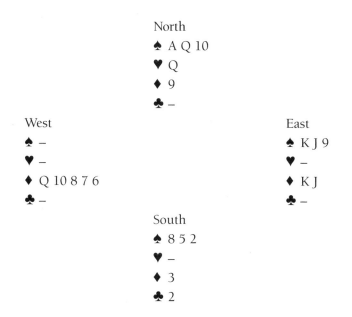

North
♠ A Q 10
♥ Q
♦ 9
♣ –

West
♠ –
♥ –
♦ Q 10 8 7 6
♣ –

East
♠ K J 9
♥ –
♦ K J
♣ –

South
♠ 8 5 2
♥ –
♦ 3
♣ 2

On the heart queen South threw his diamond loser. East was in trouble. If he threw a spade, South could play that suit and establish his 12th trick. East therefore threw a diamond, but that was no better. Lazard ruffed a diamond and took a spade finesse, scoring two spade tricks at the finish to make his slam.

This tour de force gained 17 imps, for in the replay North-South reached a normal six-spade contract and failed by two tricks. Lazard was grateful for the 5-0 spade break: If West had held a singleton spade he could have led it effectively.

In Europe, the great veteran is Henri Szwarc of France, who is the same age as Lazard. He won two world team titles, the most recent was the World Teams in Rhodes, Greece, in 1996, at the age of 66. He is still eager to win more, and fully capable of doing so. His favorite deal was played in a Paris club in 1956.

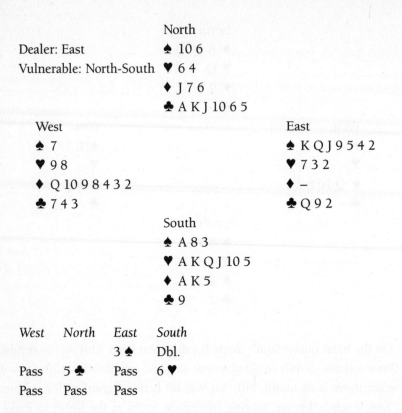

North
Dealer: East   ♠ 10 6
Vulnerable: North-South   ♥ 6 4
                                ♦ J 7 6
                                ♣ A K J 10 6 5

West   East
♠ 7   ♠ K Q J 9 5 4 2
♥ 9 8   ♥ 7 3 2
♦ Q 10 9 8 4 3 2   ♦ –
♣ 7 4 3   ♣ Q 9 2

South
♠ A 8 3
♥ A K Q J 10 5
♦ A K 5
♣ 9

West	North	East	South
		3 ♠	Dbl.
Pass	5 ♣	Pass	6 ♥
Pass	Pass	Pass	

North was slightly irritated when he put his dummy down. "I had 100 honors, partner," he pointed out.

Szwarc, as South, was not impressed. He had 150 honors of his own. He could count 11 tricks, but was not sure where to find the 12th. He won the spade lead with the ace, drew trumps, and cashed the diamond ace.

There was a crackle of electricity between the defenders when East showed out.

"How was I to know you were void?" demanded West.

It is true that a diamond lead would have beaten the slam, and the invaluable slam double devised by Theodore Lightner would have saved the day for the defenders.

But even as it was, Szwarc was worrying about his 12th trick. He did not wish to rely on a club finesse, and careful counting allowed him to solve the problem.

He knew that East had begun with seven spades, three hearts, and a void in diamonds. The clubs were therefore split 3-3. Light dawned, and he found a way to make his slam whatever the position of the club queen. He cashed dummy's top clubs, and dramatically discarded his diamond king.

He was now down to 10 winners, but when he ruffed a club dummy had winners in that suit. West was reduced to nothing but diamonds, and the lead of the diamond five settled the issue. West had to win with the queen and lead a diamond, so South was able to throw his spade losers on the diamond jack and a club winner. That was a play to remember for a lifetime.

A clue to this remarkable durability, of the Szwarcs, the Jacobys, the von Zedtwitzes, came in a famous study of nuns, which found that those who were mentally active lived longer than those who were not. "Many researchers," said the Alzheimer's Association National Newsletter, "believe that lifelong mental exercise can nourish growth of new connections between brain cells and can in effect cushion the brain against developing early symptoms of dementia."

Bridge seems to be specifically desirable in this context. In 1999, a professor of integrative biology at the University of California-Berkeley demonstrated that playing bridge leaves people with higher numbers of immune cells. It seems to be the first evidence that the human cortex—which is subject to voluntary control—can play a role in stimulating the immune system.

Marian Cleaves Diamond, who usually experiments with rat and mouse brains, decided to test players over 70 years of age at the women's bridge club in Orinda, Calif. The reason was "Bridge players plan ahead, they use working memory, they deal with sequencing, initiation and numerous other higher-order functions with which the dorsolateral cortex is involved."

Blood tests before and after the games showed a significant increase in the number of the white blood cells that seek and destroy viruses and other invaders of the human body. The increase was the only change visible in the tests, a result that Diamond found to be exciting and encouraging.

So playing bridge is positively good for your health. If you do not have anyone to play with, use a computer. Keep playing, enjoy yourself, and improve your chance for a long life.

Glossary

ADVANCE   An action by the partner of an overcaller or a takeout doubler.

APPEAL   A request that a committee review a situation involving some problem at the table, such as a hesitation.

ARTIFICIAL   A bid with a specialized meaning, unrelated to the named strain.

ASKING BID   An artificial bid inquiring about some feature of partner's hand.

AUCTION   A series of bids, ending with three passes, to determine the contract.

BALANCE   To bid when a pass would end the auction.

BALANCED   An even hand pattern, typically with the suits divided 4-3-3-3, 4-4-3-2, or 5-3-3-2. These are suitable for a one no-trump opening bid. 6-3-2-2, 7-2-2-2 and 5-4-2-2 can also be considered balanced, since they have no singleton or void.

BID   An announcement offering to take a given number of tricks more than six. One club, meaning seven tricks with clubs as trump, is the lowest bid, and seven notrump is the highest.

BIDDING   The first stage of the play, in which one or more bids decide the final contract.

BIDDING BOX   A box containing bidding cards, allowing silent bidding in duplicate play.

BLACKWOOD   A conventional bid of four notrump, asking partner to indicate how many aces he has.

BREAK   The way the cards in a suit are divided in the opposing hands.

CALL   A bid, double, redouble or pass.

CASH   To take one or more obvious tricks.

CHEATING   A deliberate attempt to circumvent the laws of the game, usually by agreement between partners.

CLAIM   To terminate the play in an obvious situation, by exposing the cards to the opponents.

COMPETITIVE   A bid that just outranks an opposing action, without intention of going higher.

CONTRACT   The last bid of the auction, determining the declarer's target in the subsequent play. Strictly speaking, this is the Final Contract.

CONTROL   Ability to win the first lead in a suit (first-round control) or the second lead (second-round control). In some conventions, an ace counts as two controls and a king as one.

CONTROL-BID   A high-level action showing control of a suit to suggest slam possibilities.

CONVENTION   A specialized bid, often artificial, that should be explained to the opposition.

COUNTING   The art of calculating the distribution of unseen hands. Also, the calculation of points in the unseen hands.

CROSSRUFF   To take two or more ruffs in opposite hands.

CUE-BID   A low-level bid in an opponent's suit, announcing a desire to reach game. Traditionally, a high-level bid showing a control and suggesting slam, but the modern term for that is CONTROL BID.

DEAL   To distribute the cards to the four players, or the result of such distribution.

DEALER   The player who makes the first call. The deal passes in rotation, and is predetermined in duplicate.

DECK   The set of 52 cards used in bridge. The English word is pack.

DECLARER   The player who wins the auction and aims to make a specified number of tricks, controlling the dummy. (The last bid may have been made by his partner, supporting him in a suit or in notrump.)

DEFENDER   A player who is opposed to the declarer, combining with his partner in the hope of defeating the contract.

DEFENSE   Playing against the declarer, in the hope of defeating the contract.

DIRECTOR   The official who plans a duplicate game or tournament, and is called to the table if any problem arises concerning procedure, laws or ethics.

DISCARD   A play of a card, other than a trump, when unable to follow suit.

DISCOURAGING   In the bidding, a suggested final contract. Partner usually passes. In the play, a suggestion to shift.

DISTRIBUTION   The way the cards are divided in a hand, or around the table in a suit.

DOUBLE   An bid that approximately doubles the stakes for a particular deal. It often has an artificial meaning. See TAKEOUT DOUBLE.

DOUBLETON   A suit with exactly two cards.

DRURY   After an opening bid of one spade or one heart, an artificial reponse of two clubs by a player who has previously passed. It shows a strong raise, with 9–11 points.

DUCK   Playing a low card, and thus allowing an opponent to win a trick that you could win. The usual purpose is to preserve an entry.

DUMMY   The partner of the declarer. He takes no part in the play. Or that player's cards, which are faced on the table after the opening lead.

DUPLICATE　Any form of bridge competition in which a deal is played more than once, making possible comparison between players with equal opportunities.

ECHO　A high-low signal.

ELIMINATION　To strip opposing cards to prepare for the endgame.

ENCOURAGING　A bid or play that suggests continuing.

ENDGAME　The final stage of the play, usually with fewer than six cards in each hand.

ENTRY　A card that will allow a player to transfer the lead between partnership hands.

ENTRY-CREATING PLAY　A maneuver to establish a line of communication between partnership hands.

ETHICS　The proprieties of the game, which include barring a player from taking advantage of partner's hesitations, facial expressions or other actions.

FAVORABLE VULNERABILITY　Being not vulnerable against vulnerable opponents. A good time for aggressive preemptive bidding and for saves.

FINAL CONTRACT　See CONTRACT.

FINESSE　A play made in the hope that one or more opposing cards are lying favorably. Example: Lead small toward A-Q and the play the queen, hoping that the second player has the king.

FORCING　A bid (or pass) that, by agreement, requires partner to continue. It may be forcing for one round, requiring one more move, or forcing until game is reached.

GAME　A contract that earns a large bonus if successful. Minimum game contracts are three notrump, four hearts, four spades, five clubs and five diamonds. At rubber bridge, two games complete a rubber.

GRAND SLAM　A bid at the seven-level, offering to take all 13 tricks.

HAND　The cards held by one player, 13 at the start and decreasing. (Often wrongly used to describe a 52-card deal.)

HIGH-LOW　A signal by a defender, in which an unnecessarily high card is followed by a low card in the same suit.

HOLD-UP　A refusal to win a trick in a strong suit led by an opponent. The purpose is to keep control of the suit and hinder the opponents' communications.

HONOR　The top five cards in a suit: ace, king, queen, jack and ten.

HONOR TRICKS　An obsolete method of valuation.

HOYLE　A book of the rules of card games, from the name of the first compiler.

IMP　An International Match Point, the basis of scoring in team play.

INVITATION　A bid that suggests a game or a slam.

JUMP　A bid that skips at least one level.

KEY CARDS　The four aces and the king of the intended trump suit.

KNAVE　The English term for a jack.

LAYDOWN   An easy contract, which can be claimed by showing the cards to the defenders.

LAWS   The rules of the game, set out in two codes, one for duplicate and another for rubber bridge.

LEAD   The first card played to a trick, from the hand that won the previous trick.

LIMIT   A bid with a narrow strength range.

LOSERS   Cards that represent probable tricks for the opposition.

MAJOR   Spades and hearts, which can bring a game bonus by bidding and making 10 tricks.

MATCH   A head-to-head contest between two teams, usually four players against four with alternates.

MAXIMUM   The most strength a player can have in light of his bidding.

MINIMUM   The least strength a player can have in light of his bidding.

MINOR   Clubs and diamonds, which are rarely the choice for game because 11 tricks are needed.

NEGATIVE   A bid showing weakness, usually artificial in response to a forcing bid.

NEGATIVE DOUBLE   A double by responder for take-out, following a suit opening bid and an overcall.

NON-FORCING   A bid (or pass) that permits partner to pass.

NOTRUMP   A contract in which there is no trump suit. In the bidding, notrump outranks the four suits. Three no-trump, needing nine tricks, is the most popular game contract.

ONE-OVER-ONE   A suit response at the one-level, a one-round force in all standard methods unless the bidder has previously passed.

OPENING BID   The first action in the auction, other than a pass.

OPENING LEAD   The first card played in the deal, made by the player on the declarer's left.

OVERCALL   A bid following an opening bid by an opponent, or an opening bid and a response.

OVERBID   A bid that lacks the normal values for the action.

OVERTRICK   A extra trick, not required to make the contract.

PAIR   In duplicate, two players competing as a unit, against others holding the same cards at one or more other tables.

PART-SCORE   A low-level contract, below game.

PARTNER   The player across the table, with whom one cooperates.

PARTNERSHIP   Two players combining as partners.

PASS   A negative action, showing no wish to make a bid. Three consecutive passes end the bidding.

PASS-OUT   An auction in which none of the four players chooses to bid. There is no score.

PATTERN   The distribution of cards in a hand, or in a suit around the table.

PENALTY   The score recorded for defeating an opposing contract.

PETER   A high-low signal. (British.)

PLAFOND   An early version of contract bridge, developed in France.

PLAY   The second stage of a deal, in which the declarer attempts to make his contract. Also, the act of putting a card on the table.

POINTS   The standard method of assessing the potential of a hand. Ace = four, king = three, queen = two and jack = one is normal. Also, the score on a deal determined by the scoring table.

POSITIVE   A bid showing some strength, usually in response to a strong forcing opening.

PREFERENCE   A bid that returns to partner's first-bid suit.

PSYCHIC   A bid made for deceptive purposes, distorting the length of a suit, and/or the strength of a hand, and/or the location of high cards.

RAISE   To support one's partner's suit or bid of notrump. Or a bid that does this.

RANK   The way in which the suits relate to each other in the bidding. In ascending order, clubs, diamonds, hearts and spades. Notrump is higher than all.

REBID   A second bid by any player.

REDOUBLE   A bid that, if the bidding ends, approximately quadruples the stake after an opponent has doubled. It may sometimes have an artificial meaning.

RESPONSE   A reply to an opening bid by the opener's partner.

RESTRICTED CHOICE   Theory suggesting that a finesse should be taken if it is made possible by the fall of an opposing high card. Example: With A 8 3 2 opposite K 10 6 5 4, play the ace and then finesse the ten if an honor appears on the right.

REPLAY   In team games, the second playing of a deal, with team positions interchanged to permit comparison.

REVOKE   Failure to follow suit when able, a misdemeanor subject to penalty.

ROUND   A cycle of four calls, or the stages of play of a suit.

RUBBER BRIDGE   The original one-table version of the game played in clubs or social situations, usually for a stake.

RUFF   The play of a trump when unable to follow suit, winning the trick unless a higher trump is played.

SANDWICH   Possession of two cards that surround one on the right. Or an overcall when both opponents have bid a suit.

SAVE, SACRIFICE   A competitive bid made in the expectation of being defeated, hoping to save points. Example: Bid four spades over an opposing four hearts if you expect to make eight tricks. Be aggressive at favorable vulnerability, cautious at unfavorable.

SCORE, SCORING   The points on a deal, positive or negative, determined by the laws. Points for tricks made, bonuses for part-scores, games and slams, and penalties for failure are determining factors.

SCREEN, or BIDDING SCREEN   A device placed diagonally across the table, preventing a player from seeing his partner. It is half raised after the bidding to make the dummy visible.

SHIFT   In the bidding or play, a switch to a new suit.

SHUFFLE   To mix the cards ready for dealing.

SIGNAL   A play by a defender conveying an agreed message to partner.

SIGN OFF   A bid attempting to apply the brakes, and partner usually passes.

SINGLETON   A suit with exactly one card.

SLAM   A small slam is a contract at the six-level, offering to take 12 of the possible 13 tricks. A grand slam is at the seven-level, offering to take all the tricks.

SLUFF   Discard.

SMALL SLAM   (or LITTLE SLAM) A bid at the six-level, offering to take 12 tricks.

SQUEEZE   A play that gains one trick (or more) by pressuring one or both opponents to give up an important card.

STRAIN   The possible choices for a contract: clubs, diamonds, hearts, spades and notrump.

STRIP   The play of unimportant suits to prepare for the endgame. Also called ELIMINATION.

STRONG CLUB   A system based on the idea that an opening one-club bid is strong and artificial.

SUIT   One of the four divisions of the deck: clubs, diamonds, hearts and spades.

SUPPORT   To raise one's partner, or to have cards suitable for doing so.

SYSTEM   A method of bidding.

TAKEOUT   An action, usually a low-level double of a suit bid, that urges partner to do something.

TEAM   Usually, four players, with alternates, competing against others.

TOURNAMENT   Two or more bridge events played at one time and place.

TRICK   A sequence of four cards played in clockwise order. The suit that starts the sequence must be matched if possible by the other players. The highest card wins unless a trump is played. The winner of the trick starts the next trick.

TRIPLETON   A suit with exactly three cards.

TRUMP   A card of the suit selected in the final contract, or the play of such a card. This wins the trick unless a higher trump is played.

TWO-OVER-ONE   A non-jump suit response at the two-level to a suit opening at the one-level. Forcing for one round or, by agreement, to game, unless the bidder has previously passed.

TWO-WAY FINESSE   A situation in which a player can finesse against either opponent.

UNBALANCED   A hand containing a singleton or a void.

UNDERRUFF   The play of a trump lower than one already played after a different suit has been led. Also UNDERTRUMP.

UNFAVORABLE VULNERABILITY   Being vulnerable against not vulnerable. A time to be cautious, especially in preemptive bidding and saves.

UNUSUAL NOTRUMP   A notrump bid in a competitive auction to show length in the minor suits. Example: two notrump following an opening of one spade.

UPSIDE-DOWN   A signaling method in which a high card discourages and a low card encourages.

VALUATION   The worth of a hand.

VOID   A suit in which a player has no cards.

VULNERABLE   A situation in which the bonuses and penalties are greater. This is predetermined in duplicate. At rubber bridge, a partnership that has earned one game is vulnerable.

WHIST   The ancestor game of bridge, with no bidding and no dummy.

WINNERS   Cards that are certain, or virtually certain, to win tricks.

YARBOROUGH   A hand with no card higher than a nine. Loosely, any very weak hand.

Index of Persons

Index of Subjects